SAMURAI!

by

SABURO SAKAI

with

MARTIN CAIDIN

and

FRED SAITO

This book is dedicated to . . .
All those fighter pilots
with whom I fought,
and fought against,
who will never come home.

Samurai!
The Autobiography of Japan's World War Two Flying Ace

by Saburo Sakai
with Martin Caidin *and* Fred Saito

Printed in the United States of America.

ISBN: 978-1088139035

Samurai! was originally published in 1957 by E. P. Dutton and Company, Inc., New York. The original book is now in the public domain.

TYPEFACE: Athelas 10.5/13

UNCOMMON VALOR SERIES

Samurai! is part of a series entitled *Uncommon Valor,* taken from the quote by Admiral Chester W. Nimitz, U.S. Navy:

"Uncommon valor was a common virtue,"

referring to the hard-won victory by U.S. Marines on Iwo Jima. The intent of the series is to keep alive a number of largely forgotten books, written by or about men and women who survived extreme hardship and deprivation during immensely trying historical times.

Steve W. Chadde
SERIES EDITOR

ACKNOWLEDGMENTS

THE AUTHORS wish to express their appreciation to all the persons and institutions without whose assistance this book would not have been possible. Particular thanks are due to former Naval Aviation Captain Masahisa Saito; to Major General Minoru Genda, JAF; to Colonel Tadashi Nakajima, JAF; to Colonel Masatake Okumiya, G-2, Japan Joint Chiefs of Staff; to Major Shoji Matsumara, JAF; to all the former pilots and officers of Japan's wartime naval air arm who contributed details of their air combat service; we wish particularly to thank Otto v. St. Whitelock, whose editorial assistance has always been invaluable; Sally Botsford, who has worked many long hours in typing the final manuscript; Major William J. McGinty, Captain James Sunderman, and Major Gordon Furbish of the United States Air Force, who have always been most cooperative in providing historical documentation and other assistance.

HIGH FLIGHT

Oh! I have slipped the surly bonds of earth
And danced the skies on laughter-silvered wings;
Sunward I've climbed, and joined the tumbling mirth
Of sun-split clouds—and done a hundred things
You have not dreamed of—wheeled and soared and swung
High in the sunlit silence. Hov'ring there
I've chased the shouting wind along, and flung
My eager craft through footless halls of air.

Up, up the long, delirious, burning blue
I've topped the wind-swept heights with easy grace
Where never lark, nor even eagle flew—
And, while with silent lifting mind I've trod
The high untrespassed sanctity of space
Put out my hand and touched the face of God.

> —*Pilot Officer* JOHN G. MAGEE, JR.,
> American flier with the Royal
> Canadian Air Force. Died in
> aerial combat on December 11, 1941

At Hankow Air Base in 1939, I posed before my Claude *fighter. The next day I attacked twelve SB bombers.*

FOREWORD

SABURO SAKAI became a living legend in Japan during World War II. Pilots everywhere spoke in awe of his incredible exploits in the air.

Sakai enjoyed a singular and most cherished reputation among fighter pilots. Of all Japan's aces, Saburo Sakai is the only pilot who never lost a wingman in combat. This is an astounding performance for a man who engaged in more than two hundred aerial melees, and it explains the fierce competition, sometimes approaching physical violence, among the other pilots who aspired to fly his wing positions.

His maintenance crews held him in adulation. It was considered the highest honor to be a mechanic assigned to Sakai's Zero fighter. Among the ground complement it is said that during his two hundred combat missions Sakai's skill was such that he never overshot a landing, never overturned or crash-landed his plane despite heavy damage, personal wounds, and night flying conditions.

Saburo Sakai suffered disastrous wounds and intense agony during air fighting over Guadalcanal in August of 1942. His struggle to return in a crippled fighter plane to Rabaul, with paralyzing wounds in his left leg and left arm, blinded permanently in his right eye and temporarily in his left eye, with jagged pieces of metal in his back and chest, and with the heavy fragments of two .50-caliber machine-gun bullets imbedded in his skull is one of the greatest air epics, a deed which I believe will become legendary among pilots.

These wounds were more than enough to have ended the combat days of any man. Ask any veteran fighter pilot of the appalling difficulties which face a combat flier with only one eye. Especially when he must return to the arena of air battle in a suddenly obsolete Zero fighter against new and superior American Hellcats.

After long months of physical and mental anguish, during which he despaired of ever returning to his first love, the air, Sakai again entered battle. Not only did he again assert his piloting skill, but he downed four more enemy planes, bringing his total score to sixty-four confirmed kills.

The reader will doubtless be surprised to learn that Saburo Sakai never received recognition by his government in the form of medals or decorations. The awarding of medals or other citations was unknown to the Japanese. Recognition was given only posthumously. Where the aces of other nations, including our own, were bedecked with rows of colorful medals and ribbons, awarded with great ceremony, Saburo Sakai and his fellow pilots flew repeatedly in combat without ever knowing the satisfaction of such recognition.

The story of Saburo Sakai provides for the first time an intimate look into the "other side." Here are the emotions of a man, a former enemy, laid open for our world to see. Sakai represents a class of Japanese we in America know little of, and understand even less. These are the celebrated Samurai, the professional warriors who devoted their lives to serving their country. Theirs was a world apart from even their own people. Now, for the first time, you will be able to listen to the thoughts, share the emotions and feelings of the men who spearheaded Japan in the air.

In writing this book, I had the opportunity to speak to many of my friends who flew our fighter planes in the Pacific theater during World War II. Not one among them has ever known the Japanese fighter pilots whom they opposed as more than an unknown entity. They have never been able to think of the Japanese fighter pilot as another human being. He has been remote and alien.

As were our fighter pilots to men like Sakai.

SAMURAI! will do much to bring the Pacific air war into new perspective. The wartime propaganda efforts of our country have distorted the picture of the Japanese pilot into an unrecognizable caricature of a man who stumbles through the air, who has poor eyesight, who remains aloft only by the grace of God.

This attitude was on too many occasions a fatal one. Saburo Sakai was as gifted in the air as the best of pilots from any nation; he ranks among the greatest of all time. Sixty-four planes went down before his guns; the toll, except for his severe wounds, would have been much higher.

The conduct and courage of our men during the trials of World War II require no apologies. We also had our share of the great and the mediocre. However, many of our "documented" victories in the air are conquests on paper only.

A case in point is the celebrated story of the heroic Captain Colin P. Kelly, Jr. The reader will find not a little interest in Sakai's version of Kelly's death, on December 10,1941, in these pages. The story surrounding his death—that he attacked and sank the battleship Haruna, that he fought his way through hordes of enemy fighters, and that he made a suicide plunge into a Japanese battleship and that he received the Congressional Medal of Honor—is an erroneous one, owing to the inaccuracies of combat observation and the passionate desire of the American people after Pearl Harbor to find a "hero."

At the time of the reported battle with the Haruna that ship was on the other side of the South China Sea, engaged in support of the Malayan campaign. There were no battleships in the Philippines at the time. The warship Kelly did attack, but did not strike, according to Sakai and the pilots who flew air cover over the vessel, was a light cruiser of the 4,000-ton Nagara class. Kelly's attack was over and his plane fleeing the area before the enemy even discovered his presence. He did not make a suicide dive, but a bombing run from 22,000 feet and later was shot down—by Saburo Sakai—near Clark Field in the Philippines. Kelly was awarded, not the Congressional Medal of Honor, but the Distinguished Service Cross.

It is ironic, and a disservice to the memory of this fine young officer, that Colin Kelly is not remembered for the actual deed of bravery which is his son's heritage. Kelly and his copilot remained at the controls of their flaming bomber in order that their crew might abandon safely their stricken bomber and live. This was his sacrifice.

To obtain the full record and the story of Saburo Sakai, Fred Saito spent every week end for nearly a year with Sakai, digging into the combat past of Japan's greatest living ace. As soon after the war as conditions allowed, Sakai prepared voluminous notes on his experiences. These notes, plus the thousands of questions posed by Saito, an experienced and capable Associated Press correspondent, recreated Sakai's more personal story.

Saito then searched through the thousands of pages of official records of the former Imperial Japanese Navy. He toured the islands of Japan to interview dozens of surviving pilots and officers, to cross-check the accounts given by these men. All ranks have been polled, from enlisted men of the maintenance crews to general officers and admirals, in order to produce this authentic record. Indeed, several of Sakai's battle accounts have been omitted simply because a search of official Japanese and/or American records failed to produce documentation.

Of especial value was the personal fighting log of former Naval Aviation Captain Masahisa Saito. Captain Saito, who commanded Sakai's fighter wing at Lae, kept an elaborate log during his combat service in this area. Since it was a personal diary which had not been submitted for Imperial Headquarters, Fred Saito and I consider it the single most valuable document of the Pacific air war.

It is a human failing that military officers at times do not report every difficulty within their front-line command to rear headquarters. This especially was true within the military system of the Japanese Navy. Captain Saito's personal diary, for example, lists in detail the precise number of Japanese planes which returned or failed to return from their almost daily sorties in the New Guinea theater. The log is at direct odds at times with the overwhelming claims for victory of many of our pilots. Captain Saito survived the war, and the long interviews with him proved invaluable to this book.

Ex-Naval Aviation Commander Tadashi Nakajima, whom you will meet throughout this book, is today a colonel in Japan's new Air Force. Many hours were spent with Colonel Nakajima, to provide some of the most interesting parts. Also of great assistance has been Major General (formerly Naval Aviation Captain) Minoru Genda, who commanded Sakai's wing during the latter part of the war. At this writing, Genda is the only Japanese general officer who is a rated jet fighter pilot, and who has logged many hours in types as the F-86.

We are also deeply indebted to Colonel Masatake Okumiya, who is today Chief of Intelligence, Japan Joint Chiefs of Staff. Colonel (formerly Commander) Okumiya, one of my coauthors on *ZERO!* and *THE ZERO FIGHTER*, was in more air-sea battles than any other Japanese officer, and for the last year of the war commanded the homeland air defense of Japan. Through his efforts we were able to secure the necessary records from the archives of the defunct Imperial Navy Ministry.

I believe it is important here to tell of Sakai's attitude toward his present position as Japan's greatest living ace. Sakai feels that he was simply fortunate to survive the losing war, the devastating air battles fought from 1943 on. There were many other great Japanese aces— Nishizawa, Ota, Takatsuka, Sugita, and more—who fought until the long odds of incessant air battles caught up with them.

This is Sakai's own statement of the postwar period:

"In the Imperial Japanese Navy I learned only one trade—how to man a fighter plane and how to kill enemies of my country. This I did for nearly five years, in China and across the Pacific. I knew no other life; I was a warrior of the air.

"With the surrender, I was thrown out of the Navy. Despite my wounds and my long service, there was no possibility of a pension. We were the losers, and pensions or disability payments are received only by the veterans of the victor nation.

"Occupation rules forbade me even to sit at the controls of an airplane, no matter what its type. For the seven long years of the Allied occupation of 1945 to 1952, I was banned from obtaining any public position. It was all quite simple; I had been a flier in combat. Period.

"The end of the Pacific War only opened a new, prolonged, and bitter struggle for me, a struggle far worse than any I had ever known in combat. There were new and deadlier enemies—poverty, hunger, sickness, and all manner of frustration. There was the ever-present barrier raised by the occupation authorities which prevented my gaining any public post. There was only one opportunity, and I snatched at it eagerly. Two years of the hardest manual labor, with primitive living quarters, with rags for clothes, and barely enough food.

"The ultimate crushing blow was the death of my dearest wife from illness. Hatsuyo had survived the bombs and all the danger of war; she could not, however, escape this new enemy.

"Finally, after the years of self-imposed privation, I scraped together enough money to open a small printing shop. By working day and night it was possible to make ends meet, and even to get a little ahead.

"Soon I succeeded in reaching the widow of Vice-Admiral Takijiro Onishi, a person I had sought out for many months. Admiral Onishi committed *harakari* immediately after the surrender in 1945. He chose death in this fashion rather than remaining alive, when so many of his men—men he had ordered out to die—were never to return. For it was none other than Onishi who had instituted the devastating *Kamikaze* attacks.

"Mrs. Onishi was even more to me than the admiral's widow; she is the aunt of Lieutenant Sasai, the best friend I ever had. Sasai flew to his death in combat over New Guinea while I was in a hospital in Japan.

"Mrs. Onishi had for several years scratched out the barest subsistence by peddling on the street. I was enraged at the sight of her shuffling along in her tattered rags, but there was no way to help.

"Now, with a small printing shop, I persuaded her to accept a position as manager. Soon our business was expanding; I searched diligently and brought into the business several other widows and brothers of my close friends who flew with me during the war and who met their death.

"Fortunately, things have changed. It is now more than a decade since the war's end. Our business has continued to expand, and the people who work together in my shop are again well on their economic feet.

"The later years have been strange, indeed. I have been invited as a guest of honor aboard several American carriers and other warships, and the incredible changes in present-day jet fighters from the old Zeros and Hellcats is astounding. I have met men against whom I fought in the air, sat and talked with these men, and found friendship. This to me is truly the most impressive fact of all; these same people who, for all I know, came under my guns so long ago, sincerely offered friendship.

"On several occasions I have been approached with offers to accept a commission with the new Japan Air Force. These offers I have declined. I do not wish to return to the military, to relive all which has passed.

"But to fly is just like swimming. You do not forget easily. I have been on the ground for more than ten years. If I close my eyes, however, I can again feel the stick in my right hand, the throttle in my left, the rudder bar beneath my feet. I can sense the freedom and the cleanliness and all the things which a pilot knows.

"No, I have not forgotten how to fly. If Japan needs me, if Communist forces press too closely against our nation, I will fly again. But I pray fervently that it is not for this reason that I return to the air."

SABURO SAKAI
Tokyo, 1956

MARTIN CAIDIN
New York, 1956

CONTENTS

CHAPTER ONE

ON the southernmost main Japanese island of Kyushu, the small city of Saga lies midway between two major centers which in recent years have become well known to thousands of Americans. At Sasebo, the United States Navy based most of its fleet which participated in the Korean War; from the airfield runways at Ashiya, American fighters and bombers took off for flights over narrow Tsushima Strait to attack the Chinese and Red Koreans on the disputed peninsula.

Saga City is no newcomer to military expeditions across Tsushima Strait. My own ancestors were members of the Japanese forces which in 1592 invaded Korea from Saga. Nor is the unpleasant outcome of the modern Korean conflict without its precedent; the medieval Korea-Japan War choked to a stalemate in 1597 after the Ming Dynasty of China threw its strength onto the side of the North Koreans, just as modern Red China has brought about the current Korean impasse.

Thus my family has a warrior's origin, and for many years my forbears served faithfully the feudal lord of Saga until, under a government centralization plan in the nineteenth century, he committed his estate to the Emperor's keeping.

In the feudal times when four castes divided the Japanese people, my family enjoyed the privilege of the ruling class known as the *Samurai,* or Warriors. Aloof from the mundane problems of everyday life, the Samurai lived proudly, without personal concern for such matters as income, and devoted their time to local government administration and to constant preparedness for emergencies which would make demands upon their fighting prowess. The Samurai's living necessities were underwritten by his lord, regardless of farm depressions or other outside influences.

The nineteenth century abolition of the caste system proved a crushing blow to the proud Samurai people. In a single stroke they were stripped of all their former privileges and forced to become merchants and farmers, and to adopt patterns of life under which they were ill suited to prosper.

It was to be expected that most of the Samurai became destitute, struggling to eke out a living through the most menial labor or through dawn-to-dusk work on their small farms. My own grandfather fared no better than his friends; he finally accepted a small farm on which he struggled bitterly to scratch out the necessities of life. My family was then, and is today, one of the very poorest in the village. It was on this farm that I was born on August 26, 1916, :he third of four sons; my family also included three sisters.

Ironically, my own career closely paralleled that of my grandfather. When Japan surrendered to the Allies in August of 1945, I was at the time the leading live ace of my country, with an official total of sixty-four enemy planes shot down in aerial combat. With the war's end, however, I was dismissed from the defunct Imperial Navy and barred from accepting any government position. I was penniless and with no skill I could employ to adapt myself to a world which had crashed all about me. Like my grandfather, I lived by dint of the crudest manual labor; only after several years of bitter struggle did I manage to save enough to set up a small printing shop to serve as a means of livelihood.

The task of tilling the one-acre household farm near Saga City fell heavily on the shoulders of my mother, who also had the problem of rending her seven children. To add to her unceasing labors, she was widowed when I was eleven years old. My memories of her at that time are of a woman steadfastly at work, my youngest sister strapped to her back as she bent over for hour upon hour in the fields, toiling under brutal conditions. But at no time do I recall hearing any complaint pass her lips. She was one of the bravest women I have ever known, a typical Samurai, proud and stem, but not without a warm heart when the occasion demanded

I sometimes returned home from school, whimpering after having been thoroughly beaten by older and larger schoolboys. She had no sympathy for my tears, only scowls and admonishing words. "Shame on you," was her favorite retort. "Do not forget that you are the son of a Samurai, that tears are not for you."

In the village primary school I worked hard at my studies and, throughout the six years, remained at the head of all my classes. But the future presented apparently insuperable problems to my further education. While the primary schools were government-financed, the majority of the more advanced institutions required the student to be supported by his family. This arrangement was, of course, impossible for the Sakai family, which barely met its needs for food and clothing. However, we had not reckoned with the generosity of my uncle in Tokyo, who offered, incredibly, to underwrite all my school expenses. He was a successful official in the Ministry of Communications and his offer included adoption and a complete education. We gratefully accepted our good fortune.

In all Japan, the feudal clan of Saga occupied one of the poorest of the self-sustaining provinces. Its Samurai class had for ages lived an austere life, and was famous for its Spartan discipline. We were the only province in all the land which lived religiously by the Bushido code, *Hagakure,* the main theme of which was: "A Samurai lives in such a way that he will always be prepared to die." *Hagakure* during the war became a textbook for every school in the country, but it was the code under which I had always lived, and its severity served me well, both in my new school life and in the years to follow in combat.

Everything in Tokyo bewildered me. I had never known a city larger than Saga, with its 50,000 people. The milling throngs in Japan's capital were incredible, as were the constant turmoil, the noise, the large buildings, and all the activities of one of the world's greatest centers. I was also to find that Tokyo in 1929 was a stage of fierce competition in every field; not only were new graduates competing bitterly for jobs, but even the young children had to fight for the comparatively few openings in the select schools.

I had thought my life on the farm difficult; I had thought myself exceptional as the leading student of my school for six entire years. But I had never encountered school children who studied literally day and night, who crammed every available moment in order to beat out their fellow students! The select Tokyo high schools, such as the Tokyo First or the Tokyo Fourth, all chose their entrants from the outstanding students of the primary schools. Furthermore, of every thirty-five applicants, only one received admission.

It was clearly out of the question for a country boy such as myself, bewildered as I was with this strange and tempestuous atmosphere, even to aspire for enrollment in these famed schools. I accepted gladly a student's place in the Aoyama Gakuin, established years before by American missionaries. Not equal in reputation to the better known institutions, it was not, however, without repute.

My new home life could not have been better. My uncle, however, was overly serious and of the opinion that the less seen or heard of children, the better. This was not the case with my aunt or her son and daughter, who could not have been kinder or more friendly. Under these pleasant circumstances I began high school, burning with ambition and enthusiasm, fully determined to retain always my comfortable place as the "head of the class."

It took less than a month for these dreams to vanish. My expectations of again leading all the students were rudely shattered. It was obvious, not only to my teachers but to myself as well, that many of the other boys—never leading students in their primary schools—bested me in studies. I found this difficult to believe. Yet, they knew many things of which I was totally ignorant; despite desperate studying into all hours of the night, I was unable to learn as quickly as the others.

The first semester ended in July. My school reports, which placed me in the middle of the class, were a heavy disappointment to my uncle, and the cause of despair for me. I knew that my uncle had accepted all my expenses because he felt I was a promising child, and could maintain student leadership. There was no denying his unhappiness at my failure. Summer vacation therefore became a period of intense home study. While my classmates went on their holidays, I crammed through the summer months, determined to make up my scholastic deficiencies. But the opening of the school year in September proved the futility of my efforts; there was no improvement.

These repeated failures to gain scholastic prominence caused a feeling of sheer desperation. Not only had I become merely average in my studies; in sports, as well, I found myself outclassed. There could be no doubt that many of the boys in the school were more agile, more capable than myself.

The disillusioned state which followed was unforgivable. Instead of continuing the attempt to surpass those students who had clearly indicated their scholastic superiority. I chose friends of mediocre abilities, lost no time in asserting leadership over these other youngsters, and then went on to pick fights with the biggest of the school seniors. Hardly a day passed when I did not, through one means or the other, goad a senior into a fight, during which I thoroughly pummeled my adversary. Almost every night I returned to my uncle's home covered with bruises, taking care, however, to keep these adventures secret.

The first blow fell after the end of my first year at the Methodist school, when a letter from my teacher informed my uncle that I had been branded as a "problem pupil." As best I could, I passed off as unimportant the fights, but made no attempt to discontinue what had become a most satisfying means of proving, to myself at least, that I was "better" than the older students. The teacher's letters became more frequent and, finally, my uncle was summoned to the school for a direct verbal report of my disgraceful conduct.

I finished my second year in school almost at the bottom of the list. It was too much for my uncle. He had become increasingly angry in his lectures to me and, now, decided finally that there was no further use in continuing my stay in Tokyo.

"Saburo," were his final words, "I weary of scolding you, and shall not do so further. Perhaps I am to blame for not supervising you more closely, but, whatever the cause, I seem to have made the child of the proud Sakai family into a delinquent. You are to go back to Saga. Obviously," he added wryly, "Tokyo's life has spoiled you." I could not say one word in defense, for everything he said was true. The blame was all mine, but it did not make my return to Saga—in shame—any less bitter. I was determined to keep my embarrassment a secret, particularly from my uncle's daughter Hatsuyo, of whom I was very fond. I passed off my departure as a visit to my family in Kyushu.

That night, however, as the train glided out of the Tokyo Central Station for the 800-mile trip to Saga. I could not prevent the tears from coming to my eyes. I had failed my family. and I dreaded the return home.

CHAPTER TWO

I RETURNED as a disgrace to my family, and to the entire village as well. To complicate matters, my home suffered from increased poverty and misery. My mother and my oldest brother tilled the tiny farm from sunup to sundown. They and my three sisters were clad in tattered rags, and the small house in which I had been raised was shockingly neglected.

Every person in the village had spurred me on with good wishes when I left for Tokyo; they would have a feeling of sharing my success. Now, although I had failed them, no one would reproach me face to face or utter words of anger. Their shame was in their eyes, however, and they turned aside to avoid embarrassment for me. I did not dare to walk through the village because of this reaction of my own people; I could not endure their silent admonitions. To flee this place of disgrace became my most fervent wish.

It was then that I recalled a large poster in the Saga Railway Station calling for volunteers to enlist in the Navy. Enlistment seemed the only way out of an unhappy situation. My mother, having already suffered from my absence for several years, deplored my determination to leave once again, but she could offer no alternative.

On May 31, 1931, I enlisted as a sixteen-year-old Seaman Recruit at the Sasebo Naval Base, some fifty miles east of my home. It was the beginning of a new life of monstrously harsh discipline, of severity beyond my wildest nightmares. It was then that the strict *Hagakure* code under which I had been raised came to my aid.

It is still difficult, if not altogether impossible, for Americans and other westerners to appreciate the harshness of the discipline under which we then lived in the Navy. The petty officers would not for a moment hesitate to administer the severest beatings to recruits they felt deserving of punishment. Whenever I committed a breach of discipline or an error in training, I was dragged physically from my cot by a petty officer.

"Stand to the wall! Bend down, Recruit Sakai!" he would roar. "I am doing this to you, not because I hate you, but because I like you and want to make you a good seaman. Bend down!"

And with that he would swing a large stick of wood and with every ounce of strength he possessed would slam it against my upturned bottom. The pain was terrible, the force of the blows unremitting. There was no choice but to grit my teeth and struggle desperately not to cry out. At times I counted up to forty crashing impacts into my buttocks. Often I fainted from the pain. A lapse into unconsciousness constituted no escape however. The petty officer simply hurled a bucket of cold water over my prostrate form and bellowed for me to resume position, whereupon he continued his "discipline" until satisfied I would mend the error of my ways.

To assure that every individual recruit in the station would do his utmost to prevent his fellows from committing too many errors, whenever one of us received a beating, each of the fifty other recruits in the outfit was made to bend down and receive one vicious blow. After such treatment it was impossible to lie on our backs on our cots. Furthermore, we were never allowed the indulgence of even a single satisfying groan in our misery. Let one single man moan in pain or anguish because of his "paternalistic discipline," and to a man every recruit in the outfit would be kicked or dragged from his cot to receive the full course.

Obviously, such treatment engendered no fondness for our petty officers, who were absolute tyrants in their own right. The majority were in their thirties and seemed destined to remain in the rank of petty officers throughout their careers. Their major obsession was to terrorize the new recruits—in this case, ourselves. We regarded these men as sadistic brutes of the worst sort. Within six months the incredibly severe training had made human cattle of every one of us. We never dared to question orders, to doubt authority, to do anything but immediately carry out all the commands of our superiors. We were automatons who obeyed without thinking.

Recruit training melted into a blur of drilling, studying, training, the vicious swings of the sticks and the always painful buttocks, the bruised and blackened skin, the wincing upon sitting down.

When I completed the recruit training course. I was no longer the ambitious and zealous youth who had several years previously left his small farm village to conquer the Tokyo school system. My scholastic failures, the family disgrace, and the recruit discipline all combined effectively to humble me. I recognized the futility of questioning official authority; my egotism had been knocked out of me. But never, while I was in training or later, has my deep-rooted anger at the brutality of the petty officers abated.

Upon completion of land training, I was assigned as an apprentice seaman to the battleship *Kirishima*. Life at sea proved a shock to me; I had thought that, with my initial training behind me, the harsh treatment of my immediate superiors would abate. But it did not; if anything, it was worse than before. All this time I had doggedly maintained my desire to get ahead, to better myself, to rise above the lowly position of a volunteer seaman. I had no more than an hour of free time each day, but into this period of grace I crammed textbook study. My goal was enrollment at a Navy special training school. Only thus could a volunteer attain the special skills and techniques so indispensable to promotion.

In 1935 I passed successfully the competitive entrance examinations for the Navy Gunners School. Six months later I had received a promotion to Seaman, and was assigned to sea duty again, this time to the battleship *Haruna,* where I worked in one of the main 16-inch gun turrets. Things were improving; after several months aboard the *Haruna* I was a noncommissioned officer with the rank of Petty Officer, Third Class.

CHAPTER THREE

THE Imperial Japanese Services were divided into two armed forces, the Army and Navy. Both commands operated their individual air fleets; an independent air force was never even considered before or during World War II. Neither were there Marines, in the sense that the United States enjoys an autonomous Marine Corps. Picked elements of the Army and Navy were trained for amphibious operations and performed the functions of the Marine units of foreign powers.

In the mid-thirties all naval fliers received their training at the Navy Fliers School at Tsuchiura, fifty miles northeast of Tokyo. Three classes of students attended the school—ensigns graduated from the Naval Academy at Eta Jima in Western Japan, noncommissioned officers already in service, and boys in their teens who were willing to begin their naval careers as student pilots.

After Japan engaged in all-out war with the United States, the Navy expanded its pilot-training facilities in a desperate attempt to produce combat pilots almost on a production-line basis. In 1937, however, this mass-training concept was wholly unknown. Pilot training was a highly select affair, and only the most qualified candidates in the entire nation could hope even to be considered. Tsuchiura accepted only a fraction of its applicants; in 1937, the year I applied, only seventy men were selected for the pilot class out of more than 1,500 hopefuls.

My jubilation knew no bounds when I discovered my name on the list of the seventy noncommissioned officers accepted for training. There was grim satisfaction in my acceptance, for entry to Tsuchiura would wipe out the disgrace of my failure at the Tokyo school. It would return honor to my family and my village, and would vindicate the faith which had been placed in me.

My pleasure in returning to my uncle's home in Tokyo on my first holiday leave can well be imagined. No longer was I the frustrated and disobedient teenager afraid to face squarely my scholastic and social problems. I was a young man of twenty, fairly bursting with pride, immaculate in new naval flier's uniform, bedecked with seven shining buttons, and willing—most willing!—to accept happily the congratulations of my uncle's family. The sight of my cousin Hatsuyo startled me. The young schoolgirl had disappeared, and in her place was an exceptionally attractive high-school student, fifteen years old. Hatsuyo greeted me with more than family warmth.

I had a long discussion with my uncle, who had always displayed such a strong interest in my life, and I was gratified to notice his pleasure at the outcome of my seaman apprenticeship, of studying on my own time, of rising through the ranks. All his pride had returned, no small thing for me after I had failed him so badly in the past. My visit to his home, with the family and Hatsuyo, was one of the most pleasant interludes in many years. After dinner we spent the evening in the sitting room where, after considerable prompting from her family, Hatsuyo honored me with a piano recital.

Hatsuyo was by no means a piano virtuoso, for she had begun her lessons only three years previously. However, I was not a music critic, and her playing seemed beautiful to me. The slow movements of Mozart, my first visit to a home in so many long months, the cordiality of Hatsuyo's greeting were incredibly pleasant. Here for the first time in a seeming eternity was beauty and affection and comfort in place of the harsh brutality of naval training. The mood was almost overwhelming. The visit, however, was a brief one, and I soon returned to the school.

The Tsuchiura training facilities were located by a large lake, and bordered an airfield with two runways of 3,000 and 2,200 yards. Hundreds of airplanes could be stored at one time within the huge hangars, and there was always the bustle of activity at the base.

Apparently I was never to cease being surprised at what awaited me in each new naval training program. Hardly had I arrived at the new school than I discovered that my prior experiences with naval discipline were minor ones. I was amazed to realize that the disciplinary customs of the Sasebo Naval Base were pleasant interludes in comparison with those of Tsuchiura. Even the Navy Gunners School was hardly more than a kindergarten alongside the Fliers School.

"A fighter pilot must be aggressive and tenacious. Always." This was our initial greeting from the athletic instructor who called together our first wrestling class. "Here at Tsuchiura we are going to instill those characteristics into you, or else you will never become a Navy pilot." He lost no time in showing us his ideas of how we were to become indoctrinated with constant aggressiveness! The instructor at random selected two students from the group and ordered them to wrestle. The victor of this clash was then allowed to leave the wrestling mat.

His opponent who had lost the important match had no such luck. He remained on the mat, prepared to take on another pilot trainee. So long as he continued to lose, he remained on that mat, tiring with every bout, slammed about heavily and often sustaining injuries. If necessary, he was forced to wrestle every one of the other sixty-nine students in his class. If, at the end of sixty-nine consecutive wrestling bouts, he was still able to resume standing, he was considered fit—but for only one more day. The following day he again took on the first wrestling opponent and continued until he either emerged a victor or was expelled from the school.

With every pilot trainee determined not to be expelled from the fliers course, the wrestling matches were scenes of fierce competition. Often students were knocked unconscious. This, however, did not excuse them from what was considered an absolute training necessity. They were revived with buckets of water or other means and sent back to the mat.

Following a month's basic ground training, we began our primary flying lessons. Flight lessons were held in the morning, classroom and other courses in the afternoon. Following dinner, we had two hours in which to study our subjects until the lights were turned out.

As the months wore on, our numbers diminished steadily. The training course demanded perfection from the students, and a trainee could be dismissed for even the slightest infraction of rules. Since the naval pilots were considered the elite of the entire Navy, of all the armed forces, there was no room for error. Before our ten-month course was completed, forty-five out of the original seventy students had been expelled from the school. The instructors did not follow the violent physical-discipline system of my former training installations, but their authority to dismiss from the school any student, for any reason, was feared far more than any mere savage beating.

The rigidity of this weeding-out process was forcibly brought home to us on the very eve of our graduation; on that same day, one of the remaining students was expelled. A shore patrol discovered him entering an off-limits bar in the town of Tsuchiura to celebrate his "graduation." He was premature in more respects than one. Upon his return to the billet he was ordered to report at once to his faculty board. By way of apology the student knelt on the floor before his officers, but to no avail.

The faculty board found him guilty of two unpardonable sins. The first, every pilot knew. That was that a combat pilot shall never, for any reason, drink alcoholic beverages the evening before he flies. As part of the graduation exercises, we were to pass over the field in formation flight the next day. The second of the two crimes was more commonplace, but equally serious. No member of the Navy was ever to disgrace his service by entering any establishment marked "off limits."

The physical training courses at Tsuchiura were among the severest in Japan. One of the more unpleasant of the obstacle courses was a high iron pole which we were required to climb. At the top of the pole, we were to suspend ourselves by one hand only. Any cadet who failed to support his weight for less than ten minutes received a swift kick in the rear and was sent scurrying up the pole again. At the end of the course, those students who had avoided expulsion were able to hang by one arm for as long as fifteen to twenty minutes.

Every enlisted man in the Imperial Navy was required to be able to swim. There were a good number of students who came from the mountain regions and had never done any swimming at all. The training solution was simple. The cadets were trussed up with rope around their waists and tossed into the ocean, where they swam—or sank. Today, thirty-nine years old and with pieces of shrapnel still in my body, I can swim fifty meters (162 feet) in thirty-four seconds. At the Fliers School, swimming that distance in less than thirty seconds was commonplace.

Every student was required to swim underwater for at least fifty meters, and to remain below the surface for at least ninety seconds. The average man can, with effort, hold his breath for forty or fifty seconds, but this is considered inadequate for a Japanese pilot. My own record is two minutes and thirty seconds below the surface.

We went through hundreds of diving lessons to improve our sense of balance, and to aid us later when we would be putting fighter planes through all sorts of aerobatic gyrations. There was special reason to pay strict attention to the diving lessons, for once the instructors felt we had received enough assistance from the boards, we were ordered to dive from a high tower to the hard ground! During the drop we somersaulted two or three times in the air, and landed on our feet. Naturally, there were errors—with disastrous results.

Acrobatics formed an important part of our athletic instruction, and every requirement laid down by the instructors was fulfilled—or the student was expelled. Walking on our hands was considered merely a primer. We also had to balance ourselves on our heads, at first for five minutes, then ten, until finally many of the students could maintain position for fifteen minutes or more. Eventually I was able to balance on my head for more than twenty minutes, during which time my fellow trainees would light cigarettes for me and place them between my lips.

Naturally, such circus antics were not the only physical requirements of our training. But they did permit us to develop an amazing sense of balance and muscular coordination, traits which were to have lifesaving value in later years.

Every student at Tsuchiura was gifted with extraordinary eyesight; this was, of course, a minimum entry requirement. Every passing moment we spent in developing our peripheral vision, in learning how to recognize distant objects with snap glances—in short, in developing the techniques which would give us advantages over opposing fighter pilots.

One of our favorite tricks was to try and discover the brighter stars during daylight hours. This is no mean feat, and without above-average eyes it is virtually impossible to accomplish. However, our instructors constantly impressed us with the fact that a fighter plane seen from a distance of several thousand yards often is no easier to identify than a star in daylight. And the pilot who first discovers his enemy and maneuvers into the most advantageous attack position can gain an invincible superiority. Gradually, and with much more practice, we became quite adept at our star-hunting. Then we went further. When we had sighted and fixed the position of a particular star, we jerked our eyes away ninety degrees, and snapped back again to see if we could locate the star immediately. Of such things are fighter pilots made.

I personally cannot too highly commend this particular activity, inane as it may seem to those unfamiliar with the split-second, life-or-death movements of aerial warfare. I know that during my 200 air engagements with enemy planes, except for two minor errors I was never caught in a surprise attack by enemy fighters, nor did I ever lose any of my wingmen to hostile pilots.

In all our spare moments during our training at Tsuchiura we sought constantly to find methods by which we could shorten our reaction time and improve our certainty of movement. A favorite trick of ours was to snatch a fly on the wing within our fists. We must have looked silly, pawing at the air with our hands, but after several months a fly which flew before our faces was almost certain to end up in our hands. The ability to make sudden and exact movements is indispensable within the cramped confines of a fighter-plane cockpit.

These improvements in reaction time came to our aid in a totally unexpected way. Four of us were racing in a car at sixty miles an hour along a narrow road when the driver lost control of the car and hurtled over the edge of an embankment. The four of us, to a man, snapped open the car doors and literally flew from the vehicle. There were some scrapes and bruises, but not a single major injury among us, although the car was thoroughly demolished.

CHAPTER FOUR

THE twenty-five students of the Thirty-eighth Noncommissioned Officers Class, including myself, graduated near the end of 1937. I was selected as the outstanding student pilot of the year, to receive as an award the Emperor's silver watch.

Our group of twenty-five men was all which remained of seventy students, hand-picked out of 1,500 applicants. We had undergone intensive and often grueling training. However, before we were to be committed to action in China, where the war was launched in July of 1937, we were to receive additional in-service training.

Despite our excellent and arduous instruction, several men from my group were later killed by enemy pilots before gaining even a single victory. Even I, with unusual flying aptitude, would have met death during my first air combat if my opponent had been even slightly more aggressive in his maneuvers. There can be no doubt that I faltered clumsily through my first dogfight, and nothing less than the support of my fellow pilots and a lack of skill on the part of my enemy saved my life.

To me a dogfight has always been a difficult, grueling task, with almost unbearable tension. Even after my first combats were behind me and I had several enemy planes to my credit, I never emerged from the wild aerial melees without being soaked in perspiration. There was *always* the chance of committing that one slight error which meant flaming death. Through all the aerial maneuvers, the vertical turns, stalling turns, spins, half rolls, rolls, slow rolls, spirals, loops, Immelmanns, dives, zooms, falling leafs—through all these and more, one slight error could bring extinction. Of my twenty-five-man class, eventually I was the only man left alive. The long and difficult air war, so much to our advantage in the early days, degenerated into a vicious nightmare in which we struggled hopelessly against a rising enemy tide impossible to overcome.

During the 1930's, the Japanese Navy trained approximately 100 fliers every year. The rigid screening and expulsion practices reduced the many hundreds of qualified students to the ridiculously low total of 100 or fewer graduated pilots. Had the Navy received additional funds for its training program and had it eased its intolerant attitude toward selecting pilot trainees, I believe our path during World War II would have been eased considerably. Doubtless the outcome would have been unaltered, but the brutal beating suffered by our air units during the last two years of war might have been somewhat alleviated. Only after the war began in the Pacific, and the attrition of experienced pilots emphasized the alarming need for an increased flow of replacements, did the Navy abandon its unreasonable training policies. By then it was too late. The caliber of the pilots produced during the wartime years was at best questionable. I know that the forty-five pilots expelled from my own student class at Tsuchiura were superior to those men who completed wartime training.

Our graduation was followed with assignment to various air squadrons for service training. My orders sent me to Oita and Omura Naval Air Bases in Northern Kyushu. Both installations stressed flying from land fields as well as from aircraft carriers. My introduction to the skill of the carrier pilots left me fairly quaking. Their aerobatics were astonishing, and were carried out with the most consummate skill. I doubted my own ability, even after years of training, to duplicate their superb airmanship.

Carrier landings proved particularly difficult for me to master. A month's hard grind of approaches and touchdowns, approaches and touchdowns, over and over again, dispelled my troubles. Strangely enough, after this training I never took off or landed on a carrier in combat. All my combat flying was done from land installations.

Following three months of intensive carrier and land training, I received orders to transfer to the Kaohsiung Air Base on Formosa Island, then Japanese territory. The tempo of naval life had changed. The China War was already raging over sprawling battlefronts, and there was a sudden urgent need for more fighter pilots, even green pilots such as myself.

From Formosa I moved up to Kiukiang in Southeastern China, and in May of 1938 I tasted my first combat . . . with hardly an auspicious start. The Kiukiang Wing commander disdained the use of green pilots in regular air sorties, feeling that their inexperience would mark them clearly to the veteran pilots flying for the Chinese. So for several days I flew low-level missions in support of Army operations. The sorties were anything but dangerous; the Japanese Army was smashing aside all enemy opposition on the ground, and there was little opposition in the air. As the weeks passed I chafed at my restriction to support flights only. I was zealous and ambitious, proud of my rank as a Naval Aviation Pilot, Second Class, and determined to storm into enemy aircraft with great valor. On May 21 I was overjoyed to find my name among the fifteen fighter pilots selected to fly over Hankow on a regular patrol the following day. Hankow promised action, since it was the main air base of Nationalist China at the time.

In 1938 the Zero fighter plane, which I later came to know so well, was not yet available for combat use. We flew the Mitsubishi Type 96 fighter plane, later given the Allied code-name identification of Claude. These were slow and restricted in range. The landing gear was fixed, and we flew with open cockpits.

Our fifteen fighters left Kiukiang early on the morning of the twenty-second, adopting a formation of five V's as we climbed. Visibility was excellent. The ninety-minute flight from our air base northwest to Hankow was like a leisurely training cruise. No interceptors arose to attack our formation, and not a single antiaircraft gun disputed the air with us. It seemed incredible that a war raged below.

From 10,000 feet the Hankow airfield was remarkably deceptive. Bright green grass stood out clearly under the morning sun, and the enemy's major air base in the area looked for all the world like a sprawling, well-tended golf course. But fighter planes do not use such sporting facilities, and those three dots I saw racing over the ground, rising toward our own planes, were enemy fighters.

Then suddenly they were at our altitude, big, black, and powerful. Without warning—to my astonished mind, at least one of the enemy planes whipped out of his formation and bored in with alarming speed at my own fighter. Abruptly all my careful plans of what I would do in my first combat evaporated. I felt my over-taut muscles twitch nervously and, although it is unpleasant to relate this now, I am certain

I trembled with excitement and the shock of the other plane using me for his target!

I have often believed that I acted stupidly during those crucial moments, and the reader may well share this opinion. I must emphasize, however, that our mental reactions at 10,000 feet, after some ninety minutes at this height without oxygen, were hardly as reliable as when we were on the ground. The air is thin, with correspondingly less oxygen reaching the brain. The engine noise in the open cockpit is deafening, as is the streaming cold wind racing past the glass windshield. And there is no such thing as relaxing at the controls; I was turning my head, trying frantically to look in all directions to avoid being caught unawares, working the control stick, the rudder pedals, the throttle, and other controls and instruments. In short, I was completely confused!

The habits instilled during my training came to my aid. And the one instruction which overrode all others for the fledgling in combat was: "Always stick to the tail of the lead fighter in your V formation." In a blur of hand movements I tightened the straps on my oxygen mask (with only two hours' oxygen. supply, we used the masks only in combat or during flight above 10,000 feet) and shoved the throttle as far forward as it would go. The engine responded with a roar and the little fighter leaped ahead. All about me fuel cells tumbled wildly through the air as the other Japanese pilots jerked the cockpit toggles. I had completely forgotten to jettison the highly explosive tank below my fuselage and my hand trembled as I reached out to hit the lever. Mine was the last to drop free.

By now I was completely upset. I had done everything in a slipshod fashion, had ignored almost all the basic rules of aerial combat. I failed to see anything going on to the sides or behind me. I couldn't see a single enemy plane and had not the slightest idea whether or not I was being shot at. All I saw was the tail of my leader's plane; in desperation I swung after his fighter, my plane looking for all the world as if it were tied to the other.

When finally I had swung into the proper wingman position, behind and to the side of the lead fighter, I regained my senses and no longer fumbled around clumsily in the cockpit. Taking a deep breath, I chanced a quick look to the left. None too soon! Two sleek enemy fighters raced in against my plane. They were Russian-made E-16s, with retractable landing gear. Higher powered than our own Claude fighters, the E-16s were also faster and more maneuverable.

Again I faltered—and in that second I was given a new lease on life. My hands hesitated in the air; I actually didn't know what to do next. Instead of snapping away to the side or clawing for altitude, I simply continued flying as before. By all the rules of air war I should have met my end at that moment. But,—unexpectedly, when they had me dead in their sights, the two Russian fighters rolled over and away! For the life of me I could not understand this miraculous turn of fortune.

The solution was simple enough. Anticipating that I might fumble with my controls in my first combat—as I did!—the flight leader had assigned one of the veteran pilots to cover my plane from behind. It was his fighter, whipping about in a tight turn and plunging at the enemy planes, which caused them to break off their attack.

And still I was incapable of any original action. I came out of a death trap, flying blindly, not even realizing that the abrupt change of position had placed my fighter 450 yards to the rear of one of the fleeing Russian planes. I simply sat in my cockpit, trying to reason with myself, trying to do *something*. At last I broke out of my stupor and reached forward.

I had the Russian fighter dead in my sights, and squeezed the gun trigger. Nothing happened. I jerked the trigger, back and forth, cursing the two jammed machine guns until, with acute embarrassment, I noticed that I had failed to complete arming the guns before engaging with the enemy planes.

The petty officer flying the fighter to my left finally gave up in despair when he saw me fumbling in the cockpit and forged ahead, firing at the escaping enemy fighter. The burst didn't take the E-16, which had steadily been veering to the right, fortunately for me, only 200 yards in front of my own guns. This time I was ready and jammed down on the trigger. The shells arced out but were wasted. I had lost another golden opportunity.

This time, I swore I would shoot down the Russian plane if I had to close in and ram. Under full throttle I narrowed the distance between the two fighters; the enemy pilot rolled, looped, and spiraled in violent maneuvers, successfully evading every burst I fired at him. His sharp turns and attempts to catch me in his own sights were surprisingly poor flying; his own tracers scattered wildly through the air. Actually, the enemy never had a chance. I was unaware of it, but several of the other Claudes circled high over our individual dogfight, prepared at a moment's notice to plunge down upon the Russian fighter should I be caught in a dangerous situation.

This the enemy knew, and concentrated his attention primarily on escape, rather than on my destruction. It was his undoing. I came out of a tight loop to find the E-16 only 150 yards ahead of me and poured bullets into the fighter's engine. The next moment oily black smoke gushed from the nose and the plane plunged earthward. Not until the enemy fighter erupted into mushrooming wreckage far below did I realize I had exhausted all my ammunition, something else I had been warned not to do. Every fighter pilot did his utmost to retain some ammunition for his return flight, in the event he was caught by patrolling enemy fighters.

I looked frantically about me, searching for the other Mitsubishis, and felt my heart drop when I discovered myself to be entirely alone in the air. I had strayed from the group. My victory was little more than a hollow mockery, for it had been given me on a silver platter by my wingmates, the same men I had lost in pursuing the Russian plane. My humiliation at my own absurd actions virtually choked me and I was close to actually bursting into tears. And that is exactly what I did do when, after looking around again, I saw fourteen Claudes circling slowly in formation, waiting patiently for me to gain my bearings and to join them. I think that for five minutes I must have cried with shame.

At Kiukiang again, I climbed exhausted from my cockpit. My flight commander stormed up to my plane in a rage, his face flushed from his anger. "Sakai! Of all the..." he spluttered. "You are a dammed fool, Sakai! It is a miracle you are alive at all! I have never seen such clumsy or ridiculous flying in all my entire life! You ..." He couldn't go on. I stared down at the ground, sorry and penitent, indeed. I hoped, I fairly prayed, he would lose his temper and in his rage kick and beat me. But he was too angry for physical violence.

The captain did the worst thing possible. He turned his back on me and walked away.

CHAPTER FIVE

TO this day we cannot prove the nationality of the enemy fliers who piloted China's Russian-made fighters. There was good reason to believe that Russian "volunteers" accompanied the Soviet aircraft across the border, but we failed ever to recover from the wreckage of the enemy planes the body of a Russian pilot.

Our Navy had strong evidence that a "Foreign Legion" of pilots manned China's air force. These men from all nations flew a mixed conglomeration of fighter-plane types, for we met in the air not only Russian planes but those of American, British, German, and other manufacture as well. Sometimes, of course, Chinese nationals were flying these aircraft.

Proof positive that an American pilot was flying an American-built fighter was established when the airplane crashed near Shanghai. Our troops rushed quickly to the site of the wreck and returned with the pilot's body; his papers identified him conclusively as American.

My own victory over the Soviet fighter soon overcame the dejection caused by my poor combat performance. The day following the flight I lost no time in painting a blue star on the fuselage of the Claude fighter, for a total of six stars on the airplane. The Japanese pilots, especially enlisted men as myself, did not fly the same plane on each mission. There were not enough fighters to go around, and we took whatever ships were available when it was our time to fly. More than once this arrangement came to the aid of an inexperienced pilot; enemy fliers, upon sighting the dozen or more blue stars on the fuselage, wanted no part of a plane with a double or triple ace at the controls—so they thought!

The conflict in China was an incredible war. Among our forces it was never referred to as a "war," but rather as the Sino-Japanese Incident. I suppose the same situation existed when America threw so much military strength into Korea; since the American Congress had not officially declared war, it was a "police action." Many years prior to this modern straggle, our government felt precisely the same way. We had not actually declared war; therefore, it was an "incident."

As soon as it was feasible, we instituted a puppet government under Wang Ching-wei, a prominent Chinese who had split openly with Generalissimo Chiang Kai-shek's Kuomintang, or Nationalist Party. The most startling aspect of the conflict, however, was the savage internal straggle between Chiang's forces and those of the Communist Chinese. At every opportunity the latter would strike at Nationalist forces when they were retreating before our own troops.

Opposing the Japanese land and air forces in China were vast enemy armies of millions of men, hopelessly outnumbering our own troops. This disparity in numbers, however, rarely worked to the Chinese advantage, for their troops were poorly trained and ill equipped. Time after time hordes of enemy troops would advance against our well-armed forces, only to be thrown back with shattering losses. Even the flood of Allied assistance to China, in the form of supplies rushed through Burma, Mongolia, and Sinkiang, failed to offset our qualitative superiority. These supplies helped the enemy, of course, especially in permitting Chiang to effect an orderly withdrawal to Chungking, but never allowed him to mount any worthwhile offensive against us. It was strictly a one-sided war until the Japanese surrender to the Allies in August of 1945.

This does not mean, however, that Japan ever conquered—or attempted to conquer—the vast Chinese population, or to occupy its tremendous land area. This would have been absolutely impossible. Instead, our troops occupied key walled towns at strategic areas, cutting enemy communications, and then exacted tolls and taxes from the millions of Chinese peasants within the authority of the occupying Japanese forces.

But outside the protection of these major walled towns violent death awaited all but the most powerful Japanese formations. Chiang's guerrillas, as well as those of the Chinese Communists, waited in savage ambush where they would do their utmost to annihilate those troops which fell into their hands. It also was obvious to our officers that those Chinese officials within the occupied cities, despite their fawning and seeming cooperation, remained in constant touch with agents of the guerrilla bands roaming the open countryside and the mountains. And, in many instances, to facilitate the problems of occupying enemy cities, such contacts were maintained with the direct acquiescence of the Japanese commanders!

It was, indeed, a strange war.

Many times I flew land-support missions and was astonished at the sights below me. I saw Chinese farmers tilling their farms, paying no attention to pitched hand-to-hand battles or blazing firefights between Chinese and Japanese troops less than a mile away. On several occasions I flew low over the streets of walled towns that were surrounded and under fierce bombardment by our artillery. On those streets rows of stores were operating under "business as usual" conditions, although the blood of the defending Chinese garrison stained the streets red.

For the Japanese air units, however, China duty was by no means hard or unpleasant. It was strictly an air war waged in our favor. Sixteen months after my arrival at Kiukiang, our ground forces stabbed deeply into enemy territory and secured for us the more elaborate airfield installations at Hankow. The entire unit moved up the line.

By now the newspapers in Japan had reported the details of my first victory over an enemy fighter. A letter arrived from my mother, and the pride in her words was balm, indeed. Of almost equal interest was a letter from Hatsuyo Hirokawa, my uncle's daughter, now sixteen years old. She wrote: "Recently my father was appointed the postmaster here in Tokushima, Shikoku. I am now studying in the Tokushima Girls' High School, and you can imagine that it is a big change from Tokyo. Your letter thrilled me. It brought great pleasure to all my classmates. Every day, we pore through the newspapers in search of more news about you. We want to be sure that we do not overlook any news about your air victories in China.

"Incidentally, Saburo, I wish to introduce to you my closest friend here in Tokushima, Mikiko Niori. Mikiko is the most beautiful girl in my class, and she is also the brightest. Her father is a professor in Kobe College. Of all my classmates to whom I showed your letter, she was the most excited, and she has begged me to introduce her to you."

The letter included a picture of Hatsuyo and Mikiko together, and also a letter from this girl I had never met. She was certainly as pretty as Hatsuyo claimed, and it was interesting to read her charming description of her town, and of her family.

The letters from home were a tremendous boon to my morale, and I went about my work singing. I remember the day with absolute clarity—October 3, 1939. I had just finished reading my mail, and was servicing the machine guns of my fighter plane. Everyone at the field was relaxed; what was there to worry about? We had whipped the Chinese and international pilots in almost every combat.

Abruptly the silence was broken by frenzied shouts from the control tower. In the next instant, without any further warning, the world erupted into a series of shattering roars. The earth heaved and shook, and blast waves smashed at our startled ears. Someone bellowed—unnecessarily—*"Air Raid!"* and then the sirens shrieked a useless, belated warning.

There was no time to try and run for the shelters. The blasting crescendo of exploding bombs was a constant thunder now; smoke rose over the field and I heard the shrill scream of bomb fragments cutting through the air. Several other pilots ran frantically with me from the machine shop for shelter. I crouched low to escape the whistling pieces of steel, and dove headlong onto the ground between two big water tanks. I was none too soon. A nearby machine-gun storage shed went up in a roaring blast of fire and smoke, and then a stick of bombs walked across the field, hammering at our ears, sending up great spouts of smoke and earth.

A second's delay in diving for the ground would have meant my end. The nearby series of bomb explosions suddenly ended and I lifted my head to see what had happened. Above the steady *crump!* of bombs exploding all across the field I heard anguished cries and groans. The men lying all about me had been badly wounded, and I started to crawl toward the nearest pilot when I gasped from a knife-like pain in my thighs and buttocks. I reached down with my hand and felt the blood seeping through my trousers. The pain was bad, but, fortunately, the wounds were not deep.

And then I lost my head. I was on my feet and running again, but this time I ran back toward the airstrip, glancing up at the sky as I moved down the runway. Overhead I saw twelve bombers in formation, very high, wheeling about in a wide turn at a height of at least 20,000 feet. They were Russian SB twin-engined planes, the main bombers of the Chinese Air Force. And there was no denying the incredible effectiveness of their sudden surprise attack. We had been caught totally unprepared.

Not a single man had any warning until the bombs were actually released from the Russian planes and shrieking in their descent. What I saw on the airfield itself was a shock.

The majority of the 200 Navy and Army bombers and fighters parked wing to wing on the long runways were burning. Great sheets of flame burst outward from the exploding fuel tanks, sending billowing clouds of smoke into the air. Those planes still safe from the flames were leaking gasoline from shrapnel holes in their fuselages. The flames traveled from one plane to the other, fed upon the dripping gasoline, and, one by one, long rows of bombers and fighters mushroomed into blinding crimson. Bombers were exploding like firecrackers, and the fighters flared like matchboxes.

I ran around the burning planes as if I were crazed, seeking desperately just one undamaged fighter. Miraculously, a few Claudes in a separate group had escaped the carnage, and I clambered into the cockpit of one plane, started the engine, and without waiting for it to warm up gunned the fighter down the runway.

The bombers were gaining height gradually as my faster fighter steadily overtook their formation. I held the throttle against the firewall, coaxing every bit of speed from the protesting Mitsubishi. And, twenty minutes after take-off, I was almost up to the enemy planes, climbing steadily so that I could open fire into the unprotected bellies of the bombers.

I paid little attention to the fact that I was the only fighter plane in the air. It was obvious to me that the lightly armed Claude could not by itself prove a serious threat to the twelve bombers. Below me was the city of Ichang on the Yangtze River, still held by defending Chinese troops. Being shot down here, even if I escaped death in a crash, meant certain and horrible death at the hands of Chiang's men. But there was no delaying the attack. This was why I had been raised in the Samurai tradition, and there was no thought other than to wreak all the damage I could.

I closed in from behind and below the trailing bomber of the formation, not without notice by the enemy, as the flickering guns in the tail proved. The enemy gunner failed to hit the Claude and I pressed as close as possible to the plane, concentrating my fire against the left engine. As I passed by and climbed above the bomber I noticed smoke trailing from the engine I had worked over. The bomber dropped out of formation and began losing altitude as I swung into a diving turn to finish off the cripple. But I never followed the advantage. Even as I pushed the stick forward to go into a shallow dive, I remembered that Ichang was at least 150 miles west of Hankow. Any additional flight in pursuing the bomber meant that I would not have enough fuel to return to base and would mean a forced landing in enemy territory.

There is a difference between risking battle against great odds and in throwing away a life and an airplane. To continue the attack would be suicide, and there was no call for drastic action of that sort. I turned for home. Whether or not the Russian bomber reached its own field successfully I do not know, of course, but at the worst it would have crashed among friendly troops.

Back at Hankow, the terrible destruction wrought by only twelve enemy planes was incredible. Almost all of our planes had been destroyed or wrecked. The commander of the base lost his left arm, and several of his lieutenants, as well as pilots and maintenance crews, were killed or maimed.

I had forgotten my own wounds; the heat of the pursuit and my battle excitement had overcome the pain temporarily. I walked a few feet from my airplane and collapsed on the runway.

The wounds healed slowly. A week later, while I was still in the hospital, I received a letter from Hatsuyo, with personal news no less devastating than the airfield attack.

"I am very, very sorry that I must write this letter," Hatsuyo wrote, "with all its painful news to you. My dearest friend, Mikiko, died suddenly in a traffic accident on October third. I am at a loss as to what to say. I am bewildered and hurt. I was almost angry at God. Why, why did such a wonderful person as Mikiko have to die at sixteen, and through no fault of her own! I hate myself that I must bring this news to you, one of our fighter pilots who is in combat. But there is no one else who can tell you...."

Hatsuyo's letter contained a sealed note from Mikiko's mother, who wrote:

"Poor Mikiko has been talking about you with Hatsuyo-san and our family every day, and she has been looking forward most anxiously to your reply to the letter she forwarded through Hatsuyo-san. But your own wonderful letter did not arrive here until the day of Mikiko's funeral. Oh, how happy I would have been to have had her read your letter before her death! She was a wonderful daughter, so good-natured, so bright, so angelic!

"Maybe that is why she has been taken by the Almighty so early. I do not know. I have been crying for days. I know that you would have wanted to know that your letter was placed in her bier and accompanied her to Heaven. Please accept my husband's and also my deepest thanks for having written to her. We now earnestly pray to God that Mikiko's spirit will protect you in the skies from enemy bullets."

I did not know what to think, i was dazed and helpless. Several hours later, after lying on my cot and staring at the ceiling, I wrote a long letter to Mikiko's mother to express my sympathy at her loss. In this letter I enclosed a token sum of money for her family to make some offering at her tomb, in accordance with ancestral tradition.

For several days I was terribly homesick, yearning for the sight of my family, for my mother and my brothers and sisters.

I did not have to wait long before I would again see Japan. Two days later I received rotation orders, directing me to report to the Omura Wing, the air base nearest to my home village. My departure was hardly jubilant. The personnel captain, stony-faced, warned me, "Because of security, you will not tell anybody back in Japan about the disaster. Do you understand?"

"Yes, sir. Because of security I will not tell anybody back in Japan about the disaster," I intoned. Then I saluted and walked out to the field to board the transport plane which would take me home.

CHAPTER SIX

I RETURNED to the Omura base in a dark mood. The devastating attack on the airfield, with the loss of many close friends, Mikiko's death, and my own wounds all contributed to a general despondency. Furthermore, despite the proximity of the airbase to my home, I would not be allowed to visit my family until my wounds were completely healed.

I viewed with misgivings my first meeting with the Personnel Commander at Omura. When I was assigned here the previous year, his contempt for and unfriendliness toward all trainees was painfully apparent, and this distaste embraced me as well. To my surprise, the commander grinned broadly at me when I snapped rigidly to attention before his desk. For a few moments he stared at me, surveying my uniform, my face, my eyes, which stared directly ahead. He actually beamed at me! I did not know it, but the news of my solo attack against the twelve Russian bombers, despite the negative results, had preceded my return to Japan. No longer was I the contemptible trainee to be shunted around; the commander informed me that I would be able to rest easily at Omura, that for the time being I was not even to be given any specific assignments. This turn of events was astonishing; enlisted men were not entitled to such treatment.

At the mess hall I realized that my flights in China, with my air victory and the attack against the Russian bombers added for zest, had made me a minor hero to the pilot trainees at the base. It was a wonderful and strange feeling to have these men crowd around me, eager to hear about the air war on the Asian mainland.

For a week I relaxed, sleeping as much as I desired, and watching the students on their training flights. Then I received a letter from a girl whose name I failed to recognize, Fujiko Niori. She wrote:

"I am the sister of Mikiko, and I wish to take this opportunity to thank you with all my heart for your letter to my mother and also for your kind words and attention to my younger sister. Your letter to my family was a ray of sunshine when we were all despondent over Mikiko's death. I am not ashamed to tell you that we all cried that Mikiko should be lost to us when she was the happiest.

"I must confess that, until your letter arrived, I held the illusion that all fighter pilots were interested only in combat, and that they lacked warmth and emotion. Your letter has, of course, changed that opinion. If it is to be permitted, I wish sincerely to become your friend, especially on behalf of my sister. My happiness will be complete if you will answer this letter."

In the envelope was a portrait of Fujiko. If anything, the eighteen-year-old girl was even prettier than her sister.

I replied immediately, telling her that I had sustained slight wounds in China, and was now back in Japan to complete my recovery. I told her that the doctors felt I would soon be able to fly again and that, once healed, I hoped I would be able to see her soon afterward.

Her second letter was in my hands in a matter of days. Fujiko wrote at length of her life and the daily events in her town of Tokushima on Shikoku Island. For the next month, with little to do at the Omura air base, I spent much of my time in writing letters to Fujiko, and reading hers several times over. Her correspondence was extremely well written, and I wondered whether or not her initial letter drafts had been edited by her mother, a not uncommon practice!

In November of 1939 I received my first overnight leave in a year, in order to visit my mother and family. With my wounds completely healed, I was anxious to make the trip home. The train ride would be barely more than an hour. At home, I knew, the rice harvesting was over. The paddies and fields would be desolate as winter approached, but this was of little consequence to me. After the drab Chinese mainland, my home province would appear to be nothing less than a garden and, as the train rolled toward the village, I watched the beautiful Kyushu mountains towering into the sky, rich and green with the thick forests, the streams sparkling in the last afternoon sunlight.

I could not believe my eyes as I walked down the road to my old, small house. A big crowd milled about in the yard and, spying me in the road, surged out in a throng to shout their greetings. I was astonished to see my mother accompanied by no less a dignitary than the Village Master! Not only was this esteemed gentleman on hand to welcome me personally, but almost every village official crowded about to extend his hands in warm welcome.

The Village Master in a loud voice proclaimed: "Welcome home, Saburo, the hero of our modest village!" I actually blushed. I had never dreamed that such a thing could happen! I stuttered and tried to tell the Village Master that I was anything but a hero, just a petty officer who had shot down a single Russian fighter.

"Tut, tut," he interrupted, "enough of your denials. It is all very well to be modest, but we all know that you are the winner of the Emperor's silver watch in the Navy Fliers School, and that you were selected as our nation's most promising airman!"

I couldn't say a word. The events of five years ago flashed into my mind, when I shuffled down this same road, a family and village disgrace, with my own lifelong friends turning their eyes away in shame. Had they known, these people, of how I fumbled, almost helplessly, in my cockpit in that first combat! Or how my captain had been speechless with rage at my conduct. And now ... all this! It was overwhelming.

Then a grand barbecue began in the narrow yard. There were heaps of food and many bottles of sake, rice wine. I was still upset and bewildered by the unexpected welcome, until my mother called me aside to whisper, "They have all been so good to us, and all this food has been contributed by them in honor of your homecoming! Do not frown and scowl so; return the honor by being pleasant in your manner."

Everyone present insisted on hearing everything that had happened in China, and they kept interrupting to demand that I tell all the details of my combat against the Russian fighter and how I attacked the Russian bomber formation. It was strange to hear these elderly folk, the most respected of our village, professing their admiration of what I had done. But most wonderful of all were the shining eyes of my mother, who fairly burst with pride for her son. And the rest of the family, my three brothers and my sisters, adorned in their best clothes, sat happy and smiling, just watching the events of the evening. I had precious little time in which to speak to my mother; the festival lasted the better part of the night.

When our guests took their leave, however, I soon realized that our family was still as impoverished as when I left for the Navy. My mother stilled my fears with the assurance that the entire village had helped her in her labors, that our neighbors could not have been kinder.

During my stay in China I had sent the better part of my salary home to the family. There was little use for money in that country. I never drank, or indeed, entertained any girls. Both were considered vices for fighter pilots, and I wished no criticism leveled at me.

"Saburo," my mother continued, "we are grateful for the continued help you have given us by sending home most of your pay. But now I wish you to stop. You have been contributing too much of the funds you need for yourself. It is now time that you began to think more of yourself, and to begin saving for your marriage one day."

I protested heatedly. I had managed to save a tidy sum myself, and had no plans for marriage for a good many years to come. Suddenly I recalled Fujiko, with whom I had been corresponding daily. It occurred to me that, had I remained in my own village instead of enlisting in the Navy and rising to pilot, her family position would not have permitted her to more than speak to me!

Back at Omura, the personnel commander returned me to flying status, and I began a series of intensive training flights, regaining a sure hand at the controls of the fighter planes. The second week in January of 1940, I found my name posted on the bulletin board, with orders notifying me that I had been selected with several other pilots to make an exhibition flight over the large industrial city of Osaka on February 11, our National Foundation Day.

I rushed a letter off to Fujiko, telling her of the flight. Her return letter asked me where we would be staying in Osaka, for "my parents and myself wish to visit you in Osaka on this day." A visit from the family! It was an honor indeed, for it required a full day's journey from Tokushima across the Island Sea to Osaka.

The exhibition flight went off easily. Japan looked beautiful from the air, with the neat and orderly fields and rice paddies, the cultivated gardens and parks. I saw school children in their yards, forming characters which read, *"Banzai!"* as our formation passed overhead. Late that afternoon, with the flight completed, we moved into our rooms in an Osaka hotel.

I had barely shaved and changed into a fresh uniform when one of the noncommissioned pilots dashed down the hall and bellowed lustily, "Pilot Sakai! Get a move on! Your fiancee is downstairs waiting to see you!" Everyone laughed and cheered as I reddened and hurried out.

Fujiko Niori was stunning. I stopped on the stairway and just stared at her, holding my breath. She was dressed in a beautiful kimono, and waited for me with her parents in the portico. I could hardly speak, and it was an effort to take my eyes away from the girl. I stuttered and bowed.

That evening the Niori family took me as their guest for dinner to one of the famous restaurants in downtown Osaka. I had never even been in such a restaurant before!

Fujiko's parents were wonderful to me, and did their best to make me feel comfortable. But I could not avoid feeling self-conscious, for it was obvious—to them, Fujiko, and myself—that I was being studied and examined as their daughter's potential groom. Increasing my anguish was the knowledge that the Niori family was one of the most distinguished in Japan, that they came from one of the outstanding Samurai groups in the country, and that Fujiko's father had attained eminence as a college professor. During the dinner I refused a cup of sake poured for me by Mr. Niori. He smiled and urged me on until I informed him that, as a fighter pilot, I did not drink. My reply, it was obvious, was pleasing to the entire family.

The night ended all too quickly, and the good-byes at the hotel were to be the last for a long time to come. It ended, however, with unspoken but obvious approval of me as Fujiko's suitor.

Back at Omura, I resumed the dawn-to-dusk training. Spring passed, and then the summer had come and gone. I was still at Omura, cursing the delays which kept me at the training field. What buoyed me up were the letters which came uninterruptedly from Fujiko; in that respect I was filled with hopes and dreams.

But I had become depressed. I received letters from my former pilot friends who still flew in China, who wrote in glowing terms of the air kills they made from week to week. Almost all of them by now were aces, pilots to be feared by the enemy as they wove a pattern of absolute air supremacy in China. The good news came at last, with orders to transfer to the Kaohsiung Air Base on Formosa. It was just one year since

I had returned from China, and I was chafing to return to action. By now Kaohsiung had become Japan's main outer air base, and a transfer there meant combat assignments soon after.

Before I left, however, I bought something I'd wanted for years, a Leica camera with a Sonar 2.0 lens, then considered the best camera in the world. The purchase of a camera would hardly be considered of special importance to most people, I imagine, but it represented more than three months of pay, and it wiped out almost my entire savings. To me the Leica was a beautiful and precision-built gem. I had a special use for this particular type of camera; our fighter planes did not carry the automatic cameras so familiar to American pilots, and the Leica was particularly well suited to aerial photography from a cockpit.

At Kaohsiung I was in for a tremendous surprise. On the airfield I saw strange new fighter planes, as different from the familiar Type 96 Claudes as night from day. These were the new Mitsubishi Zero fighters, sleek and modern. The Zero excited me as nothing else had ever done before. Even on the ground it had the cleanest lines I had ever seen in an airplane. We now had enclosed cockpits, a powerful engine, and retractable landing gear. Instead of only two light machine guns, we were armed with two machine guns and two heavy 20-mm. cannon, as well.

The Zero had almost twice the speed and range of the Claude, and it was a dream to fly. The airplane was the most sensitive I had ever flown, and even slight finger pressure brought instant response. We could hardly wait to meet enemy planes in this remarkable new aircraft.

We put the new fighter to its first test in the occupation of French Indochina, flying top cover for our Army troops which occupied key ground positions. This meant a nonstop flight of 800 miles from Kaohsiung to Hainan Island. This was an incredible distance for a fighter plane, especially with much of the flight over the ocean. It was carried out without a hitch—sheer wonder for us who were accustomed to the short-ranging Claudes.

There was no opposition, however, as we patrolled over the occupation forces moving into Indochina. Except for some minor border skirmishes caused by uninformed regional French troops, our forces moved in quietly and without trouble. The occupation, of course, was conducted "peacefully" after agreement with local French authorities that prevented open war.

The Zero's combat trials were postponed until we were rotated back to the Hankow Air Wing in May of 1941. Back in the China theater, we discovered that the enemy pilots had lost heart for fighting. No longer were they aggressive and quick to attack, as were the three Russian fighters which jumped our fifteen Claudes in my first fight. The enemy pilots eluded us at almost every opportunity, and would engage only when they had the advantage of plunging out of the sun in a surprise attack. Their timidity forced us to invade deeper and deeper inland to force them to do battle.

On August 11,1941, I was assigned to one such mission, with the express purpose of forcing the enemy into a fight. It was an 800-mile nonstop flight, from Ichang to Chengtu. This was familiar territory; it was over Ichang, then enemy-held, that I had challenged the twelve Russian bombers.

On our penetration flight we escorted seven twin-engined Mitsubishi Type 1 bombers, better known during World War II as Bettys. The bombers took off from Hankow shortly after midnight, and we picked them up over Ichang. The night was pitch black, and our only landmark was the whitish Yangtze Valley winding its way across the dark country. We arrived at Wenkiang airstrip before dawn, circling slowly until daybreak. Finally the sky lightened. No enemy fighters appeared. We watched the flight leader bank his Zero and dive. That was the signal to strafe.

One after the other we plummeted from the sky toward the airfield, where I saw Russian fighters already moving along the runways on their take-off runs. Their ground crews were running frantically over the field, heading for the trenches.

I pulled out at low altitude, coming up behind one E-16 fighter as it rolled down the field. It was a perfect target, and a short cannon burst exploded the fighter in flames. I flashed across the field and spiraled sharply to the right, climbing steeply to come around for another run. Tracers and flak were to left and right of me, but the Zero's unexpected speed threw the enemy gunners off.

Other Zero fighters dove and made strafing passes over the runways. Several of the Russian fighters were burning or had crashed. I pulled out of a dive to catch another plane in my sights. A second short cannon burst and there was a mushrooming ball of fire.

There was nothing left to strafe. Our attack had cleared the field of enemy planes, and not a single Russian aircraft was able to fly. The majority either were burning or had exploded. Back at 7,000 feet, we noticed the hangars and other shops burning fiercely from the regular bombing attack. It was a thorough job. We were disappointed in the lack of air opposition, and continued to circle, hoping the towering smoke would draw the enemy planes.

Three Zeros suddenly dropped out of formation and raced for the earth. Far below me I saw a brightly colored biplane hedge-hopping over the ground. In a flash the three fighters had jumped the enemy plane, hurling bullets and cannon shells without success as the skillful enemy pilot rolled right and left, snapping his slow but agile plane through wild gyrations to evade the slugs and shells. All three fighters screamed up and away from the unscathed biplane.

Now it was my turn, and I caught the biplane dead in my sights and squeezed the trigger. He was gone, rolling violently off to the left, cutting around in a turn too sharp even for the Zero to follow. Another Zero joined the fray, and the five of us slewed desperately through the air to catch the elusive enemy in our sights. That pilot was an absolute master. The biplane was almost like a wraith as it snap-rolled, spiraled, looped, and turned through all sorts of seemingly impossible maneuvers. We were completely unable to catch him in a solid burst.

Then suddenly we neared the summit of a low hill west of Chengtu. The biplane pilot had no choice but to clear over the hill, slow-rolling as he climbed. It was the one mistake, the one fatal error which no pilot is allowed. His belly flashed before my sights, and the cannon shells tore through the floor boards into the cockpit. The biplane fell off into a wild spin, even as another Zero threw useless shells into the ship with a dead man at the controls. It crashed into a hill and exploded.

That made two, and my first with the Zero.

That was our last combat action in the China theater. Shortly thereafter we moved up to Yuncheng, a small city far up the Yellow River. During several weeks of air patrol we failed to encounter any enemy aircraft.

Early in September all naval pilots were returned to Hankow, where we were surprised by the appearance of Vice-Admiral Eikichi Katagiri, the Naval Air Force Commander in China. The admiral told us that we were to be transferred back to Formosa, where we would "fulfill a most important mission." The admiral did not elaborate, but it was obvious to us all that open war with the great Western powers seemed imminent.

In September we were back on the island. A total of 150 fighter pilots and an equal number of bomber crewmen moved from the Kaohsiung air base to Tainan, where we were organized into the new Tainan Flotilla.

The entire Pacific was about to explode.

CHAPTER SEVEN

ON the second of December Vice-Admiral Fushizo Tsukahara, Commander of the 11th Air Fleet, sent the first reconnaissance planes over the Philippine Islands. They returned on the fourth and fifth to take photographs of Clark and Iba Fields, and of other major installations near Manila, from a height of 20,000 feet. The photographs of Clark Field shown to us clearly revealed thirty-two B-17 bombers, three medium-sized aircraft, and seventy-one small planes. The Navy estimated that on Luzon there were some 300 combat planes, of all types, a figure which we discovered later was twice as high as the number of planes actually in the Philippines.

Our reconnaissance planes were not alone in this type of activity. American PBY Catalinas were seen on a number of occasions over Formosa. The twin-engined flying boats came in on cloudy days, flying slowly at an elevation of 1,500 feet, leisurely snapping pictures of our ground installations and aircraft.

The American pilots were amazing. With their lumbering, slow airplanes, they should have proved easy prey, but we failed ever to intercept a single PBY. Whenever the air-raid alarms shrieked, dozens of our pilots scrambled into the air, but invariably the Catalinas slipped into the heavy cloud cover and escaped unscathed. Their pictures, taken at such low altitude, must have told the Americans everything they wanted to know about our air units.

When we reached Tainan as part of the new flotilla, we began a new and intense training period. All the men were restricted to their home fields. From daybreak until late at night, seven days a week, in all kinds of weather, we were engaged in training flights to learn the finer points of escort missions, mass formation flying, strafing runs, and so forth.

Our original attack plan for the Philippines called for the use of three small aircraft carriers to bring the Zeros close to the enemy islands. They were the 11,700-ton *Ryujo;* the 13,950-ton *Zuiho,* a converted submarine tender; and the 20,000-ton *Taiho,* a converted merchant ship. Theoretically the three carriers should have had a combined capacity of ninety fighters, but their actual operation figure was closer to fifty planes, and even this number was halved on windy days. Tsukahara found the three ships almost useless for his purposes.

If, however, the Zeros could fly from Formosa directly to the Philippines and return nonstop, we could then eliminate our need for the carriers. The admiral's aides doubted, however, that a single-engine fighter could carry out a mission of such range. Clark Field was 450 miles away from our own air base, and Nichols Field, another major target near Manila was 500 miles distant from Tainan. That meant, considering the factors of still-air range, fuel for fighting, and fuel for reserve, that we would be required to fly nonstop for some 1,000 to 1,200 miles! No fighters had ever flown on such combat missions before, and there were vehement arguments among the air staff as to whether even the Zero was capable of this performance. There was only one way to determine this point.

From then on we flew literally day and night to stretch the range of our planes. Apart from its range, the Zero was designed to remain in the air on a single flight for a maximum of six or seven hours. We stretched this figure to from ten to twelve hours, and did so on mass formation flights. I personally established the record low consumption of less than seventeen gallons per hour; on the average our pilots reduced their consumption from thirty-five gallons per hour to only eighteen. The Zero carried a normal fuel load of some 182 gallons.

To conserve fuel, we cruised at only 115 knots at 12,000-feet altitude. Under normal full-power conditions, the Zero was capable of 275 knots and, when over-boosted for short emergencies, could reach its maximum speed of about 300 knots. On our long-range flights we lowered propeller revolutions to only 1,700 to 1,850 rpm, and throttled the air control valve to its leanest mixture. This furnished us the absolute minimum of power and speed, and we hung on the fringe of losing engine power at any time and stalling.

These new long-range cruising methods extended the Zero's range by a remarkable figure, however, and our flight commanders reported the exciting news to Admiral Tsukahara, who then dropped the three small carriers from his plans. Two of them returned to Japan and one moved on to support our operations at Palau. As a result, the 11th Fleet became a fleet without any ships.

We were curious, of course, as to the opposition we would encounter from the Americans. We knew little of the types of planes or the performance of the American pilots, except to anticipate that they would possess even greater flying ability than the pilots against whom we had fought in China.

Not a man questioned the wisdom of launching the war. We were, after all, noncommissioned officers who had been trained—painfully—to respond immediately to orders. When we were told to fly and fight, we did so unquestionably.

At two in the morning on December 8, 1941, an orderly went through our billet at Tainan, waking my group of pilots. It had come—X-Day, as we knew the opening day of the war. The pilots slipped into their flying gear quietly and in small groups moved outside. The night was clear, moonless, with gleaming stars stretching from horizon to horizon. Over all was a deathly stillness broken only by the sounds of our boots crunching on gravel, and the low voices of the pilots as they hurried to the airstrip. Captain Masahisa Saito, our commander, told us that we would take off at 0400 hours and briefed each flight on its respective assignments for the attack on the American airfields in the Philippines. Then we could only wait. Orderlies brought us our breakfasts as we sat beside our planes on the runway.

At approximately 0300 hours a mist began to close on the airfield, a rare occurrence in this semitropical area. By four o'clock it had become a thick pea-soup fog with visibility reduced to only five yards. The loudspeakers on the control tower boomed out: "Take-off is delayed indefinitely." Our nervousness increased as the darkness wore on. We kept looking at our watches, cursing the fog. Three hours passed this way, and still the fog had not abated. If anything, it had thickened.

Abruptly, the loudspeaker crackled: "Attention! Here is an important announcement!" The pilots listened in attentive silence. "At 0600 this morning a Japanese task force succeeded in carrying out a devastating surprise attack against the American forces in the Hawaiian Islands."

A wild, surging roar went up in the darkness. Pilots danced and slapped their friends on the back, but the shouts were not entirely those of exultation. Many of the fliers were releasing their pent-up anger at being chained to the ground while our other planes were smashing at the enemy.

This attack created a factor which we must consider. The Americans were now warned of our attack plan, and it was incredible that they would not be waiting for us in strength in the Philippines. The tension increased as the morning approached. The fog had crippled our plans, worse yet, it would allow the Americans to send their bombers from Luzon and catch our planes on the ground the moment the fog lifted. We manned our defense installations. Machine gunners slipped live rounds into their weapons, and every man on the field strained for the sound of enemy bombers.

Miraculously, the attack never came! At nine in the morning the fog began to lift and the welcome sound of the loudspeakers told us that we would take off in only one hour. Every pilot and bomber crewman on the field climbed into his plane without awaiting further orders.

Exactly at ten the signal lights flickered through the last wisps of fog. One after the other the bombers rolled down the long runway. One, two, three, then six planes were in the air, climbing steadily. The seventh plane was racing down the runway, 1,200 feet from its starting point, when suddenly the right landing gear collapsed. With a great screeching roar the plane spun along the ground on its belly, flames enveloping the entire fuselage. In the harsh glare of the fire we saw the crew struggle through their hatches and jump onto the ground, then run furiously away from their plane. The next instant a tremendous blast rocked the field as the bomb load blew up. None of the crew survived the explosion.

Repair crews were on the runway in seconds, and the men proceeded frantically to drag away the twisted pieces of metal. Dozens of men raced against time to fill the smoking crater; in less than fifteen minutes the signal was given for the next bomber to resume its take-off. By 10:45 planes were airborne, fifty-three bombers and forty-five Zero fighters.

The fighters broke up into two groups, one staying with the bombers as escorts, while the other flew ahead to tackle the interceptors, which, we felt certain, after the long delay in our attack, would be awaiting us in great strength. I flew in the first wave, and our formation moved up to 19,000 feet.

Soon after passing the southernmost cape on Formosa, I sighted a nine-plane bomber formation flying directly toward Formosa, apparently an enemy force out to attack our fields. Nine pilots, including myself, were briefed before take-off to oppose any enemy aircraft discovered on our route to Luzon, while the others were to continue the attack as planned. We dropped out of the main formation and dove for the bombers. In seconds I was in firing position and closed in to take the lead plane. I started to squeeze the trigger when I suddenly realized that these were Japanese Army planes! I rocked my wings in signal to the other fighters to hold their fire. Those fools in the bombers! No one in the Army command area had taken the trouble to coordinate their flights with the Navy, and these idiots were out on a routine training flight.

We regained our formation when passing over the Batan Islands, midway between Formosa and Luzon. These were occupied by our paratroopers, shortly after we flew over the islands, to provide a haven for any planes which might be forced to ditch on their return from the Philippines. Actually we lost no aircraft through ditching. And then the Philippine Islands hove into view, a deep green against the rich blue of the ocean. The coastline slipped beneath us, beautiful and peaceful, without another airplane in the air. Then we were back over the China Sea.

At 1:35 p.m. we flashed in from the China Sea and headed for Clark Field. The sight which met us was unbelievable. Instead of encountering a swarm of American fighters diving at us in attack, we looked down and saw some sixty enemy bombers and fighters neatly parked along the airfield runways. They squatted there like sitting ducks; the Americans had made no attempt to disperse the planes and increase their safety on the ground. We failed utterly to comprehend the enemy's attitude. Pearl Harbor had been hit more than five hours before; surely they had received word of that attack and expected one against these critical fields!

We still could not believe that the Americans did not have fighters in the air waiting for us. Finally, after several minutes of circling over the fields, I discovered five American fighters at a height of about 15,000 feet, some 7,000 feet below our own altitude. At once we jettisoned the external fuel tanks, and all pilots armed their guns and canon.

The enemy planes, however, refused to attack, and maintained their own altitude. It was a ridiculous affair, the American fighters flying around at 15,000 feet, while we circled above them. Our orders precluded us from attacking, however, until the main bomber force arrived on the scene.

At 1:45 p.m. the twenty-seven bombers with their Zero escorts approached from the north and moved directly into their bombing runs. The attack was perfect. Long strings of bombs tumbled from the bays and dropped toward the targets the bombardiers had studied in detail for so long. Their accuracy was phenomenal—it was, in fact, the most accurate bombing I ever witnessed by our own planes throughout the war. The entire air base seemed to be rising into the air with the explosions. Pieces of airplanes, hangars, and other ground installations scattered wildly. Great fires erupted and smoke boiled upward.

Their mission accomplished, the bombers wheeled about and began their return flight home. We remained as escort for another ten minutes, then returned to Clark Field. The American base was a shambles, flaming and smoking. We circled down to 13,000 feet and, still without enemy opposition, received orders to carry out strafing attacks.

With my two wingmen tied to me as if by invisible lines, I pushed the stick forward and dove at a steep angle for the ground. I selected two undamaged B-17's on the runway for our targets, and all three planes poured a fusillade of bullets into the big bombers. We flashed low over the ground and climbed steeply on the pull-out.

Five fighters jumped us. They were P-40's, the first American planes I had ever encountered.

I jerked the stick and rudder pedal and spiraled sharply to the left, then yanked back on the stick for a sudden climb. The maneuver threw the enemy attack off, and all five P-40's abruptly rolled back and scattered. Four of the planes arced up and over into the thick columns of black smoke boiling up over the field, and were gone.

The fifth plane spiraled to the left—a mistake. Had he remained with his own group he could have escaped within the thick smoke. Immediately I swung up and approached the P-40 from below; the American half-rolled and began a high loop. At 200 yards the plane's belly moved into my sights. I rammed the throttle forward and closed the distance to fifty yards as the P-40 tried desperately to turn away.

He was as good as finished, and a short burst of my guns and cannon walked into the cockpit, blowing the canopy off the plane. The fighter seemed to stagger in the air, then fell off and dove into the ground.

That was my third kill—the first American plane to be shot down in the Philippines.

I saw no other fighters after that, but other Zero pilots caught a group of planes in the air. Later that night, back at Tainan, our reports showed claims for nine planes shot down, four probably destroyed in the air, and thirty-five destroyed on the ground. Clark Field antiaircraft guns shot down one Zero, and four others crashed during the flight home. But not a single plane was lost to an enemy aircraft.

CHAPTER EIGHT

THE second day of the war—December 9—we fought our worst battles against violent rainstorms, which came close to inflicting serious losses on our air units. Early on the ninth we took off for Luzon. The weather was so bad that the bombers were forced to remain on the ground. The storms raged over the Philippines as well as at Formosa, and at the end of the day we had shot up only a few planes on the ground.

Torrential rainstorms broke up the big fighter formation on the return flight. The rain was incredible; it lashed at the light fighter planes in the worst downpour I have ever encountered. Swirling masses of clouds drove us to the ocean surface. Finally we scattered into V's of three fighters, with each group concerned only for its own safety.

From a height of fifteen and twenty yards the water was a fearsome sight, lashed into white spray by the wind. I had no choice but to fly at this low altitude, my two wingmen hugging my tail, desperately trying not to lose sight of my plane. For hours we fought our way northward, our fuel gauges dropping lower and lower. Finally, after what seemed like countless hours, the southern tip of Formosa broke through the clouds. We circled through the downpour until we found an Army air base near the coastline and with barely enough fuel for our approach set down on the muddy runway. Thirty other fighters preceded me, and later that night we discovered that three fighters had made forced landings on a small islet near the Army field. Not a pilot was lost, however.

That evening was our first real rest in the three months since our assignment to Formosa. The shabby inn at the hot springs hamlet was a small paradise to us, as we soaked in the tubs and turned in for a long sleep.

The third day of the war is one I will long remember, for on December 10 I shot down my first Boeing B-17; it was also the first of the Flying Fortresses to be lost by the Americans in combat. After the war I found that this particular bomber was piloted by Captain Colin P. Kelly, Jr., the American air hero.

We did not take off for Luzon until 10:00 a.m. since all the fighters first had to fly on to Tainan for regrouping, arming, and new orders. We left Tainan with a formation of twenty-seven fighters. Over Clark Field, we found not a single target. For thirty minutes we circled the burned-out American base, but failed to sight a plane either on the ground or in the air.

The group turned north to fly cover for the Japanese convoy landing troops at Vigan. One light cruiser of the 4,000-ton *Nagara* type and six destroyers escorted four transports. An American account of this force, based on reports by the surviving crew of Captain Kelly's plane, grossly exaggerated the number of ships. According to the Americans, our force comprised the battleship *Haruna* of 29,000 tons, six cruisers, ten destroyers, and fifteen to twenty transports.

We maintained cover over the transports for about twenty to twenty-five minutes, flying at 18,000 feet, when I noticed three large water rings near the ships. We were too high to see water pillars from bomb explosions, but the three rings were unmistakable. A second glance showed that none of the ships had been hit, although the American report of the attack claimed that the nonexistent battleship had received one direct hit and two near misses, and was left smoking and draining oil into the water.

My fellow pilots and I were upset by the fact that the enemy had attacked despite our screening Zero fighters. We did not even see the bombers! A few moments later, after squirming around in my cockpit, I saw a lone B-17, about 6,000 feet above us, speeding southward. I called the attention of the other pilots to the single bomber, and we continued the search for the other planes we were certain had assisted in the attack. We had never heard of unescorted bombers in battle, especially a single bomber in an area known to be patrolled by dozens of enemy fighters. Unbelievable as it seemed, that B-17 had made a lone attack in the very teeth of all our planes. The pilot certainly did not lack courage.

We received the pursuit signal from our lead plane, and all but three fighters which remained behind as transport cover turned and raced after the fleeing bomber. The B-17 was surprisingly fast, and only under full throttle did we manage to get within attacking distance. Approximately fifty miles north of Clark Field we maneuvered to make our firing runs. Abruptly three Zeroes appeared—it seemed from out of thin air—and sliced across the B-17's course. Evidently they were from the Kaohsiung Wing which had strafed Nichols Field earlier in the day.

We were still out of gun range when the three Kaohsiung fighters peeled off and made their firing passes from above on the big plane. The bomber continued serenely on, almost as if the Zeros were no more bothersome than gnats. The thin air at 22,000 feet had the slight advantage of forcing a reduction of the Zero's performance.

Seven of our fighters joined up with the three Kaohsiung planes and swung into the attack. It was impossible for the ten Zeros to make a concerted attack against the bomber, for in the rarefied air we could easily over-control and collide with another plane. Instead, we swung out in a long file, and made our firing passes one after the other, each plane making its run alone. It was a time-consuming maneuver, and irritated me because of the long wait for each pass. By the time all ten Zeros had made their runs, we were flabbergasted. It appeared that not a single bullet or cannon shell had struck the bomber.

This was our first experience with the B-17, and the airplane's unusual size caused us to misjudge our firing distance. In addition, the bomber's extraordinary speed, for which we had made no allowance, threw our range finders off. All through the attack the Fortress kept up a steady stream of fire at us from its gun positions. Fortunately, the accuracy of the enemy gunners was no better than our own.

After my pass I noticed that we were over Clark Field, and it appeared certain that the B-17 pilot had called for help from American fighters. We had to destroy the plane quickly lest we be caught in a trap of our own making. But there seemed to be little purpose in continuing the long sweeping passes by diving down onto the bomber from behind. I decided to try a close-in attack directly from the rear. Greatly to my advantage, of course, was the fact that the early B-17 models lacked tail turrets, or I might never have been able to hold my course. Under full throttle I swung in behind the bomber and closed in for my firing run. Two other fighters, watching me, moved up and, wing to wing, we raced in for the kill.

The Fortress' guns flashed brightly as the pilot fishtailed from side to side, trying to give the side gunners the opportunity to catch us in their sights. But despite the frantic defensive flying the enemy tracers missed our planes. I moved in ahead of the other two fighters and opened fire. Pieces of metal flew off in chunks from the bomber's right wing, and then a thin white film sprayed back. It looked like jettisoned gasoline, but it might have been smoke. I kept up my fire against the damaged area, hoping to hit either the fuel tanks or oxygen system with my cannon shells. Abruptly the film turned into a geyser. The bomber's guns ceased firing; the plane seemed to be afire within the fuselage. I was unable to continue the attack; my ammunition was exhausted.

I banked away to let the Zero behind me have his chance. The pilot hung grimly to the B-1y's tail, pouring in a stream of bullets and cannon shells. The damage was already done, however, and even as the other fighter closed in the bomber nosed down and was speeding toward the ground. Miraculously, its wings were on an even keel and the bomber's pilot might have been trying to crash land on Clark Field. I dove after the crippled Fortress and, maintaining several hundred yards' distance, took pictures with my Leica. I managed to get in three or four shots. At 7,000 feet three men bailed out. Their chutes opened and the next moment the B-17 disappeared into an overcast.

Later we heard reports that the Americans had damned our fighter pilots for machine-gunning the crewmen who drifted to earth beneath their parachutes. This was pure propaganda. Mine was the only Zero fighter near the bomber when they abandoned their airplane, and I had not a single bullet or cannon shell left. The only thing I shot were photographs with the Leica.

No Japanese pilot actually saw the B-17 crash, so credit for the kill was denied at the time.

The bomber pilot's courage in attempting his solo bombing run was the subject of much discussion that night in our billets. We had never heard of anything like that before, a single plane risking almost certain destruction from so many enemy fighters in order to press home its attack. The discrepancies of the surviving crew's reports in no way detracted from the act of heroism. Later that afternoon, back in Formosa, we found the wings of two Zeros riddled with machine-gun bullets which had been fired by the bomber's gunners.

Thirteen years after this battle, I met Colonel Frank Kurtz, USAF, pilot of the famed bomber "Swoose," in Tokyo. Kurtz told me: "The day Colin was shot down, I was in the Clark Field tower. I saw his plane coming in, and you were right about his trying for a landing. Three open chutes came down through the overcast, and the cloud deck seemed to me to be at 2,500 feet. Then five more chutes opened. At least, it looked like five from where I was watching. Colin, of course, never got out."

CHAPTER NINE

THAT evening I found several letters from home, and a small package from Fujiko. She had sent me a cotton band to wrap about my stomach, with one thousand red stitches; this was Japan's traditional talisman against enemy bullets.

Fujiko wrote, "Today we were told that our fatherland launched a great war against the United States and Great Britain. We can only pray for our ultimate victory and for your good fortune in battle.

"Hatsuyo-san and I have stood at a street corner several hours a day for the last several days, and have begged 998 women who passed to give us each a stitch for this band. So it has the individual stitches of one thousand women. We wish you will wear it on your body, and we pray that it may protect you from the bullets of the enemy guns...

Actually, few Japanese airmen held faith in the charm. But I knew what it meant for Fujiko and my cousin to stand for long hours on the streets in the cold air of winter. Of course I would wear it, and I wrapped it about my midsection. Fujiko's letter set me to thinking; that night, for the first time, I thought of the enemy pilots I had shot down as other human beings like myself, instead of unknown entities in their planes. It was a strange and depressing reeling, but, as with every other facet of war, it was kill or be killed.

We continued our routine sorties from Formosa to the Philippines for the next ten days, and then received transfer orders to Jolo Air Base in the Sulu Islands, midway between Mindanao and Borneo, 1,200 air miles from our Tainan airfield. On December 30 I took off at 9:00 a.m. with twenty-six other fighters for the 1,200-mile nonstop flight to the new station. Here new orders awaited us, and we flew 270 miles further south to Tarakan off the eastern coast of Borneo. Our flights were uneventful; we did not encounter any enemy planes.

The enemy struck back at our units for the first time in January. Late one night a lone B-17 caught the entire Tarakan force unawares. A string of bombs landed on the construction-crew billets, which formed a perfect target for the unseen bomber; the construction men stupidly disdained blackout procedures. The exploding bombs killed more than 100 men and injured many others, in addition to wrecking the group of buildings.

Not a Zero could take to the air, because the Tarakan airfield was one of the worst in all the East Indies. Even for daytime operations we found the slippery mud of the runways treacherous for take-off and landing. During our arrival two Zeros had overshot the sharp list of the runway and been demolished. The base commander flew into a rage, and ordered Naval Pilot I /C Kuniyoshi Tanaka and myself to fly night patrol over the airfield. Tanaka was a former China ace with twelve kills, and in the Pacific eventually shot down another eight enemy planes, flying until he was wounded and disabled.

The night-flying assignment was both difficult and dangerous. In those days the Zero was unfit for night operations, and neither Tanaka nor I were even sure what we could do should enemy bombers attack. Fortunately for us—and the air base—we were not disturbed again.

On January 21 one of our convoys steamed out of Tarakan Harbor, bound for a landing operation at Balikpapan in lower Borneo. Headquarters ordered our group to supply air support, but at the best we could maintain only a light patrol of fighters over the vulnerable transports.

Instead of the great numbers of fighters reputed to be at our disposal, in the early months of 1942 we had less than seventy Zeros available for the entire vast area of the East Indies. And since a good number of the fighter planes were always undergoing combat repairs and a thorough overhaul after 150 hours of flight, we averaged thirty fighter planes at any given time for combat action.

During mid-January, B-17 bombers began to arrive at the enemy's Malang base in Java and initiated attacks against our forces in the Philippines and throughout the East Indies. These planes proved effective in harassing surface forces on the islands, but their inadequate numbers prevented them from interfering with our operations.

During the predawn darkness of January 24 we were afforded another demonstration of the Zero's glaring inadequacies for night combat. An American surface force stormed the Japanese convoy at Balikpapan in a savage, well-executed attack, and blew several transports out of the water. We were unable, of course, to provide air cover of any sort before the American raiders were well out to sea again. And, even during daylight hours, we could mount an average patrol of only three planes over Balikpapan.

In the spring of 1942 the first B-17's with new tail turrets made their appearance in our theater. Up until this time our favorite method of attack against the big planes had been to dive from behind in a sweeping firing pass, raking the bombers from tail to nose as we flashed by. We soon discovered this had little effect on the well-constructed and heavily-armored B-17. was this knowledge—and not primarily the addition of tail armament to the Fortresses—which brought about a sudden change of tactics. We adopted head-on passes, flying directly against the oncoming B-17's, pouring bullets and cannon shells into the forward areas of the enemy bombers. This proved temporarily effective, but it was soon negated by sudden evasive maneuvers by the B-17 pilots, which brought their heavy guns to bear on our incoming planes. The final attack procedure, and the most effective, was to fly high above the Fortresses, dive vertically, then snap over on our backs and continue to roll as we dove, maintaining a steady fire into the B-17's.

During the afternoon of January 24 Tanaka returned to Tarakan with his two wingmen after a patrol over Balikpapan. The three pilots were exhausted, although none was wounded. Tanaka reported that earlier in the day his flight of three fighters had encountered eight Fortresses, flying in two close formations.

"It was incredible, out there today," Tanaka said. "We caught the Fortresses just right, and over and over I pressed home the attacks against the B-17's. At least twice I caught a bomber perfectly. I could see the bullets hitting and the cannon shells exploding in the airplanes. But they wouldn't go down!"

Tanaka looked almost haggard. "These damned bombers are impossible," he spat disgustedly, "when they work into their defensive formations."

He went on to relate how his attack had, however, disrupted the B-17s' bombing run, causing many of the bombs to fall harmlessly into the open sea. Only one ship was hit, a big oil tanker, and that was blazing fiercely when Tanaka left Balikpapan to return.

The following day I took the Balikpapan patrol, with NAP 2/C Sadao Uehara as my wingman. Our two Zeros were all that the air base could muster for the convoy shift; the other fighters were needed elsewhere. Since Tanaka had encountered the B-17's at 20,000 feet, we cruised slowly in a wide circle at 22,000 feet. Tanaka had been unable to climb quickly enough from 18,000 feet to intercept the bombers before they started to spill their missiles into the air.

Far below our planes, the tanker hit the day before still burned like a torch.

Late in the morning, several specks appeared in the sky, approaching from the general direction of Java. They came in fast, swelling in size until two formations of four planes each became clear. Fortresses, in two close flights, exactly as Tanaka had found them yesterday. The rear flight flew slightly above the lead group and, as we approached, the second group of planes moved closer to form a defensive box.

The B-17's passed about a half mile beneath me. I rolled, Uehara glued to my wing tip, and dove against the formations. I was still out of gun range, but flicked a burst as I passed them. I saw the bombs falling as I flashed by the planes. We rolled back and climbed steeply. I saw the water rings appearing on the surface. No hits; the convoy hadn't been touched. Back above the B-17s, which now were turning in a wide 180-degree sweep, we searched for a possible second wave of planes. The sky was clear.

I moved into position again, a half mile above the rear of the formations. Now I'd see what Tanaka had been up against. I shoved the stick forward and rolled as I dove. The fighter picked up speed quickly; I kept the stick hard over, in a long rolling dive, firing with both guns and cannon. No results. Everywhere around me the Fortresses seemed to be filling the sky, and tracers arced through the air as we flashed through the formation. We slipped through without damage, and I climbed again for another dive.

Again. Dive, roll, concentrate on one bomber! This time I caught one! I saw the shells exploding, a series of red and black eruptions moving across the fuselage. Surely he would go down now! Chunks of metal—big chunks—exploded outward from the B-17 and flashed away in the slip stream. The waist and top guns went silent as the shells hammered home.

Nothing! No fire, no telltale sign of smoke trailing back . . . the B-17 continued on in formation.

We swung around and up, and rolled back in for the third run. The enemy formation continued on, seemingly impregnable, as if nothing had happened. The third time down I went after the bomber I had hit before, and again I caught him flush. Through the sight I watched the shells exploding, ripping metal from the wings and fuselage, ripping the inside of the fuselage apart. Then I was past the plane, pulling out into a wide, sweeping turn, going for height.

The plane was still in formation! No fire, no smoke. Each time we dove against the B-17s their gunners opened up with heavy defensive fire which, fortunately, seemed to have been impaired by the tightness of the formation. So far I felt no damage to the Zero. I made two more passes, each time swinging down into a dive, rolling as I dropped, Uehara right with me, each of us snapping out bursts with the machine guns and cannon. And every time we saw the bullets and shells slamming into the bombers, seemingly without effect.

We had just completed the sixth firing run when the eight B-17s split into two flights. Four banked to the right and the other four wheeled away to the left. Uehara pointed excitedly to the flight bearing to the right; a thin black film trailed the left engine of the third B-17.

We *had* gotten through, after all. I turned to follow the four bombers and pushed the throttle all the way forward, closing in rapidly behind the damaged plane. He was hurt, all right, dropping behind the other three planes. As I moved in I saw tangled wreckage instead of the tail turret; the guns remained silent. At maximum speed I approached to fifty yards' distance, and held the gun triggers down. Every last round poured from my guns and cannon into the cripple. Abruptly a cloud of black smoke burst from the bomber, and he nosed down steadily, to disappear into a solid cloud layer below.

Back at Tarakan I reported the details of the day's flight to my superior, Lieutenant Shingo. The other pilots gathered around us to hear my description of the firing passes. In their opinion it was a miracle that I had come back at all, with the guns of eight Fortresses working me over all at once.

My ground crew found only three bullet holes near my fighter's wing tip. I have never been a superstitious man, but I could not help running my hand over the talisman Fujiko had sent me.

The high command credited me with a probable for the day's

action. Two days later a Japanese reconnaissance plane reported that a B-17 had crash landed on a small island between Balikpapan and Surabaya.

CHAPTER TEN

SEVERAL years after the war I read Rear Admiral Samuel Eliot Morison's heralded historical volumes, the *History of United States Naval Operations in World War II*. Morison once again shows himself to be an eloquent historian, and in his work has provided voluminous documentation.

It is regrettable, then, that a specific portion of this war history has little basis in fact. I refer to the campaign which won for us the Dutch East Indies, especially the major bastion of Java. It is the admiral's own opinion that, where this campaign is concerned, our victories were "of stealth and of strength, rather than skill." Particular attention is given to the defeat of the Dutch and Allied fleets in February of 1942; here not only Morison but other equally renowned American historians have all neglected to include in their "documented reports" details of the greatest air battle staged in the entire Pacific up to that time.

As a mere noncommissioned pilot in that fray, my perspective is of course much more confined than that of the writer who encompasses the entire vast war. However, my personal account of part of that February campaign may prove enlightening to the student of the Pacific War.

The Java campaign was virtually ended on February 26, with the defeat by Japanese warships of the Allied surface forces in the area. A major factor contributing to that defeat was the lack of air cover which the Allied ships required so desperately. But nowhere in the American versions of the war have I read that the Allies' air units were destroyed on February 19, in a wild air melee over Surabaya, when a total of nearly seventy-five fighter planes of both combatants fought their biggest air duel of the war to date. It was this fighter-versus-fighter air victory—and not raids by our bombers against enemy airfields—which denied the Allied warships their air cover, and contributed so completely to their destruction.

On February 4, 1942, I flew to the Balikpapan airfield with several other Zero pilots. The next day we established new combat patrols in the area. Action was brisk, since enemy air activity was heavy and aggressive. Official Japanese records credit me with a victory on the fifth, when we fought a series of running air battles.

The next week our reconnaissance planes brought back reports that the enemy had concentrated in the Surabaya area a total of fifty to sixty fighter planes—Curtiss P-36 Mohawks, Curtiss P-40 Tomahawks, and Brewster F2A Buffaloes—which were to resist our invasion of Java.

Our high command ordered all available land-based fighter planes in the theater to concentrate at newly captured Balikpapan. On the morning of February 19, twenty-three Zero fighters, assembled from the Tainan and Kaohsiung units, took off for Surabaya.

This was the first occasion on which we knew we would encounter heavy enemy fighter opposition. Before us was a 430-mile flight to the Dutch bastion, where there awaited a numerically superior force. No one expected to breeze through another victory as we had done in the Philippines.

Every possible precaution was taken to aid our flight. Special ditching islands were assigned all pilots, where naval units awaited those planes which might be forced down. Weather planes preceded our flight to give constant readings, and a fast reconnaissance plane acted as a pathfinder and warning scout for our Zeros.

We reached Surabaya at 11:30 a.m., flying at 16,000 feet. The enemy force anticipating our arrival was unprecedented. At least fifty Allied fighters, flying at about 10,000 feet, maintained a large, counterclockwise sweep over the city. The enemy planes extended in a long line, composed of three waves of V groups which outnumbered us by more than two to one.

Upon sighting the enemy fighters, we jettisoned our tanks and climbed for altitude. Sighting our force, the Allied fighters broke off their circular movement and at full speed closed toward us. They were prepared and eager for a fight—unlike the American fighters we had encountered over Clark Field on December 8.

Less than a minute later the orderly formations disintegrated into a wild, swirling dogfight.

I watched a P-36 scream toward me, then flicked into a swift left roll, waiting for the enemy's reaction. Foolishly, he maintained his course. That was all for me, and I snapped around into a sharp right turn, standing the Zero on her wing, and came out directly on the tail of the startled P-36 pilot.

A look behind me showed my own plane clear, and I closed the distance to the enemy fighter. He rolled to the right, but slight control movements kept the Zero glued to his tail. Fifty yards away I opened up with the guns and cannon. Almost immediately the right wing broke off and snapped away in the air stream; then the left wing tore loose. Spinning wildly, the P-36 broke up into wreckage as it plummeted. The pilot failed to get out.

Swinging into a wide, climbing turn I headed back for the main flight. At least six planes were falling in flames. Fighters swirled crazily about in the air and abruptly the olive drab of a P-36 rolled toward my own fighter. I turned to meet his rush, but in the next moment another Zero whipped upward in a steep climb, caught the P-36 in a long cannon burst, then snapped away as the Dutch plane exploded.

To my left a P-40 closed in on the tail of a fleeing Zero, and I turned desperately to draw the enemy fighter off. There was no need to do so; the Zero whipped up and around in a tight loop which ended exactly above and behind the P-40. The guns and cannon hammered and the P-40 burst into flames.

Another P-40 flashed by, trailing a streamer of flame fully three times as long as the fighter. A P-36 flipped crazily through the air, its pilot dead at the controls.

Below me, our unarmed pathfinder plane flashed by, caught by three Dutch fighters. The Japanese pilot was corkscrewing violently to evade the enemy tracers which flashed all about his plane.

Again I arrived too late. A Zero plummeted down in a power dive, and his cannon shells exploded the top Dutch fighter's fuel tanks. Pulling out of the dive, the Zero flashed upward in a steep zoom, catching the second P-36 from beneath. It fell off on one wing even as the third pilot whipped around to meet the Zero. Too late; his cockpit erupted in a shower of glass.

The other Zero pulled alongside my plane, the pilot waving and grinning broadly, then dropped away as he escorted the reconnaissance plane out of the area.

A P-36, apparently fleeing the fight, passed over me. I slammed the throttle on over-boost and yanked the stick back, looping to come out close to the Dutchman. Still climbing, I opened up with the cannon. Too soon; the pressure of the turn threw my aim off.

The cannon gave me away; the P-36 jerked hard over in a left roll and dove vertically for the ground. I cut inside his turn and went into a dive as the Curtiss flashed by less than fifty yards away. My finger snapped down on the button, and the shells exploded in the fuselage. Thick black smoke belched back. I fired two more bursts, then pulled out as a sheet of flame enveloped the Dutch fighter.

A Zero with two blue stripes across the fuselage passed 200 yards in front of my plane. Without warning the Zero exploded in a vivid blast of fire, killing Lieutenant Masao Asai, our squadron commander. To this day I do not know what caused the explosion.

Back at 8,000 feet, I noticed about twenty Zero fighters circling in formation. The few surviving Dutch fighters were black specks disappearing in the distance. The battle was over, six minutes after it had started.

Strangely, with the air cleared of their own planes, the Dutch antiaircraft batteries remained silent as we circled over the city, waiting for any other Zeros that might have left in pursuit of the escaping Dutch fighters.

While the other fighters circled, I passed over the narrow waterway separating Surabaya from Madura Island . . . there was a well-camouflaged airstrip there! I descended slowly, marking on my map the location of the airstrip, near Djombang on the western tip of Madura. We had no reports of the existence of this secret airfield, and the information would be well received by intelligence.

I began my climb back to rendezvous with the other fighters when a single P-36 passed beneath me, low over the city. It was too good a target to miss. The enemy pilot flew leisurely at cruising speed, unaware of my approach.

My eagerness lost me a quick victory. Too far away for effective fire, I squeezed the cannon trigger. That was all the warning the Dutchman needed and he nosed down suddenly, fleeing with all his speed. Cursing my own stupidity, I slammed the throttle home and shoved the stick forward to follow the P-36. But I had afforded the enemy pilot a priceless advantage.

The flight performance of the P-36 was considerably below that of our own fighters; the Zeros were faster, had superior maneuverability, armament, rate of roll and climb. But the Zero was never designed for high-speed dives, and my premature burst enabled the P-36 to extend the distance between our two planes to 200 yards. I could get no closer.

The enemy pilot could have made good his escape had he begun his dive at a greater height, but the uprushing ground forced him to pull out into level flight. Now I could use the Zero's superior speed to advantage.

The Dutchman hedge-hopped and zig-zagged frantically. Every rime he turned I cut inside his turn, narrowing the distance between our two planes. He flew lower and lower in a desperate attempt to escape, barely clearing trees and houses, hoping to elude me until a shortage of fuel would cause me to break off the attack.

And I was close to that mark. In a final bid for speed I pushed the engine on over-boost even as the Malang Air Base came into sight. Fifty yards away I concentrated on the P-36 cockpit and squeezed the trigger. The cannon were empty, but two streams of machine-gun bullets tore the pilot apart. The fighter crashed into a rice paddy and flipped over on its back.

I was the last pilot to rejoin the other fighters, circling at 13,000 feet twenty miles north of Madura.

We had lost Lieutenant Asai and two other pilots. Back at Balikpapan the pilots claimed a total of forty enemy fighters shot down and probably destroyed. I have always been inclined to discount by 20 or 30 per cent the claims of any group of pilots after a wild battle such as we had fought over Surabaya; in the confusion of a dogfight, two or three pilots shoot at the same enemy plane, and each will claim that fighter for his own.

This time, however, it appeared that there was little exaggeration in our claims, for from that day on we met practically no opposition from Dutch fighters.

There was more good fortune. Intelligence officers sent out a bombing group to attack the secret air base at Djombang, and the unexpected bombing destroyed most of the remaining enemy planes—P-40s, Buffaloes, and British Hurricanes—on the ground.

We returned the next day to Java to attack any fighters encountered in the air and to strafe available targets on the ground. The enemy antiaircraft which had remained silent the day before now opened up with a vengeance, and we lost three of our eighteen Zeros.

Each night we heard Allied claims of five or six Zero fighters shot down in battle by the enemy during the day. It was remarkable, considering that our group flew the only Zeros in the area, and that our greatest casualties occurred on February 19 and 20, with six planes and pilots lost.

On the twenty-fifth eighteen Zeros left Balikpapan with orders to mop up the Malang Air Base, where intelligence believed the enemy was servicing several Allied bombers staging a last-ditch defense of the islands. En route to Malang we encountered a Dutch float-plane, and I broke formation long enough to send him crashing into the ocean.

If the Dutch had any fighters left at Malang, they refused to do battle. After circling the field for six minutes, our flight leader led us down to strafe three B-17s on the field. Antiaircraft fire was intense, but we saw all three bombers exploding in flame. The Dutch ground gunners holed several fighters, but failed to bring down any Zeros.

My next kill—officially my thirteenth—came on the last day of February. I flew as part of the escort of twelve fighters shepherding twelve Betty bombers from Macassar to attack the Allied forced evacuation of Tjilatjap. The enemy ships had cleared the harbor before our arrival, and the fighters cruised slowly while the bombers dumped their missiles into the port installations. The attack was uneventful for us and, after escorting the bombers back to the Java Sea, we turned toward Malang in search of enemy planes.

Luck was with us today. Four fighters, of a type we had not yet encountered, circled in the air near a tremendous cumulonimbus cloud which towered to 25,000 feet. As we approached, we identified the enemy planes as Dutch Buffaloes. I have never understood the lack of caution on the part of these Dutch pilots; even before they knew we were in the vicinity, we closed in and one Zero set a Buffalo blazing with a long burst. I rushed the second fighter, which whipped around in a tight turn; he was willing enough to fight! I cut easily inside the Buffalo's turn, heeling over in a vertical bank and coming out of the turn 200 yards from the enemy plane. I rarely fired when still in a turn, but this time I jabbed impatiently on the button. Several bullets hit the Buffalo's engine and smoke burst back from the plane. It seemed as if the pilot had also been hit, for the Brewster went into a series of repeated slow rolls until it disappeared into the cloud. It appeared impossible for the crippled fighter to survive the violent thermal inside the cloud, but, as I did not actually see the plane crash, I was credited only with a probable.

For the next several months we moved from one air base to another. We returned to the Philippines and flew support missions for the Army as they wore Corregidor's defenses to the breaking point. Then our unit transferred south to Bali Island in Indonesia, to prepare for the next major operation to the south.

I have never understood the American versions of the aerial combats of those days. Especially astonishing was a report by a Lieutenant Colonel Jack D. Dale, who claimed that his P-40 squadron shot down seventy-one Japanese aircraft with a loss of only nine P-40 pilots in forty-five days of fighting in Java. This is an incredible figure, as our actual losses were less than ten Zeros in combat during this period.

According to Dale, his P-40 pilots used a split-S maneuver, descending 6,000 to 8,000 feet when encountering Zeros, and then returning to fighting position. He claimed that in this fashion he could make his sixteen fighters appear as forty-eight. In all my combat with American P-40 fighters, I never once encountered this maneuver as described by Colonel Dale. Especially against the P-40, a fighter plane markedly inferior in performance to the Zero, my own group invariably terminated combat in a heavy victory for our own pilots.

Also confusing is Dale's report that "one night we heard Radio Tokyo say: 'Hundreds of P-40s were attacking out of nowhere. They are a new type of Curtiss, armed with six cannon.' " Katsutaro Kamiya, who at the time was in charge of Radio Tokyo's shortwave English broadcasts, told me that there was never any such broadcast as quoted by the American colonel. There was little need for such statements, Kamiya added, for then we had nothing to report but victories.

Colonel Dale's reports of air victories held as little truth as did the "sinking" of the *Haruna* by Captain Kelly.

CHAPTER ELEVEN

IN early March of 1942 the 150 pilots of the Tainan Fighter Wing, who had been scattered over a wide area of the Philippines and Indonesia, reassembled in Bali Island in the East Indies. The complete occupation of Indonesia itself appeared imminent. One company of Japanese army troops constituted the entire military occupation force of the island. Occupation is a misleading term, for our forces found the Bali natives friendly to the Japanese.

Bali seemed like a paradise. The weather was perfect, and the local scenery the most colorful and beautiful I have ever seen anywhere in the Pacific. Lush vegetation grew around our airfield, and we delighted in the hot springs which bubbled from the rocks. Since we were grounded for a while, we turned, at least for the moment, to more personal pleasures.

One afternoon we were lounging inside our "club" when we were startled by the sound of a heavy bomber approaching the field. One pilot ran to the window, then jerked his head back, his eyes wide. "Hey! B-17! And it's coming down!"

We ran to the window, crowding for a look. There it was, the impossible! A giant Flying Fortress, its landing gear and flaps extended, engines throttled back, easing out of its approach path for a landing. I rubbed my eyes; this just couldn't be true. Where could the plane have come from?

But... there it was, bouncing slightly as the wheels hit the earth. The squeal of brakes came to our ears. In a moment we were rushing through the door, excited with the prospect of being able to study in detail the defenses of the powerful American bomber. That ship out there could only be a plane we had captured!

The roar of machine guns brought us up short. Someone pointed—the Army troops! The B-17 wasn't captured! Its pilot had landed in error at our field, and some idiotic soldier was firing at him even before the plane stopped rolling!

Hardly had the machine gun spit out a dozen rounds when the bursting roar of four engines suddenly rammed to full power thundered over the field. The B-17 raced down the runway, streaming dust behind as its pilot fought the plane into the air. And then it was gone.

We were stunned. A B-17, intact, right in our hands, and the priceless opportunity had been thrown away by some trigger-happy baboon of a machine gunner! In a group we ran to the Army revetments. Several of the pilots could barely restrain themselves. One noncommissioned officer lost his temper. "What damned stupid fool son-of-a-bitch fired that gun?" he roared.

An indignant sergeant stood up. "Why?" he asked. "That was an enemy plane. Our orders are to shoot at enemy planes, not to make them welcome!"

We had to restrain the pilot; white with anger, he might have tried to kill the sergeant. The Army unit's lieutenant heard the shouting and came running up. When the full story unfolded, he bowed deeply and could only state, "I do not know how to apologize for my men's stupidity."

For the next several days we cursed the Army and bemoaned the loss of the enemy bomber. Today, of course, the incident provokes humor, but not in 1942, when the Flying Fortress was the most formidable opponent among all the Allied planes.

As the week passed tension between the Navy pilots and the Army garrison increased acutely. We did no combat flying during this period, and our tempers grew short. The unhappy situation exploded one night when, lying on my cot, I forgot the blackout and lit a cigarette.

Immediately a voice called from outside. "Cut out that smoking in there, you stupid bastard! Don't you even know what the regulations are?"

The pilot next to me, NAP 3/C Honda, jumped to his feet and dashed out the door. In an instant he had grabbed the soldier by the throat and was cursing him soundly. Honda, my wingman, was always too quick to take offense at any slight to me. I ran after him, but I was too late. Honda lost all control and before I could reach him there was the sound of a fist against flesh, and then a thud as the soldier fell unconscious to the ground.

Honda raged. He ran from the billet and stood on the grass, shouting as loudly as he could. "Come on, you Army bastards! Here I am, Honda of the Navy! Come on out and fight, morons!"

Two soldiers rushed from their barracks and jumped Honda. I saw him grin as he spun about and with a shout of glee leaped upon the Army men. There was a brisk scuffle, the sound of blows struck quickly, and Honda rose to his feet, standing triumphantly over two more prostrate forms.

"Honda! Stop it!" I called, but without effect. More soldiers came running out and Honda happily turned to do battle. But the Army lieutenant was hard on the heels of his own men, and herded them back to their own area. He said not a word to us, but we could hear him cursing out his troops. "You are here to fight the enemy, idiots, swine!" he spat. "Not our own countrymen. And if you must fight, pick a quarrel with someone you can finish. Those pilots, every one of them is a Samurai, and they like nothing better than to fight."

The following morning the lieutenant entered our club, and we braced ourselves for the expected complaints for our behavior. Instead he smiled and said, "Gentlemen, I am happy to bring you the news that another Army contingent at Bandung in Java has captured a B-17 bomber intact and flyable." A loud cheer went up. A B-17 we could fly!

The lieutenant waved his hands for silence. "Unfortunately, Tokyo has ordered the bomber sent to Japan at once. I did not receive news of the capture until the B-17 took off for the home islands this morning."

Disappointed voices and curses met this last report. "However," the lieutenant added hastily, "I assure you I will try to obtain as much information as possible about the captured aircraft for you." He saluted and left the room quickly.

We despaired of ever getting a single scrap of information concerning the captured B-17. As far as the Army and Navy were concerned, the left hand never knew what the right hand was doing at any moment.

Another week went by, and we were still grounded. Even the peaceful atmosphere of Bali began to grate on our nerves. Perhaps under other circumstances we could have enjoyed the inactivity, but we had come here to fight. For years I had done nothing but learn how to fight, and all I and the other pilots wanted to do was to get back into the air.

Then one morning a pilot rushed breathlessly into our billet with startling news. Rotation! That was the rumor, and it appeared as if some of us would be sent back to Japan. Everyone began to total up his overseas time.

I felt that, of all the men to be sent home, I would be the first to leave. I had left Japan for China in May of 1938 and, deducting my one year of recuperation after being wounded, had been overseas for thirty-five months. When I realized I might actually see my home again, I became acutely homesick. I spent all afternoon reading through the letters from Fujiko and my mother. They had written me at great length about the elaborate celebrations at home when Singapore fell in February, and of the many other festivities which our continued victories occasioned. All Japan was flushed with the sensational conquests of our forces, especially in the air. I yearned to again look at Fujiko, the most beautiful girl I had ever known. Only once had I gazed at her, and the thought that possibly—or even probably—she would become my bride made me burst with happiness.

Unlike most rumors, the news of rotation turned out to be true. On the twelfth of March, Lieutenant Commander Tadashi Nakajima arrived from Japan, and informed the squadron that he was relieving Lieutenant S. G. Eijo Shingo as squadron commander. "Lieutenant Shingo is relieved for rotation," he said. "I will now read off the names of those pilots ordered to return to Japan."

Not a sound interrupted Nakajima's voice as he began reading down the list of pilots' names. The first man was not, as I had hoped, myself. Neither was the second, nor the third. I listened with disbelief as the commander ran through the list of more than seventy names, none of which was mine. I was baffled and hurt. I could not understand why I had been dropped from the list of pilots who were to return to Japan. And I had been overseas longer than most!

Later, I approached the new commander and asked, "Sir, I understand that my name was not among those of the pilots to be sent home. Would you be kind enough to tell me of the reason? I do not believe I. . ."

Commander Nakajima interrupted me by waving his hands in the air and grinning. "No, you do not go home with the other men. I need you, Sakai, to go with me. We are advancing to a new air base, the foremost post against the enemy. We shall move to Rabaul at New Britain. So far as I am concerned, you are the best pilot in this squadron, and you will fly with me. Let these other men go home to defend the homeland."

And that was that. The conversation was ended. Under our Navy system, I dared not even question the commander further. I returned to my billet, upset, miserable with the world, and despairing of ever seeing Fujiko and my family. I did not learn until many months later that Commander Nakajima's preference for me as one of his pilots in reality saved my life. Those pilots who returned home transferred later to the Midway Task Force, which suffered a crushing defeat at the hands of the enemy navy on June 5. Almost all those men who left Bali were killed.

The next several weeks were among the worst I have ever spent. Never have I suffered so much illness, dejection, and despondency crowded into such a brief period of time.

Our next destination, Rabaul, was 2,500 miles east of Bali, too great a distance for the Zero fighter to fly. Instead of transferring our group of pilots by transport plane or flying boat or even on a fast warship, we were horrified to find ourselves herded like cattle into a small, old, and decrepit merchant freighter. More than eighty of us were jammed into the stinking vessel, which crawled sluggishly through the water at twelve knots. For protection we were given only one small 1,000-ton sub chaser.

Never have I felt so naked or exposed to the enemy as I did on that horrible vessel. We could not understand the workings of the high command's mind. Just one torpedo from a lurking submarine, one 500-lb. bomb from a diving bomber, and the thin-skinned freighter would blow into a thousand pieces! It was inconceivable, but true, that our commanders would risk half of the theater's fighter pilots, especially those with the most experience, in such a seagoing monstrosity! Discontented and unhappy, I finally succumbed to my low spirits and became really ill. I was confined to my bunk in the hold of the ship for most of the two-week voyage from Bali to Rabaul.

The ship creaked and groaned incessantly as it wallowed along in its zigzag pattern. Every time we passed the wash of the escorting subchaser we heeled over, rolling drunkenly. Inside the vessel conditions were torturous. The heat was almost unbearable; I did not spend a single dry day during the entire two weeks. Sweat poured from our bodies in the humid and sultry holds. The smell of paint was gagging, and every single pilot in my hold became violently ill. After passing Timor Island, already occupied by our troops, the lone naval escort turned and disappeared rapidly in the distance. By now I was seriously ill. At times I felt I was dying, and I believe I would have welcomed the release from my engulfing misery.

But even the worst of experiences can have its rewards. At my side for most of the trip was a young lieutenant, recently assigned to lead my flight in combat. Lieutenant J/G Junichi Sasai was one of the most impressive men I have ever met. A graduate of the Japanese Naval Academy, he should have remained aloof from the problems of the noncommissioned officers. So strict was the Navy caste system that, even had we been dying in the holds, he would not have been required, indeed, would not have been expected, to enter those stinking quarters. Sasai, however, was different. He paid no attention to the unwritten law that officers did not make friends with enlisted men. While in delirium I groaned and cried, lying in the reek of sweat and body odors, Sasai sat beside my cot, anxiously tending me as best he could. Every now and then I opened my eyes to gaze into his, clear and compassionate. His friendliness and ministrations pulled me through the worst of the voyage.

At last the ship chugged its way into Rabaul Harbor, the main port of New Britain. With a gasp of relief, I staggered from below decks to the pier. I could not believe what I saw. If Bali had been a paradise, then Rabaul was plucked from the very depths of hell itself. There was a narrow and dusty airstrip which was to serve our group. It was the worst airfield I had ever seen anywhere. Immediately behind this wretched runway a ghastly volcano loomed 700 feet into the air. Every few minutes the ground trembled and the volcano groaned deeply, then hurled out stones and thick, choking smoke. Behind the volcano stood pallid mountains stripped of all their trees and foliage.

As soon as we were off the ship, the pilots were taken to the airstrip. The dusty road over which we traveled was inches deep in pumice and bitter volcanic ash. The airstrip was desolate and forbidding. Dust and ashes rose into the air directly behind us. Mutters of despair rose from the pilots when they found among the parked fighters several of the long-obsolete, open-cockpit, fixed-landing-gear Claude fighters! It was all too much for me. I became ill again and collapsed. Lieutenant Sasai rushed me to the half-completed hospital on a hill bordering the airstrip.

I learned early the next morning that Rabaul was by no means the place of exile I believed it to be. Instead of being isolated from the war, Rabaul was rapidly being sucked into its very center.

The air-raid alarm jerked me out of a drugged sleep. Through the window I saw a dozen Marauders, twin-engined bombers, streaking low over the harbor and expertly pouring bombs into the *Komaki Maru*, the ship which had brought us here from Bali. Her crew, unloading cargo when the B-26 bombers struck, scattered across the pier and dove into the water. In a few moments the burning and gutted ship was sinking. The bombers, all bearing Australian markings, then worked over the runway and the planes parked there. For three successive days the Marauders returned to blast the field and anything which moved. They cruised slowly at low altitude, their gunners enjoying a field day of strafing. No man was safe above the ground, for he was sure to draw the fire of several heavy machine guns.

The attacks were the best possible tonic for me. At least Rabaul promised action to jerk me out of the stupor into which I had sunk from so many weeks of being grounded. I begged the doctor to discharge me from the hospital at once; I fairly itched to get my hands at the controls of a Zero again.

The doctor laughed. "You stay here, Sakai, for another few days. There's no use letting you out now. We haven't any fighters for you to fly. When our planes come in, I'll let you go."

Four days later, greatly improved, I left the hospital. With nineteen other fighter pilots I climbed into a four-engined flying boat which had arrived only that morning. We were soon to be flying again, for the seaplane was from the converted carrier *Kasuga* which had brought twenty new Zero fighter planes for our squadron. Constant enemy reconnaissance and bombing prevented the *Kasuga* from entering Rabaul, and she waited near Buka Island, 200 miles away, for the seaplane to transport us there.

Two hours later we were back at Rabaul, grinning like school children with our twenty new fighters, all armed and ready for combat. That same day, however, a reconnaissance plane saw our fighters on the ground and disappeared before we could take off. Rabaul became quiet, except for the volcanic eruptions which continued unabated.

For the next several weeks there was a constant flow of fighters and bombers into Rabaul. We rapidly accumulated new strength for the growing offensive to be directed against Australia and Port Moresby in New Guinea. We were told that Japanese plans called for the complete occupation of New Guinea.

Early in April, thirty of us from the Tainan Wing transferred to a new air base at Lae, on the eastern coast of New Guinea. Captain Masahisa Saito led our group to the new installation. Then began some of the fiercest air battles of the entire Pacific war. Only 180 miles away from the Allied bastion of Port Moresby, we began our new assignments by flying escort almost daily for our bombers, which flew from Rabaul to hammer the enemy installations in the critical Moresby area. No longer was the war entirely one-sided. As often as we lashed out at Moresby, Allied fighters and bombers came to attack Lae. The valor of the Allied pilots and their willingness to fight surprised us all. Whenever they attacked Lae, they were invariably intercepted and several of their planes were damaged or shot down. Our attacks on Moresby also contributed to the Allied losses.

The willingness of the Allied pilots to engage us in combat deserves special mention here, for, regardless of the odds, their fighters were always screaming in to attack. And it is important to point out that their fighter planes were clearly inferior in performance to our own Zeros. Furthermore, almost all of our pilots were skilled air veterans; coupled with the Zero's outstanding performance, this afforded us a distinct advantage. The men we fought then were among the bravest I have ever encountered, no less so than our own pilots who, three years later, went out willingly on missions from which there was no hope of return.

CHAPTER TWELVE

ON APRIL 8 I flew with eight other pilots from Rabaul to our new base on Lae. I groaned when I circled the field. Where were the hangars, the maintenance shops, the control tower? Where was anything but a dirty, small runway? I felt as though I were landing on a carrier deck. On three sides of the runway there towered the rugged mountains of the Papuan peninsula; the fourth side, from which I approached, was bordered by the ocean.

Twenty-one other pilots, who had preceded us by several days, awaited us at the end of the runway as we taxied off the strip. Honda and Yonekawa, my wingmen in the Java theater, were the first to greet me.

"Welcome home, Sakai!" Honda shouted, grinning. "The world's most wonderful place greets you!"

I looked at Honda. As usual, he was joking, although I could find little cause for humor in this forsaken mudhole. The runway was 3,000 feet long at the most, and ran at a right angle from the mountain slope almost down to the water. Adjacent to the beach was a small aircraft hangar, riddled with shrapnel and bullet holes. Three shattered Australian transport planes lay in a tangled heap on the floor, and demolished equipment littered the area. The hangar and its contents had been bombed and strafed by our planes during landing operations the previous month.

The Lae airdrome had been hacked out by the Australians to airlift supplies and gold ore to and from the Kokoda Mine, which lay deep within the formidable Owen Stanley Mountains. Overland access to the mine was almost impossible, since thick, steaming jungles and precipitous mountain slopes barred the way to foot travel. The seaport was as desolate as the airfield. A single merchant ship of 500 tons, also Australian, lay in the harbor mud, its stem and a mast jutting from the water, near the primitive pier. And that was the only vessel in sight. I was convinced that Lae was the worst airfield I had ever seen, not excluding Rabaul or even the advanced fields in China.

However, nothing could dampen Honda's spirits. "I tell you, Saburo," he insisted, "you have come to the best hunting grounds on the earth. Don't let this field or the jungle fool you. We have never had better opportunities to bag game than we have here." He was still grinning. Honda was serious; he liked. being here. He went on to explain that the isolated air base had seen brisk action for three consecutive days before my arrival. On April 5, four Zeros from Lae escorting seven bombers raided Port Moresby and shot down two enemy fighters with the loss of a Zero. On the next day, the same number of planes went out, and the fighter pilots came home jubilantly with claims for five enemy planes shot down. Yesterday, the seventh, two Zeros intercepted three enemy bombers over Salamaua and in a running fight shot down two, in addition to one probable. The enemy gunners took one Zero with them.

To Honda, action was the most important thing in life. He was indifferent to the pesthole from which we flew; that was unimportant.

That afternoon we assembled for briefing in the airfield Command Post. I use the words Command Post freely. The CP was ridiculously inadequate. It failed to deserve even the name "shack," for it had no walls! Mats hung from flimsy overhead beams to serve as walls, curtains, and doors. The room was barely large enough to hold all thirty fliers when they huddled closely together. In the center was a large, crude table hewn from local timber. A few candles and one kerosene lamp served for illumination. Our electricity for telephones came from batteries.

After we had been briefed by Captain Saito, we went to our billets. Outside the CP I saw all the vehicles assigned to Lae. These consisted of an ancient, rusty, creaky Ford sedan, one decrepit truck, and one fueling vehicle. They served the entire base. There were no hangars. We lacked even a control tower! However, my obvious disappointment at Lae failed to dampen the spirits of Honda and Yonekawa. Honda grabbed my duffel bag and sang gaily as we walked to the billets; on the way Yonekawa pointed out the base facilities.

Two hundred sailors manned flak positions beyond the airstrip. They provided the entire combat garrison. These 200 men, plus 100 maintenance personnel and the thirty pilots, comprised the entire Japanese strength at Lae. During our stay, and until Lae's capture by the Allies in 1943, no attempt was made to improve our facilities, nor were any ground reinforcements brought in.

Twenty noncommissioned officers and three enlisted fliers were packed into a single shack. This so-called building was six by ten yards. In its center there rested a large table, which we used alternately for eating, for writing, and for reading. On both sides of the room cots were jammed together. A handful of candles provided our only light. The billet was a typical tropical hut with a floor raised five feet off the damp ground. A rickety staircase at its front provided entry to our "home." A big water tank lay behind the billet. The men cut an empty fuel drum open and shaped it into an impromptu bathtub. It was an unwritten law that every other night each man would bathe. Other fuel drums were cut open and bent into different shapes for use as cooking facilities and washbasins.

One orderly attended the kitchen. He was a harried man, for the task of providing sixty-nine meals a day alone kept him busy. But, despite the intense combat of later weeks, every man took special pains to wash out all his underclothes in the basins every day. We might be living in a pesthole, but no man wished his own body to become filthy.

Near the row of drums the men had dug a crude dugout for an air-raid shelter. When the enemy bombers came, flying swiftly and low over the trees in surprise attacks, the dugouts were filled in amazingly short time by men leaping from the billets, bath, or latrine.

We were quartered some 500 yards east of the airstrip and walked or ran to the runway to reach our planes. The luxury of motorized transportation appeared only when we had orders to scramble. Then the Ford snorted its way down to pick us up.

Five hundred yards northeast of the strip lay the officers' quarters. Their billet was exactly the same as ours. Their only advantage was that ten officers comprised their total strength; they had the same facilities for half the number of men. The base commander, his deputy, and an assistant crowded into a smaller shack adjoining the officers' billet.

Our daily schedule for the four months following our arrival settled into an almost unvarying routine. At 2:30 a.m. the maintenance crews were aroused from their sleep to prepare our fighters. One hour later the orderlies woke all the pilots.

Breakfast was taken either at the billet or, occasionally, around the Command Post. Our menu was monotonous and unvarying. A dish of rice, soybean-paste soup with dried vegetables, and pickles comprised breakfast. For the first month the rice was mixed with an unsavory barley to stretch out our supplies.

After four weeks of steady combat, however, the barley was stopped. At its best, our chow at Lae was pitifully inadequate.

Following breakfast six pilots waited by their planes, their fighters warmed up and ready for take-off. These were to be scrambled for interception, and they stood at the end of the runway, poised for immediate flight. We never flew scout missions at Lae, and radar was something unknown. But the six fighters could be moving in seconds.

Those pilots not scheduled for the scramble flight waited around the CP for orders. With little to discuss except aerial tactics, we resorted to chess and checkers to pass the time.

At eight in the morning a formation of Zeros went aloft for patrol. On a fighter sortie, they took the shortest route for the enemy area, down Moresby Alley. If the mission was bomber escort, we flew southeastward along the Papuan coastline and joined the bombers over the usual rendezvous of Buna.

Usually we were back at Lae by noon for lunch. It was hardly anything to come home for. The meals were unchanging and exactly the same fare we would have for supper. Lunch consisted of bowls of steaming rice and canned fish or meat. The officers were only slightly better off; their rations were the same, but the five orderlies assigned to them took special pains to disguise the food as "different" dishes.

Between the regular three meals, all pilots were fed fruit juice and various types of candy to compensate for the deficiency of vitamins and calories in our regular meals.

About five o'clock each evening, all the pilots assembled for daily gymnastics—a required athletic course designed to keep our bodies agile and our reflexes sharp. After the group training, all men off emergency stand-by returned to their billets for supper and bathing, and spent two or three hours reading or writing letters home. By eight or nine we were in bed.

Our recreation was all improvised. The pilots often took out their guitars, ukuleles, accordions, or harmonicas, and joined together to play our national songs.

While the Rabaul base hired many natives to work as coolies, our own force at Lae had no natives to do our work. The nearest village was two miles away, and no coaxing or coercion could force the inhabitants to expose themselves to the attacks which came almost daily. They were terrified by the roaring planes, the machine guns, and die shattering thunder of bombs.

So this was Lae. The chow was poor, the daily schedule harsh and unchanging. We had no post exchange, or any other recreation facilities. Women? At Lae, everyone asked, "What are those?"

Yet, our morale was high. Certainly, we lacked the physical comforts—and even some of the so-called necessities—of everyday life, but this was little cause for complaint. We were here not to have our personal requirements met but to fight. We wanted to fight; what were we fighter pilots for, except to engage enemy planes in combat? At Bali, with a paradise at our disposal, the men bitched unceasingly. At Bali we had been grounded, and clipping the wings of our group was the worst possible punishment.

It must be remembered that the pilots' garrison at Lae was unlike those of other air bases. Every one of us was hand-picked from our Air Force. At Lae our officers had collected the men whose only desire was to be squeezing the gun trigger in a Zero while riding an enemy fighter's tail.

On April 11 I was back in combat. It was a most auspicious return, for on that day I scored my first "double play." The prospect of returning to combat after nearly two months of enforced idleness excited me. The day before, April 10, I was not scheduled to fly, and had to remain on the ground while the other pilots enjoyed a field day. Six of our fighters escorted seven bombers to Moresby, shot down two enemy bombers caught trying to flee the enemy field, and probably shot down a third. Later the same day three stand-by Zeros scrambled from the Lae runway to make a timely interception of several enemy bombers over Salamaua; of the latter, one was shot down and the others damaged.

Our flight on the eleventh was more of a familiarization mission. With eight other new arrivals to Lae we took off and formed into three V's, flying toward Moresby. During the run along the coastline we pulled steadily for altitude. The weather was perfect, and the white sandy beach looked like a mass of bleached bones ground up and scattered along the edge of the island. Then the Owen Stanley Range towered in front of us, jutting 15,000 feet above the ocean. Despite their extreme height, no snow capped their peaks, and the slopes resembled vast walls of fearsome jungle.

At 16,500 feet we crossed the mountain ridgeline. And, abruptly, we were in a new world: the enemy's. I failed to sight even a single ship on the vast, deep blue surface of the Coral Sea. The water was an incredible indigo-marble sheet, stretching as far as the eye could see. The mountains before us sloped down to the southern coast in a decline more gradual than their drop to our airstrip. Otherwise it was all the same.

Forty-five minutes after the take-off, the Moresby base slipped beneath my wings. I could see a large number of planes of different types on the ground. Many were being rushed from their exposed positions on the field to jungle revetments hidden from the air by the thick foliage surrounding the enemy strip. The antiaircraft guns remained silent—perhaps we were above their effective range. It seemed to be a perfect setup for a strafing attack—we could hit the planes on the ground long before they could be in their revetments and safe from our guns. But the orders were for a familiarization flight—air combat only, and no strafing.

We passed Moresby, and turned out to the Coral Sea. After a while we retraced our former course, again passing over the enemy base. We were amazed that the enemy gunners and pilots seemed to ignore our presence and offered no resistance.

We passed over the airfield, this time with the sun directly behind us, cruising slowly when we finally sighted the enemy's planes, four P-39s, the first Airacobras I had ever seen. They were flying almost directly at us, some three miles off and to our left. It was impossible to tell yet whether or not we had been sighted. I jettisoned my fuel tank and poured power to the engine, my two wingmen right with me. I pulled alongside our lead fighter, and signaled my discovery to Lieutenant Sasai, requesting cover for our attack. He waved his hand forward. "Go ahead. We'll cover you."

Not a move from the four Airacobras yet. We were in luck. With the blinding sun directly before them, the American pilots failed to pick out our approaching fighters. The P-39s flew in two pairs, the first two planes preceding the others by about 300 yards.

I moved Honda behind and above me, and signaled the less experienced Yonekawa to follow directly behind my fighter. Then we were only 500 yards from the enemy planes, heeling over to the left. In a few seconds we would be ready to strike. If only they continued to be blinded by the sun, we could hit them before they even knew we were in the air.

Even as I was ready to roll over for the attack, I changed my approach. If I pulled up to come in from a dive, I would lose the advantage of having the sun behind me. Instead, I shoved the stick forward and dove, Honda and Yonekawa sticking to me like glue. We went down and then came around in a sharp, fast turn, in perfect position.

The last two fighters were now above and ahead of me, unaware of our approach. They were still blinded, and I closed the distance steadily, waiting until it would be impossible to miss the target. The two P-39s were almost wing to wing, and at fifty yards they were clear in my range finder. *Now!* I jammed down on the cannon button, and in a second the first Airacobra was done for. The shells converged in the center of the fuselage; pieces of metal broke off and flipped away. A fountain of smoke and flame belched outward.

I skidded and brought the guns to bear on the second P-39. Again the shells went directly home, exploding inside and tearing the fighter into bits. Both Airacobras plummeted out of control.

I brought the Zero out of its skid and swung up in a tight turn, prepared to come out directly behind the two lead fighters. The battle was already over! Both P-39s were plunging crazily toward the earth, trailing bright flames and thick smoke. They had been shot down as quickly as the two I had caught so unawares. I recognized one of the Zeroes still pulling out from its diving pass, Hiroyoshi Nishizawa, a rookie pilot at the controls. The second Zero, which had made a kill with a single firing pass, piloted by Toshio Ota, hauled around in a steep pull-out to rejoin the formation.

It was incredible that in less than five seconds the fight was over, and four enemy fighters were smashing on the surface far below. It was remarkable that two of the kills were registered by Nishizawa, twenty-three years old, and Ota, only twenty-two.

A word of explanation is proper here. As stated before, all the pilots at Lae were hand-picked. Foremost among the reasons for their selection was their flying aptitude; both these two young pilots stood out, even among the men with whom we flew. Many of us were combat veterans, and the newcomers were especially quick to learn. Nishizawa and Ota proved to be brilliant at the controls. They went on to become, with myself, the leading aces of the Lae Wing. Often we flew together, and were known to the other pilots as the "cleanup trio."

I can think of Nishizawa and Ota only as pilots of genius. They did not fly their airplanes, they became a part of the Zero, welded into the fiber of the fighter, an automaton which functioned, it seemed, as a machine capable of intelligent thought. They were among the greatest of all Japanese fliers.

Both men were devoted solely to their roles as fighter pilots. Everything was subordinated to their fighting function. Their skill made them particularly dangerous opponents. Even against a fighter airplane of superior performance—such as we were to encounter later in the war—their prowess enabled them individually to invite attack by several enemy planes and still emerge victorious.

Hiroyoshi Nishizawa became Japan's greatest fighter ace. He did not look the part, indeed, one had only to look at Nishizawa to feel sorry for him; one felt the man should be in a hospital bed. He was tall and lanky for a Japanese, nearly five feet eight inches in height. He had a gaunt look about him; he weighed only 140 pounds, and his ribs protruded sharply through his skin. Nishizawa suffered almost constantly from malaria and tropical skin diseases. He was pale most of the time.

Despite the worshipful attitude of his pilots, Nishizawa rarely returned the offers of intimate friendship. He cloaked himself in a cold, unfriendly reserve almost impossible to penetrate. Often he spent an entire day without speaking a word; he would not even respond to the overtures of his closest friends, the men with whom he flew and fought. We became accustomed to seeing him strolling alone, disdaining friendship, silent, almost like a pensive outcast instead of a man who was in reality the object of veneration. If there is such an expression, Nishizawa was "all pilot." He lived and breathed only to fly, and he flew for two things; the joy which comes with the ownership of that strange and wonderful world in the sky, and to fight.

Once he had taken wing, this strange and phlegmatic man underwent a startling transformation. His reserve, his silence, his spuming of his associates vanished almost as quickly as the darkness vanishes before dawn. To all who flew with him he became the "Devil." He was unpredictable in the air, a genius, a poet who seemed to make his fighter respond obediently to his gentle, sure touch at the controls. Never have I seen a man with a fighter plane do what Nishizawa would do with his Zero. His aerobatics were all at once breathtaking, brilliant, totally unpredictable, impossible, and heart-stirring to witness. He was a bird, yet he could fly in such a way as no bird could imitate.

Even his eyesight was unusual. Where we could see only sky, Nishizawa, with almost supernatural vision, could catch the specks of enemy planes still invisible to us. Never in his long and brilliant career as a warrior of the skies was this man caught unaware by the enemy. He fulfilled truly his title of Devil—only he was a devil of the blue and the clouds, a man so gifted as to make us all, even myself, envious of his genius in the air.

Toshio Ota was exactly the opposite. A brilliant youngster, Ota was amiable and friendly, willing to join in the fun and festivities of the group, quick to laugh at our jokes, instantly at the side of a fellow pilot in need of help, either in the air or on the ground. He was taller and heavier than. I was and, like Nishizawa, was inexperienced in combat on his arrival at Lae. Despite his amiability and stark contrast to Nishizawa, his talent at his controls was quickly recognized and Ota flew always as cover wingman for the squadron commander's own fighter.

Ota was hardly the typical hero type. He was too quick to grin and laugh, too quick to be friendly. The aura of hero worship could not be attached to this smiling young man, who appeared more at home, I am sure, in a nightclub than in the forsaken loneliness of Lae. Yet this intimacy with his friends in no way detracted from the great respect which his flying skill inspired; even the rough-and-ready men like Honda held him in high regard, although Honda, as well as Yonekawa, feared and shunned the Devil.

CHAPTER THIRTEEN

THE Allies poured an unceasing flow of men and materiel into their bastion at Port Moresby, and our high command called on us for more and heavier strikes against the growing complex of airstrips, ground installations, and harbor facilities.

On April 17 I flew my first escort mission to the enemy area. Thirteen Zero fighters, instead of the usual six or seven, covered the bombers; our reconnaissance reports indicated a strong Allied fighter build-up and we anticipated stronger opposition than in the past.

I was worried about my pilots. NAP 1/C Yoshio Miyazaki looked almost emaciated after a long bout with diarrhea, and I did not think him fit for duty. Despite my protestations, Miyazaki refused to stay grounded.

I was worried lest his feverish feeling affect his ability to hold the weave pattern when we flew escort, but as we neared Moresby my apprehension vanished. Miyazaki navigated perfectly with my group of six fighters, which flew top Cover for the bombers and the seven other fighters.

With the bombers at 16,000 feet and my own group 1,500 feet higher, we crossed the Owen Stanley Range. Moresby slid into view. The seven Zeros closest to the bombers suddenly broke their protecting weave and wheeled around in a tight climbing turn, still bunched together. P-40s, dropping from higher altitude to hit the bombers, had been seen too soon, and the wedge of climbing Zeros split their ranks, spilling the fighters away from the lumbering heavyweights.

The seven fighters returned to their original position. Angry blossoms of flame and black smoke burst into being below the bombers; the flak was some 1,500 feet low. However, the bursts were a roaring sign of danger. Immediately we broke formation and rolled frantically to escape. Barely in time; a second flak barrage exploded thunderously above us, but not close enough to damage our planes.

Even as we rolled back into formation, the bombers and their fighter escorts were clawing in a maximum-power climb. We knew the third flak barrage would have caught the bombers dead center if they had maintained their original course. And there it was, exactly where the bombers would have been, the violent, cracking sounds of the antiaircraft shells materializing out of nowhere. For some unknown reason the Americans refused to alter the change-of-range settings for their antiaircraft shells. They followed a pattern we could anticipate almost exactly. So precise was their battery range-setting formula, and so unchanging its use, that evading the American flak at high altitude was almost no problem.

The bombers passed over Moresby and swung into their wide, slow turns, coming back this time for their bombing run, the sun now behind the pilots and the bombardiers. Hardly had the bombers slipped into their target runs when six fighters came at us from high altitude. I hauled back on the stick, standing the Zero on its tail. The other five fighters were glued to me as we turned directly into the enemy attack. We had no chance to fire; the enemy fighters rolled away and scattered, still diving. We returned to our escort weave positions, but only two fighters slipped into their wingman positions. Miyazaki and his other two fighters had apparently gone crazy; they were swerving down, below the bombers.

I had no time to worry about Miyazaki. The enemy flak was trying to find the range, and a snarl of shells thundered 1,500 feet below the bombers. They could not evade the shells this time; they were on their runs and the bombardiers held every plane tightly in place. I kicked the rudder bar and skidded away from the expected barrage. Then the bombers were gone, hidden completely by a series of bursting shells which spewed out thick smoke. For a moment it looked as though the shells had struck dead center. But then—miraculously, it seemed—the seven planes emerged in formation from the boiling smoke. Their bays were open and the black missiles tumbled through the air. I watched them curve, picking up speed; they erupted in fountains of smoke, the blast waves from each bomb bursting outward in a flash of light as it struck.

Their bellies empty, the bombers picked up speed amid the continual bursts of flak, then wheeled hard over to the left. Miyazaki was flying some 1,500 feet below the bombers. He was in a fantastic position. Without radio (they had been ripped out to increase our range), I could not call him to return to position, and we dared not leave the bombers unprotected.

We passed Moresby and the bursting flak fell behind. I sighed with relief. Too soon! Nearly a mile above us, a single P-40 fighter dove with incredible speed. He came down so fast I could not move a muscle; one second he was above us, the next the lone plane plummeted like lightning into the bombers. Six hundred yards in front of me, I watched the fighter—he was going to ram!

How that plane ever got through the few yards' clearance between the third and fourth bombers of the left echelon, I shall never know. It seemed impossible, but it happened. With all guns blazing, the P-40 ripped through the bomber formation and poured a river of lead into Miyazaki's plane.

Instantly the Zero burst into flames. With tremendous speed the P-40 disappeared far below us. Miyazaki's plane drifted slowly down, trailing flame. Brilliant fire flared out and an explosion tore the Zero into tiny pieces of wreckage. We failed to see even a piece of metal falling. Everything had happened in three or four seconds. We maintained our course for home. Over Buna our fighters broke, abandoned their roles as escort, and turned for Lae.

Miyazaki's loss was a painful lesson to all of us. I am firmly convinced that in those early days of the war the individual skill of our pilots was definitely superior to that of the men flying the Dutch, Australian, and American fighters. Our training, which was conducted in prewar Japan, was more meticulous than that of any other nation. Flying meant everything to us, and we spared no effort to learn every aspect of air-to-air combat. And, of course, we flew a fighter superior in most respects to those of the enemy. In the air battles of World War II, however, individual skill was not enough to insure continued survival. There were many instances, of course, when planes met in individual dogfights, and a pilot's prowess gave him victory. This was not, however, the general rule, but the exception. Our greatest failing in aerial combat lay in the fact that we lacked teamwork, a skill, unfortunately, which the Americans developed so thoroughly as the war went on.

Miyazaki's loss, as well as that of three other Zero pilots shot down early in April, I can attribute only to the inability of our fighter pilots to function as a closely knit team. When encountering enemy fighters, our pilots were more apt to scramble in all directions for a wild free-for-all, one plane against another, much as in the days of World War I. To the Japanese pilots of the late thirties, the most valued quality of a fighter plane was its ability to cut inside an enemy fighter's turn. Maneuverability was desirable above all other characteristics.

And it worked well—under certain conditions, and for a certain time. But the value of the individual dogfight technique evaporated when the enemy refused to fight your own kind of battle, or when his tenacious adherence to a preconceived plan reduced the effectiveness of the lone-wolf attack.

Two days after Miyazaki's death, seven B-26 bombers attacked Lae. Fortunately, we received sufficient advance warning and had nine fighters in the air to meet the planes as they stormed in at a height of only 1,500 feet. For an hour we fought a bitter running battle with the Marauders; in the end only one bomber went down, with another fleeing as a cripple. It was the clumsiest air fight I had ever seen. The nine Zeros lacked organization. Instead of making concerted attacks against one or two planes, and using massed firepower to cut the B-26s apart, our pilots were overzealous and threw themselves all over the sky. Repeatedly several planes jerked frantically out of their firing passes to avoid a collision with another Zero or to evade the fire of a friendly fighter. It was incredible that none of our planes rammed into another or shot any of us down.

I fairly exploded in anger back at Lae. I jumped from the Zero's cockpit, brushing aside my ground crew, and shouted at every pilot to stand and listen. For perhaps fifteen minutes I cursed their clumsy stupidity, pointing out to each man his errors and stressing the unpleasant fact that only a miracle had brought them all back to Lae alive. From that night on, we held sessions every evening to improve our teamwork. These classes continued for the first week during a strange and unexpected lull in the air war.

On April 23, Nishizawa, Ota, and I made a reconnaissance flight to Kairuku, a new enemy base north of Moresby, shooting up and burning several carrier planes on the airstrip. We had been ordered to carry out only a reconnaissance mission, but the temptation was too much—especially after our recent poor showings in the air.

Our report brought us orders to launch a fifteen-plane strafing attack on the following day. We swooped down on six B-26 bombers, fifteen P-40s, and one P-39, all of which seemed to be evacuating the field. We tallied two bombers and six P-40s as definite kills, with a probable for the P-39. After the one-sided air battle we continued up to Moresby, strafing and burning one anchored PBY. Perhaps my emphasis on teamwork was the fault—especially since I rode close herd on the other fighters—but I ended the day without being able to claim a single plane. Neither could Nishizawa, to his great disgust.

The next day we returned to Moresby. Despite their heavy losses in the one-sided fight of the previous day, the enemy put up stiff resistance. Seven P-40s challenged our fifteen fighters; before the wild melee was over, six enemy fighters plunged earthward in flames. We suffered no losses and, with the air cleared, strafed Moresby and Kairuku, burning five B-26s and two P-40s.

Apparently our new attempt to achieve teamwork was effective. However, it failed to benefit me or Nishizawa. After two consecutive battles in which the other pilots scored heavily, we returned unable to claim a single kill. We argued late into the night in an attempt to analyze each other's actions in the air, to try to discover what we were doing wrong. Everything *seemed* all right, but the cold fact of the matter was that we were not getting our bullets home.

Another air battle followed on the twenty-sixth. Again, I returned scoreless. Again, Nishizawa was unable to claim a single victory, although three of seven P-40s had gone down.

Nishizawa was baffled. Ignoring his range finder, he had clung grimly to a P-40 whose pilot was frantically trying to elude the Zero glued to his tail. At point-blank range Nishizawa, chasing the P-40 all over the sky, poured bullets and cannon shells into the enemy fighter. The latter nevertheless escaped.

April 29 was Emperor Hirohito's birthday, and our commander planned a modest celebration in honor of the special event. All sailors with any cooking experience joined the kitchen staff and prepared the best possible breakfast from the limited supplies available. The Allies had made almost no effort to attack Lae in the preceding few days. This lull in battle, plus our feeling of well-being on this special occasion, threw us off guard, as the enemy had probably hoped it would. We were just finishing our morning meal at seven o'clock when sentries screamed, *"Enemy planes!"* Immediately a blaring, discordant sound shattered the morning stillness. Buckets, drums, hollow logs, and the like were struck as warning signals. Two bugles blew shrilly to add to the racket—our air-raid warning system.

We raced for the runway too late. The bombs had already fallen, and done their work. We looked up to see our old friends, the B-17s. Three of them cruised at 20,000 feet. They dropped only a few bombs, but, considering their great height, with as excellent accuracy as I have ever witnessed. Five Zeros lay in flaming wreckage. Four others were seriously damaged, riddled throughout with jagged bomb splinters. Of the six stand-by fighters, only two were in flying condition.

Ota and one other pilot reached the planes first. In seconds they had gunned their motors and were racing down the runway. By the time the rest of us reached our planes, it was too late to take off. The three B-17s and the two Zeros were out of sight and, with their amazing speed, the B-17s were beyond our reach. The time passed slowly, and we cursed the bombers and fretted over Ota's return. An hour later a single Zero dropped in for a landing. It was Endo. "We attacked while climbing," he explained, "and worked over the B-17s as much as possible. Ota crippled one bomber and was still shooting up the airplane when my ammunition ran out. So I left for home."

Another hour passed without Ota. We were worried about his safe return. Ota, the friend of one and all, the brilliant pilot, attacking at least two heavily armed B-17s alone. Endo became frantic, and mumbled morosely about having left Ota because of his lack of ammunition.

Fifteen minutes more went by, then Captain Saito stuck his head out of the CP and shouted joyously to us, "Hey! He's safe! Ota just called from Salamaua. He got one Fortress definitely. He landed for fuel; he'll be home soon."

Wonderful news! But there was still unfinished business at hand. Six fliers, including Nishizawa and myself, were selected to "return the Emperor's birthday greetings" to Moresby. We would have felt better had there been sixteen Zeros, but our six fighters were the only machines fit for combat. The enemy undoubtedly expected a reprisal for his attack against Lae. To forestall running into a storm of waiting antiaircraft fire, we cleared the mountain ridge at 16,000 feet and then, instead of continuing toward Moresby at high altitude, dove immediately once we were past the crest. We flew a steep triangle, hitting its top point as we cleared the mountain range and then diving steeply at the enemy air base. It was perfect! The enemy timing was thrown off completely; no one expected us to attack in this new fashion.

We hit the field in a wide sweep just above the ground. Dozens of maintenance men were crowded around bombers and fighters which appeared ready for take-off. That meant full fuel tanks and bomb bays, made to order for the surprise strafing run.

They were like sitting ducks, and we sprayed bullets and shells down the runway. I could see the men on the ground staring at us in amazement, hardly believing their eyes. Six Zeros out of nowhere!

The initial pass was perfect. Not a gun had been fired at us. At the end of the runway, with the surprised gun batteries still silent, we pulled up into a steep turn and dove immediately for another run. The view on the way back was excellent. Three fighters and a bomber were burning fiercely. This time we worked over another row of aircraft, parked neatly in a long line. We hadn't expected this kind of cooperation! Again we fired in a long, running pass, strafing the enemy planes. We hit four bombers and fighters, although none burned. Men ran frantically in all directions as we screamed down for our second strafing run, and dozens remained on the ground, riddled by our bullets. We made three passes in all and then raced away at high speed. Not until we were on our way out of the area did the first antiaircraft gun open up. I grinned; let them waste their ammunition!

But at 5:30 the next morning the enemy repaid us with a visit of his own with three Marauders, coming in low and fast, no higher than 600 feet. The earth shook and heaved as the B-26s dumped their bombs directly onto the airstrip. As the smoke cleared we saw five of our stand-by fighters tearing for altitude. They were hardly off the ground when the enemy raiders turned and came back again, thundering over the field before the fighters could close with them. Then they were gone, disappearing into the breaking dawn. They had done well; one Zero burned brightly and another was smashed wreckage. Four other fighters and a bomber were badly holed with bullets and bomb fragments.

For the next several days the tempo of the air war increased furiously. The Allies returned our next strafing attack with a beautifully executed run by twelve P-39s against our airfield, and heavily damaged nine bombers and three fighters. We caught the Airacobras on their withdrawal, and shot down two without losses on our part. But, again, neither Nishizawa nor I was able to bring down a plane.

I broke out of my slump—as did Nishizawa—the day after the strafing attack by the P-39s. Nine of us flew to Moresby, spoiling for a fight. We got one. Nine enemy fighters, P-39s and P-40s, waited for us over the enemy airstrip, willing to fight!

Hardly were we in sight when they broke off their circle and roared head on against our planes. I took on the first enemy fighter. The P-40 rolled into a turn as he came at me, hoping for a belly shot. I cut sharply inside him and fired. I could not have timed it better; the P-40 staggered into the burst. Instantly the enemy pilot snapped over in a left roll, but he was already too late. Another burst and the fighter exploded in flames.

But he had friends and I jerked out of my turn as a P-39 dove on me. No need to run for it; I drew a split-S and the enemy pilot walked right into the trap. For a moment his belly hung before my guns as he tried to loop away. I needed only that moment, and I squeezed the cannon trigger. The shells caught the enemy fighter while it was still pulling up, and the plane fell apart in the air.

He was sure, I knew, to have a wingman, and even as I fired my burst I had the stick hard back and the rudder bar all the way down, horsing the Zero back into the tightest turn I could make. It worked; I came out in line for a quick burst. The startled pilot tried to disengage by diving, but too late. I rolled out of the turn in time to snap out another burst. The enemy fighter flew directly into my fire, staggered, then plunged in a dive.

I shouted with joy! I was out of the slump. Three fighters in less than fifteen seconds! My first "triple play"!

The fight was over, and I had scored the only kills. Six enemy fighters fled in wild power dives, too fast for our fighters to catch up, although Nishizawa and the seven other Zeros were attempting to do so. It was impossible; the American P-39s and P-40s could always escape us by diving.

Back at the Lae airstrip, my mechanics came running to me excitedly. They were amazed to find that I had fired only 610 rounds of ammunition during the day's air battle, an average of just over 200 rounds for each enemy fighter. Nishizawa climbed from his plane with his face black with angry disappointment.

The next day, May 2, we flew back to Moresby with a force of eight Zeros. Thirteen enemy fighters waited for us, cruising slowly at 18,000 feet. Nishizawa spotted them first, and jumped the gun. We followed his lead as he swung around in a wide turn, coming up to the enemy formation from their left and rear. What was the matter with these pilots? Didn't they ever look all about them? We hit the thirteen planes before they even knew we were in the air. Before they could roll away in evasive action, several enemy fighters were falling in flames. Our total bag for the day came to eight P-39s and P-40s, of which I claimed two.

Nishizawa leaped from his cockpit as the Zero came to a stop. We were startled; usually he climbed down slowly. Today, however, he stretched luxuriously, raised both arms above his head, and shrieked, "Yeeeeooww!" We stared in stupefaction; this was completely out of character. Then Nishizawa grinned and walked away. His smiling mechanic told us why. He stood before the fighter and held up three fingers. Nishizawa was back in form!

On May 7, after several days of rest back at Rabaul, I flew in what I called a "dream sweep." Four Zeros were ordered out for reconnaissance over Moresby, and, when each pilot saw who his wingmates were, he shouted happily. We were the wing's leading aces. I had twenty-two planes to my credit; Nishizawa had thirteen; Ota now had eleven; and Takatsuka trailed us with nine. Our four best aces! What a day to mix it up with the enemy! We knew we could count on each other to cover anyone in trouble. And certainly any enemy fighter pilots wouldn't know they were flying into the worst hornet's nest possible! I hoped we'd run into opposition today.

We found them. We were circling over Moresby when Nishizawa rocked his wings in signal and pointed at ten fighters in a long column, coming at us from the sea, about 2,000 feet higher than our group. Nishizawa and Ota formed a wedge of two planes, with Takatsuka and myself immediately behind and a little lower. Four P-40s separated from the enemy formation and dove at us.

All four Zeros nosed up in a rapid, almost vertical climb, instead of rolling away and scattering as the enemy pilots expected. The first P-40 went up in a wild loop, trying to get away from his own trap. The belly Hashed in front of me and I snapped out a burst. The shells caught him and tore a wing off. I came out of the climb in an Immelmann and saw each Zero hammering away at a P-40. All burst into flames. The remaining six fighters were on us. We scattered to the right and left, coming up in tight loops and arcing over. It worked! All of us came out with a fighter beneath us. Three more P-40s disintegrated and burned; one escaped. The three remaining fighters stuck their noses down and ran for it.

On May 8 and 9 I destroyed two more enemy fighters, a P-39 and a P-40, in sweeps over Moresby. On the tenth I shot down a P-39 with a record low consumption of ammunition—only four cannon shells. It was the best shooting I had ever done, and the lowest number of ammunition rounds ever required to destroy an enemy plane. I was flying over the Coral Sea with Honda and Yonekawa as my wingmen. After some fifteen minutes of patrolling we noticed a lone Airacobra flying about 3,000 feet over our fighters, cruising slowly. The pilot seemed oblivious to everything; he maintained his course as we approached from behind and below.

I kept gaining altitude from directly beneath his belly, where the pilot was completely blind unless taking evasive action in a deliberate search for other planes. Honda and Yonekawa were about 200 yards below me, flying cover position.

Incredibly, the P-39 allowed me to close in. He had not the slightest idea that I was coming up on him. I kept narrowing the distance until I was less than twenty yards beneath the enemy fighter. He still had no idea I was there! The opportunity was too good to waste: I snapped several pictures with my Leica. My speedometer showed 130 knots, and I marked this figure down as the cruising speed for the P-39.

The amazing formation flight of my Zero and the P-39 continued. With Honda and Yonekawa sliding up to catch the Airacobra if he should catch sight of me and dive, I climbed slowly until I was off to the right and slightly below the enemy plane. I could see the pilot clearly and I still could not understand his stupidity in not searching the sky around him. He was a big man, wearing a white cap. I studied him for several seconds, then dropped below his fighter.

I aimed carefully before firing, and then jabbed lightly for a moment on the cannon trigger. There was a cough and (I discovered later) two shells from each weapon burst out. I saw two quick explosions along the bottom of the P-39's right wing, and two others in the center of the fuselage. The P-39 broke in two! The two fuselage halves tumbled crazily as they fell, then disintegrated into smaller pieces. The pilot did not bail out.

CHAPTER FOURTEEN

SEVERAL weeks at Lae taught me a new respect for the luxury of sleep. Life at the airdrome was reduced to its simplest terms. During the day we either flew fighter missions or waited on stand-by alert. At night we wished only to sleep. The enemy, however, had other ideas about the matter, and almost unfailingly his bombers punctured the darkness to string rows of bombs against the field and to send ribbons of tracers into the ground as they passed over at low height.

We could dispense with the foods we desired most, live in shacks, and fly from a primitive field, but we could not go without sleep. And the Americans and Australians exerted every effort to keep us awake at night.

It became so bad that often we abandoned our billets. Pilots went out to the runway after dark and slept in the craters dug that same night by enemy bombs. Our theory, afforded substance by an overwhelming desire to sleep, was that there was little probability of an enemy bomb striking exactly where one had fallen previously. I have no concept of the law of probabilities involved, but I do know that less than six pilots were killed in enemy night attacks during our entire tour of duty at Lae.

The constant attacks, almost daily flying, and primitive living conditions reduced tempers to hair-trigger status. Nothing less than the most exemplary conduct on the part of our officers prevented serious friction among the pilots—and this I consider the most remarkable fact of all at our jungle outpost.

Our base commander, Captain Masahisa Saito, was a Samurai officer who maintained about himself an air of reserve and dignity— sharply different from that of the attention-demanding, caste-conscious Army officers who surrounded General Hideki Tojo at Tokyo. Quiet, yet authoritative, Saito was regarded with devoted respect by all his men. He was careful always to be the last man to enter shelter when enemy bombers attacked Lae. Despite the sluggishness of some of us, we never failed to see Captain Saito waiting—sometimes impatiently, if the bombs were already exploding!—for a pilot to come scrambling to the dugout. The captain would walk slowly from his billet or the Command Post to the shelter trenches, look up at the skies, and scan the field to see that all of his men had taken cover. And only then would he himself seek protection. Needless to say, this action had a wonderful effect on his subordinates. It is one of those unexplainable things, but this brave officer survived the war without suffering a wound.

But the most unforgettable man of my combat life was Lieutenant Junichi Sasai, my direct superior, who led perhaps Japan's strongest fighter squadron. Under Sasai's command were four of Japan's leading aces—Nishizawa, Ota, Takatsuka, and myself. It is no exaggeration to say that every man who flew with Sasai would not have hesitated even a moment to die in defense of the young lieutenant. I have recounted how his personal intervention aided me so greatly during the unpleasant voyage from Bali to Rabaul. More than once I wondered at the time about his presence, and felt inclined to believe it was an hallucination—it was not only unprecedented, but unthinkable, that a squadron commander should reduce himself to the status of an orderly to attend a man at his sickbed. And yet, this was what Sasai did.

Twenty-seven years old and unmarried, Sasai kept in his billet an image of Yoshitsune, the legendary Japanese war hero. Sasai disdained the demands of the naval caste system, and paid no more attention to the appearance of his clothes than any of the other pilots. Again, this may seem a small point upon which to dwell, but it was a mountainous matter in the Japanese officer code.

After our arrival at Lae, I was amazed to witness Sasai's intimate interest in the welfare and health of his pilots. When a man was stricken with malaria or other tropical disease, including the vicious fungi which rotted away a man's flesh, Sasai was the first to be at his side, tending him, soothing him, and raising incredible hell with the hospital orderlies to assure his pilot's continued and constant ministrations. In order to help his men, he exposed himself without flinching to some of the worst diseases man has ever known. To us he became almost legendary. Men who did not hesitate to kill and who lusted for battle wept shamelessly when they witnessed Sasai's deeds, and pledged eternal loyalty to the young officer.

One night we watched in wonder as Sasai entered the hospital to go to the side of a pilot stricken with a fungus which was eating painfully at his flesh. Nobody knew whether or not the disease was communicable, only that it was horrible. Yet it was Sasai who tended the unfortunate; it was Sasai who forfeited sleep; it was Sasai who comforted.

And all this was done in defiance of what was probably the strictest military caste system in the world, where a breach of that caste by a subordinate could result in discipline—justified in the mind of the superior officer—by brutal beating or even by death. Even here at Lae, barely more than a jungle outpost, the hierarchy system was strictly maintained. It was unthinkable that there should be a breach of respect, no matter how slight, to an officer.

Sasai especially would have had just cause to fall back upon this caste distinction if he so wished, for he was a graduate of Eta Jima, Japan's Annapolis. Perhaps the other officers objected; I do not know. But Sasai often forfeited the more comfortable accommodations of the officers' billet with its lesser crowding, and spent much of his time with us.

He took every precaution to assure our health. One of the medical requirements at Lae was that we take quinine pills every other day for protection against malaria. Because of their bitter taste, these were unpalatable to the pilots. Sasai treated the men almost like children when he discovered them ignoring their quinine doses. He would take several of the bitter pills in his mouth, chew them, and lick his lips. The average man could not refrain from spitting these out violently, but not Sasai. No man who watched his own squadron commander go through this routine would dare to complain of the quinine's bitterness!

When I was alone with Sasai, I expressed my wonder at his ability to eat the quinine in this extraordinary fashion.

"Don't take me for a hypocrite," Sasai explained quietly, "I hate them just as badly as anyone. But my men must be kept from malaria. Actually, I'm doing for them exactly what my mother did for me when I was ill as a child."

In our many conversations Sasai told me of his childhood, of years of illness, of being bedridden. He told me with some embarrassment of whimpering at having to take medicine, of how his mother would pretend she enjoyed the medicine her sickly youngster needed in order to live.

Because of his mother's years of devotion, Sasai's health gradually improved. He made an intense effort to build his weakened body, often suffering great pain to gain stamina. In high school he lost his sickly appearance and finally became a judo champion. In the Naval Academy and at the Fliers School, Sasai had stood out as a leading student and in athletics.

As the months passed at Lae and the air battles grew in intensity, our supplies gradually diminished. Despite the excellent fighting record of our own wing of Zero fighters, we found it impossible to pin down the Allies. They appeared in ever-growing numbers in the air. Coupled with their always persistent aggressiveness, they proved a formidable force, indeed. Their fighters and bombers prowled over the islands and ocean area by day and by night, smashing at our supply ships in devastating attacks. American submarines also took a fearful toll.

As a result, our Navy was forced to hide its ships by day and resort to the cloak of darkness to move its supplies. But such movements were always inadequate and even the trickle of supplies delivered by surface shipping fell off. In desperation the Navy commandeered its submarines to deliver supplies to us. This was at best a compromise with necessity, for the submarines were severely limited in their capacity. Eventually we were reduced to shipments of only the most critical goods needed to continue fighting. As a result, even the few luxuries we had were reduced to the barest minimum. Beer or cigarettes were coveted by the men, and even these were never issued except as a reward when our pilots scored great victories in the air without loss to our own forces. The majority of the pilots did not drink. Cigarettes, however, were in great demand to meet the needs of many men who were inveterate smokers.

What galled the men was that the flying personnel were denied cigarettes except on occasions of registering a severe defeat upon the enemy in air combat. This did not, however, deter the officers from following their caste system and issuing daily to the nonflying officer personnel a regular cigarette ration. We cursed the administration officers, men who never flew, who smoked freely while the combat pilots—because of their enlisted status—could not do the same.

Captain Saito normally inspected the enlisted pilots' billets once every two weeks. On these inspections he always managed to "forget" his cigarette case on a desk or bunk. Nishizawa gratefully helped himself to about half of the base commander's supply from the case, and then distributed his "find" to the other pilots. But Saito did not come very often.

Finally I lost patience, and took a desperate chance. I sent my men to the native community with orders to buy native cigars. We were strictly forbidden to smoke the local tobacco, for fear that it might contain narcotics. With a package of the evil-smelling cheroots I summoned the other pilots to a far corner of the airfield. They looked at me in astonishment, hesitating to risk the wrath of higher authority by disobeying direct orders. "I'll take full responsibility for these cigars, and you smoke them," I told the group.

Without a word each man took a cigar from me as I passed among them. We all lit up.

I knew that when an officer sighted our group clustered together he would come over, and within fifteen minutes Lieutenant Sasai ran up to us with astonishment on his face. One look at the cigars was enough. "What are you doing? Have you all gone crazy?" he shouted. "Throw those things away!" Several of the men flushed with embarrassment at the unusual tone from Sasai, and hurled their cigars on the ground. Nishizawa and I refused to do so, and remained smoking.

Sasai's eyes opened wide at this refusal to obey orders. "What's the matter with you two?" he asked. "You know that smoking those things is against regulations!"

His questions was what I had hoped for. I took a deep breath and told Sasai exactly what I thought of the system which denied the combat pilots tobacco, but permitted officers who never subjected themselves to enemy guns to smoke freely. I rambled on for a while, telling Sasai whatever punishment he could give me was worth the smoking. Nishizawa stood by my side, silent as usual, puffing great clouds of smoke.

Sasai bit his lips in anger, and his face clouded. Another officer would not have hesitated to kick me as hard as he could. I turned away from Sasai—guilty at having treated this fine officer in such a shameful fashion—but went right back to smoking again. The other pilots stared at Nishizawa and me in wonder—they had never seen or even heard of an officer being defied so brazenly before.

Sasai disappeared. Several minutes later we saw the lone air-base sedan trailing a cloud of dust as it bore down upon our group with breakneck speed. The vehicle braked screechingly to a halt. Sasai angrily flung the door open, dragging two large duffel bags behind him.

He did not say a word as he opened the tops of the two bags, each bulging with packs of cigarettes! "Take these and divide them among yourselves," he said, "and don't ask any questions as to where they came from."

He looked out the car window as he drove off. "And throw those damned cigars away!" he shouted.

We called Sasai the "Flying Tiger." This name had nothing to do with the American Volunteer Group, the Flying Tigers, in China. Lieutenant Sasai always wore a belt with a large silver buckle on which was engraved the picture of a roaring tiger. Sasai's father, a retired Navy captain, had made three buckles before the war and presented one to Sasai, his only son, and one to each of the husbands of his two daughters, both naval lieutenant commanders. According to Japanese legend a tiger goes out for one thousand miles to prowl on his hunt, and always returns from his adventure. This was the significance of Sasai's engraved buckle.

Sasai was a talented pilot, but during April and early May he accounted for few victories in the air, a failure stemming directly from his lack of combat experience. Nishizawa, Ota, Takatsuka, and I were determined to see to it that Sasai emerged from his cocoon and blossomed into a full-fledged ace. We took special pains to teach the lieutenant the fine points of aerial combat. We spent many a long hour in our billets explaining the mistakes to avoid in the air and the means to assure a kill. Sasai especially had difficulty with adjusting his range finder during a dogfight, and repeatedly we went through mock battles to help him to overcome this deficiency.

On May 12 we found the opportunity to test the results of our instructions. Sasai responded perfectly by scoring—in a breathless diving and zooming sweep which took less than twenty seconds—three victories unassisted.

We were flying near Moresby in our regular morning patrol of fifteen Zeros in five V formations when I sighted three Airacobras about a mile to our right, and 1,500 feet below us. Their formation was unusual—the three fighters flew in a column with about 200 yards' distance between each plane. I pulled along Sasai's plane, and pointed out the enemy fighters. He nodded, and I gestured for him to go ahead and make the attack. He waved his hand and grinned, and we followed as he turned sharply to the right and dove.

He hit the first Airacobra in a perfect firing pass. His Zero pounced on the unsuspecting enemy plane from above and behind; he rolled to the right and fired his cannon as he closed in. His aim was excellent; the Airacobra burst into flames and fell apart in the air. Sasai pulled out of his dive and hauled back in a steep climb, rolling out 1,500 feet above and to the left of the second fighter. It seemed incredible, but the P-39 pilot maintained his original course. From his point of vantage Sasai dove, rolled to the right to adjust his firing course, and raked the P-39 from tail to nose. The fighter lurched, skidded into a wild spin, and plunged for the earth. The pilot failed to get out, probably dead from the cannon shells.

Sasai continued his attack in the same manner, climbing steeply and rolling over for the third attack, but the last pilot was not to be caught so easily. Even as Sasai began rolling to the right, the P-39's nose lifted steeply as the pilot began a loop, but too late. The plane was hauled up in the beginning of the loop when Sasai poured a stream of cannon shells into the fuselage and left wing. It was too much for the American plane, at the moment already under tremendous pressure from the loop. The left wing tore loose and instantly the plane whipped into a flat spin, trapping the pilot. Even I was astonished. Nishizawa grinned broadly at me from his cockpit as we rejoined the formation. Sasai was now an ace with his perfect one-two-three.

Sasai's lessons for the day were not over—but it was a different and more harrowing one he was about to learn. On the return to Lae, Sasai's fighter trio moved nearly two miles ahead of the main formation. I was so pleased with the lieutenant's new status as an ace that I failed to pay attention to the widening gulf of his V flight, a failure which had almost fatal consequences.

We were crossing the Owen Stanley Range, Sasai's fighters well ahead of us, when a lone Airacobra plunged like an arrow from a high cloud layer directly at the unsuspecting Zeros. Never did I regret our lack of radios as much as I did at that moment. There was no way to warn Sasai; despite my speed of almost 300 knots with the engine on maximum over-boost, I could not reach the P-39 in time to draw him off. Fortunately for Sasai, the enemy pilot did not make his attack from above. Instead, he chose the "submarine approach," diving below and behind the other fighters, then pulling up in a rapid zoom and firing from below.

I was less than 800 yards away when the P-39 hauled up in a screaming climb to hit Sasai from below. In desperation I jammed down on the cannon trigger, hoping the report would warn Sasai or possibly alarm the enemy pilot into breaking off his attack. The P-39 did not waver, but Sasai finally heard the cannon reports. Immediately, with his wingmen hugging his own plane, he pulled up in a loop, swinging wide in a bid for height.

That was enough for the enemy pilot. With three Zeros in front of him, and more coming up behind, he realized the danger of being trapped. The P-39 started looping over from his climb, ready to dive as he came out. But the initiative now was mine. I went down in a turning dive, prepared to catch the Airacobra just as it rolled out and started to race for the earth. The pilot, however, saw me, and jerked over wildly in a left roll, then dove. The towering mountains blocked his path, and even as he started to pull away from my plane he was forced to pull up.

The pilot was good. He whipped down the mountainside, turning and banking sharply as he just missed the crags and slopes, with me on his tail. Every time he turned I cut inside the turn and narrowed the distance between our two planes. And every time the P-39 saw a chance to wing away to the right or left he faced another Zero—my wingmen. Good men! We had the Airacobra boxed; he would have to fight.

And he did. More than once he came around in a wicked turn as he banked to avoid the mountain, firing as he closed in. Every time he did so I turned a little shorter, looped a little closer, and brought the firing range down. I caught him at a distance of 150 yards, firing in short bursts, closing in to less than fifty yards. The P-39 spit black smoke and hurtled into the jungle.

It was a shamefaced Lieutenant Sasai who came up to my plane back at Lae. My mechanics were examining with wide eyes the bullet holes in my wings, when Sasai came up to stammer his thanks.

He looked at the punctured metal, and said no more.

CHAPTER FIFTEEN

DURING the period from May 1 through the 12, our Lae Wing emerged without a single loss from every clash with the enemy. We had taken good advantage of the enemy pilots' failures to remain alert when airborne, and excellent tactics on the part of our formations chalked up an imposing string of one-sided victories.

On May 13 the damage suffered by my own fighter grounded me for the day. It gave me the opportunity to catch up on a month's mail delivered only that morning by submarine. My mother wrote that my brothers were now sharing Japan's battles. One had volunteered for the Navy Fliers School, but failed to meet their rigid requirements, and had, instead, enlisted at the Sasebo Naval Base. My other brother was drafted into the Army and already was on his way to China. He never came home: he was later transferred to Burma and was there killed in action.

But the most eagerly awaited mail was, of course, from Fujiko. She wrote at length of the great changes which were occurring at home, and surprised me with the news that she was now working in her uncle's company, which had been converted into a munitions factory.

"Nowadays not one person should stay idle, the Prime Minister has said. He has told the country that even daughters, if they remain home without contributing to the war effort, will be drafted and sent to any munitions plant where their services are needed. So my uncle, in order to keep me with the family, hired me at once to work for him." I was amazed to realize that Fujiko, the daughter of such an eminent family, had to work in a munitions factory! It was hard to conceive of my mother's small farm without the help of my two brothers; and she had been forced to labor and found it difficult even when we were home to help.

My cousin Hatsuyo had even more disturbing news. She wrote that her father had been transferred back to Tokyo from Shikoku. Several days after her return to the city, she witnessed the April 18 attack on Tokyo by American B-25 bombers.

"I know that you are in the thick of combat," she wrote, "and your successes against the enemy are of great comfort to all of us at home. The bombing of Tokyo and several other cities has brought about a tremendous change in the attitude of our people toward the war. Now things are different; the bombs have dropped here on our homes. It does not seem any more that there is such a great difference between the battle-front and the home-front. I know that I, as well as the other girls, will work all the harder to do our share at home to support you and the other pilots who are so far away from Japan."

Hatsuyo was still in school, but her afternoons and part of her evenings were spent with other schoolgirls working in factories, sewing military uniforms. The sudden change in the status at home was bewildering. My brothers in service, Fujiko working in a munitions factory, Hatsuyo in another factory... it was all so strange.

Hatsuyo did not describe the enemy bombing in detail, even though it was the first time that our homeland had been attacked. Of course, we had received the news here at Lae much earlier, the same day, in fact. Officially, the government disclaimed any heavy damage, which seemed reasonable in view of the limited number of attacking planes. But the attack unnerved almost every pilot at Lae. The knowledge that the enemy was strong enough to smash at our homeland, even in what might be a punitive raid, was cause for serious apprehension of future and heavier attacks.

I was still reading my mail when Warrant Officer Wataru Handa approached me to request the loan of my wingman, Honda, for a reconnaissance flight to Port Moresby. W/O Handa was a new arrival at Lae, and a most welcome one. Although he had not yet fought in the Pacific, he was one of Japan's most famous aces from the China theater, with fifteen enemy planes to his credit. Since his return from the Asiatic mainland he had served as a flight instructor at Tsuchiura. I saw no problem in letting Honda fly with him; certainly he would be with one of our best pilots.

Honda, however, had other ideas about the matter. Veteran ace or not, he growled at my orders. "I'd rather not go, Saburo," he mumbled. "I have been flying only with you and I don't want any changes now."

"Oh, shut up, you fool," I snapped. "Handa is a better flier than I am, and has been flying a lot longer. You go."

At noon Honda took off with five other Zeros for a reconnaissance flight over Moresby.

I was disturbed at Honda's reluctance to fly the mission and sweated out his return. Two hours later five Zeros came in for a landing: Warrant Officer Handa's lead plane and four others. Honda's plane was missing!

I ran all the way to the runway and climbed onto the wing of W/O Handa's Zero even before it stopped rolling. "Where's Honda?" I shouted, "Where is he? What happened to him?"

Handa looked at me, misery on his face. "Where is he?" I screamed, "What's happened?"

Handa climbed down from the cockpit. On the ground he took both my hands in his, bowed low, then spoke with an effort. His voice was choked. "I. . . I am sorry, Saburo," he stammered. "I am sorry. Honda, he—he is dead. It was my fault."

I was stupefied! I couldn't believe it; not Honda! He was the best wingman I'd ever flown with.

W/O Handa turned his face away from me, staring at the ground, and began to trudge to the Command Post. I followed him, unable to speak, as he continued.

"We were over Moresby," he said in a low tone. "We started to circle at seven thousand feet. The sky seemed clear of enemy planes, and I was searching the field for planes on the ground.

"It was my fault; all my fault," he murmured. "I didn't even see the fighters. They were P-39s. I don't know how many, just a few of them. They came down so fast that we had no warning. We didn't even know they were on us until we heard them firing. I went over into a roll, as did Endo, my other wingman. When I turned around for a moment I saw Honda's plane, which had been at the end of my trio, enveloped in flames. He drew the crossfire from the P-39s."

I stopped and stared at him. Handa walked away. He never seemed to recover from the blow of having lost my wingman. Although he was an ace in China, W/O Handa had apparently lost his sure touch in the air. He had never fought the American fighters, which could out-dive our planes by a considerable margin. Whatever had actually happened, Handa took personal blame for the death of my wingman. He was wan and pale for the remainder of his time at Lae. Finally he contracted tuberculosis and was sent home. Many years later I received a letter from his wife. She wrote: "My husband died yesterday from his long illness. I am writing this letter to meet his last request, that I write and apologize for him. He never recovered from the loss of your pilot at Lae. The last words he spoke before he died were: 'I have fought bravely all my life, but I cannot forgive myself for what I did at Lae when I lost Sakai's man.' "

When he died, Honda was only twenty years old. He was a strong man, in his actions on the ground as well as in the air. He was quick to fight, but was one of the most popular men in the Sasai squadron. I was very proud of him; his wing flying had been superb. I was confident that he was on his way to becoming an ace.

For the rest of the day I wandered around the base in a daze. I paid no attention to the rest of the men in the squadron who pledged revenge for the first pilot lost from our group since April 17. To me, my greatest accomplishment in air battle was the fact that I had never lost a wingman. And now, I had sent out Honda against his own wishes to fly with another man, and he was dead. I could not help thinking that my other wingman, Yonekawa, might well be killed also. For long months Yonekawa had faultlessly covered my fighter in the air; he had done so well by me that he was still without a single victory of his own. Honda had been more aggressive, and had shot down several enemy planes.

My mind was made up: Yonekawa must get his own victim. On the following day, May 14, I received NAP 3/C Hatori as Honda's replacement. Before we took off in a flight of seven fighters for Moresby, I told Yonekawa that, if we met enemy fighters, he would fly my position and I would cover him. Yonekawa's face lit up with excitement. If I had known what was in store for us that day, I would not have arranged things differently.

The Allied pilots, it appeared, had given serious study to the unexcelled maneuverability we enjoyed with the Zero fighter. Today marked their first attempt at new tactics. We saw the enemy planes over Moresby but, unlike their previous maneuvers, they failed to form into a single large formation. Instead, the enemy planes formed in pairs and trios, and were all over the sky as we approached. Their movements were baffling. If we turned to the left, we'd be hit from above and the right. And so on. If they were trying to confuse us, they were achieving their purpose.

There was only one thing to do: meet them on their own terms. I pulled up to Sasai's plane and signaled him that I would take the nearest pair of enemy fighters. He nodded and as I pulled away I saw him signaling the other four Zeros into two pairs. We split into three separate groups and turned to meet the enemy. We rushed at the two P-39s I had selected and I fired a burst at 100 yards. The first Airacobra evaded my shells and winged over into a screaming dive. I had no chance even to get near him for another burst.

The second plane was already rolling over for a dive when I rolled hard over to the left, turned, and came out on his tail. For a moment I saw the pilot's startled face as he saw me coming in. The P-39 skidded along on its back, then whipped over again to the left in an attempt to dive. He looked good for Yonekawa, who was glued to my tail. I waved my hand in the cockpit and rolled to the right, leaving the P-39 for my wingman.

Yonekawa went at the Airacobra like a madman, and I clung to his tail at a distance of 200 yards. The P-39 jerked wildly in a left roll to evade Yonekawa's fire, and Yonekawa took advantage of the bank and turn to narrow the distance between the two planes to about fifty yards. For the next few minutes the two fighters tangled like wildcats, rolling, spiraling, looping, always losing altitude, with Yonekawa clinging grimly to the tail of the enemy plane and almost leaping out of the way whenever the P-39 turned on his Zero.

It was a mistake on the part of the enemy pilot to break his dive in the first place. He had every chance of getting away, but now with Yonekawa so close to him, the dive would mean an open and clear shot for the Zero. From 13,000 feet the two planes—with me right behind them—dropped to only 3,000 feet. The enemy pilot, however, knew what he was doing. Unable to shake the Zero after him, he led the fight back to the Moresby air base and thus within range of the antiaircraft guns.

It was by no means a one-sided battle, for the P-39 pilot maneuvered brilliantly with an airplane which was outperformed by his pursuer. The Airacobra and Zero looked like whirling dervishes, both firing in short bursts, and neither pilot scoring any major hits. Soon it became obvious that Yonekawa was slowly gaining the upper hand. On every turn he hung a second or two longer to the tail of the P-39, steadily gaining the advantage. The two planes passed over Moresby and continued their running battle over the thick jungle growth.

Hatori pulled alongside my own fighter and we gained altitude, circling slowly over the two battling planes. Now they were down to treetop level, where Yonekawa could use the Zero to its best advantage. The Airacobra no longer had air space in which to roll or spiral, and could only break away in horizontal flight. As he swung out of a turn Yonekawa was on him in a flash. There was no question of his accuracy this time. The P-39 dropped into the jungle and disappeared.

Yonekawa had drawn his first blood.

CHAPTER SIXTEEN

A TORRENTIAL downpour on May 15 meant a day of rest for all pilots. But the respite was short, for before daybreak on the sixteenth several B-25s swarmed over the field at treetop level, digging craters in the runway and shooting up maintenance facilities.

For the second day in a row we remained on the ground—it would take the entire day merely to fill in the holes and patch up the field. We sat around in the billets, several pilots catching up on sleep, while the rest of us discussed the rising tempo of the enemy attacks.

A bomber pilot joined our group (he had landed at Lae for refueling, and was grounded after the attack) and listened with interest to our descriptions of attacking the enemy bombers. After a while he looked wistfully at the Zero fighters parked off the runway.

"You know," he said suddenly, "I think my greatest ambition has been to fly a fighter, not these trucks we go around in. It's funny," he mused, "we've been taking more and more punishment on our raids. Most of the men feel they'll never live to go home. I feel the same way.

"Yet," he turned to look at us, "I would be satisfied if there was one thing I could do."

We waited for him to continue. "I'd like to loop that truck I fly," he added. He grinned. "Can you picture that thing going around in a loop?"

One of the Zero pilots spoke up. "If I were you, I wouldn't try it," he said softly. "You'd never come out of a loop in one piece, even if you could get up and around into one."

"I suppose so," he replied. We watched him walk across the field and climb into the cockpit of a fighter, where he sat and studied the controls. At the time we didn't know that all of us would remember this pilot for the rest of our lives.

The day passed slowly and that night Nishizawa, Ota, and I went to the radio room to listen to the music hour which came over nightly on the Australian radio.

Nishizawa suddenly spoke up. "That music—listen. Isn't that the *Danse Macabre,* the dance of death?"

We nodded. Nishizawa was excited. "That gives me an idea. You know the mission tomorrow, strafing at Moresby? Why don't we throw in a little dance of death of our own?"

"What the devil are you talking about?" Ota snapped. "You sound like you've gone crazy."

"No, I mean it!" Nishizawa protested. "After we start home, let's slip back to Moresby, the three of us, and do a few demonstration loops right over the field. It should drive them crazy on the ground!"

"It might be fun," Ota said cautiously, "but what about the commander? He'd never let us go through with it."

"So?" was the retort. "Who says he must know about it?" Nishizawa grinned broadly.

We went off to the billet, and the three of us talked in whispers of our plans for the morrow. We had no fear about appearing over Moresby with only three fighters—among the three of us, we'd shot down a total of sixty-five enemy planes. My tally was twenty-seven, Nishizawa had twenty, and Ota had accounted for eighteen.

We hit Moresby the next day with a maximum fighter sweep of eighteen Zeros, with Lieutenant Commander Tadashi Nakajima personally heading the formation. Nishizawa and I flew as his wingmen on the mission.

The strafing was a failure. Every bomber on the field was hidden from our view. The story in the air was different. Three enemy fighter formations came at us over die field. We turned into the first group and took them in a head-on attack. In the swirling air battle, six P-39s—two of them mine—fell in flames. Several Zeros broke from the battle to shoot up the field, which proved later to be their undoing. Two fighters, badly shot up, crashed on the Owen Stanley slopes during the return trip.

After the dogfight we reformed. As soon as we were in formation I signaled to Commander Nakajima that I was going down in pursuit of an enemy plane; he waved his hand and I dropped down in a long turning dive.

I was back at Moresby in a few minutes, circling above the field at 12,000 feet. The antiaircraft remained quiet, and no enemy fighters appeared. Then two Zeros came in at my height, and we fell into formation. Nishizawa and Ota grinned at me and I waved back in greeting.

We gathered in a formation with only a few scant feet between our wing tips. I slid my canopy back, described a ring over my head with my finger, then showed them three fingers. Both pilots raised their hands in acknowledgment. We were to fly three loops, all tied together.

One last look for enemy fighters, and I nosed down to gain speed, Nishizawa and Ota hugging my own plane. I pulled back on the stick, and the Zero responded beautifully in a high arcing climb, rolling over on her back. The other two fighters were right with me, all the way up and around in a perfect inside loop.

Twice more we went up and around, dove, and went back into the loop. Not a single gun fired from the ground, and the air remained clear of any enemy planes.

When I came out of the third loop Nishizawa pulled up to my plane, grinning happily, and signaled that he wanted to do it again. I turned to my left; there was Ota, laughing, nodding his head in agreement. I couldn't resist the temptation. We dove to only 6,000 feet above the enemy field and repeated the three loops, swinging around in perfect formation. And still not a gun fired at us! We might have been over our own field for all the excitement we seemed to create. But I thought of all the men on the ground watching us and I laughed loudly.

We returned to Lae twenty minutes after the other fighters landed. We told no one of what we had done. As soon as we could get together by ourselves, we broke into loud laughter and whoops. Ota howled with glee, and even the stoic Nishizawa slapped our backs with enjoyment. Our secret, however, was not to remain ours very long. Just after nine o'clock that night an orderly approached us in the billet and stated that Lieutenant Sasai wished to see us—immediately. We looked at each other, not a little worried. We could receive serious punishment for what we had done.

No sooner did we walk into Sasai's office than the lieutenant was on his feet, shouting at us. "Look here, you silly bastards!" he roared, "just look at this!" His face was red and he could hardly control himself as he waved a letter—in English—before our faces. "Do you know where I got this thing? " he yelled. "No? I'll tell you, you fools; it was dropped on this base a few minutes ago by an enemy intruder!"

The letter read:

"To the Lae Commander: We were much impressed with those three pilots who visited us today, and we all liked the loops they flew over our field. It was quite an exhibition. We would appreciate it if these same pilots returned here once again, each wearing a green muffler around his neck. We're sorry we couldn't give them better attention on their last trip, but we will see to it that the next time they will receive an all-out welcome from us."

It was all we could do to keep from bursting out with laughter. The letter was signed by a group of fighter pilots at Moresby. Lieutenant Sasai kept us at ramrod attention and lectured us severely on our "idiotic behavior." We were ordered specifically never to stage any more flying exhibitions over enemy fields. It was a good joke, and we enjoyed every minute of our *Danse Macabre* over Moresby.

None of us knew that night, however, that the next day was to be a true Dance of Death executed without aerial histrionics. Seven Zeros from our wing escorted eight bombers for an attack on Moresby. Hardly had we reached the enemy base when at least eighteen fighter planes plummeted upon us from every direction. This was the first defensive battle I had ever fought. We were hard pressed even to defend the eight bombers from the swooping attacks of the enemy planes. Although I drove several fighters away from the bombers, I failed to shoot down any planes. Three Allied fighters fell to the other pilots. The bombers meanwhile released their missiles—none too accurately—and then shakily swung into their turn to head for home.

We saw a P-39 plunge with tremendous speed into the bomber formation, but could not move in time to disrupt the attack. One moment the sky was clear; the next the Airacobra was spitting shells into the last bomber in the flight. Then it rolled and dove beyond our range. The bomber streamed flame; the airplane seemed familiar as I closed in to watch. It was the same Mitsubishi which had landed at Lae; its pilot was the one with whom we had talked in the billet. The flames increased in fury as the bomber nosed down and skidded wildly. It lost altitude quickly, and seemed on the verge of going out of control. At 6,000 feet it was only a matter of seconds; the flames were engulfing the wings and fuselage.

Suddenly, still blazing fiercely, the nose lifted and the bomber went into a climb. I gaped at the plane in astonishment as its pilot started to draw a loop—an impossible maneuver for the Betty. The pilot—the same one who had told us he wished to loop in a fighter—hauled her back and up. The bomber went up; hung on its nose in a half loop, and then burst into a seething ball of flame which blotted it out entirely.

The flaming mass fell. Just before it struck the ground a violent explosion shook the air as the fuel tanks went off.

CHAPTER SEVENTEEN

THE three months of May, June, and July were filled with almost constant air battles. It was not until after the war that I discovered that our Lae Wing was the most successful of all Japanese fighter plane operations against the enemy and that our continued successes were by no means repeated with such regularity elsewhere. Lae was nothing less than a hornet's nest of fighter planes to the enemy. Despite its position as a major base for our bombers and for surface shipping, not even Rabaul figured so highly in the destruction of enemy aircraft as we did during the four months from mid-April to mid-August.

We flew what was then the outstanding fighter airplane of the entire Pacific theater. Our pilots enjoyed a clear-cut superiority against the enemy, many of them having gained their greater experience through combat in China and through the rigid and exacting training requirements of prewar Japan.

It was not surprising, therefore, that the enemy suffered such grievous plane losses against the Zeros which flew from Lae. To us, however, it seemed that the courage of the pilots and crews who manned the B-25 Mitchells and B-26 Marauders was deserving of the highest praise. These twin-engined raiders lacked the firepower and the armor protection of the rugged Flying Fortresses, yet, time after time, they flew against Lae and other targets minus the fighter escort our own high command deemed indispensable for the survival of bombers.

They always came in low, anywhere from 1,500 feet above the ground to such a low level that they were actually slicing through the top of tree branches, as we saw more than once. They combined with their courage the highest piloting skill, and it was unfortunate for their ability that their airplanes proved no match for the maneuverable Zero fighter. Nevertheless, on more than a few occasions, their formations endured the very worst our fighters had to offer as they fled after their attacks. They were undaunted. They continued to come, continued to hit us with everything they had. Day and night their bombs slammed into the Lae base and their gunners strafed anything which moved. Their morale was marvelous, despite the terrible toll we exacted of their ranks in the late spring and summer of 1942.

On May 23 seven Zeros caught five B-25s over Lae, and sent one into the sea thirty miles south of Salamaua. The following day six bombers returned to Lae. Unfortunately for their crews, our island warning net sighted them far from Lae, and eleven fighters stormed the hapless bombers, burning and shooting down five, and badly crippling the sixth. I flew in both interception missions, and the records of Imperial Headquarters credit me with three bombers shot down on those two days.

The tempo of attacks increased as May drew to a close. For the first time, on May 25, four B-17s attacked with an escort of twenty fighters. Over the towering Owen Stanley Mountains, all hell broke loose when sixteen Zeros plummeted into their ranks. Five enemy fighters went down, but the Fortresses escaped. Three days later five unescorted B-26s returned to Lae; I chalked up another victory. On June 9 I sent two more B-26s crashing into the ocean.

The days seemed to blur into one another. Life became an endless repetition of fighter sweeps, of escorting our bombers over Moresby, of racing for fighters on the ground to scramble up against the incoming enemy raiders. The Allies seemed to have an inexhaustible supply of aircraft. A week never went by without the enemy suffering losses, and yet his planes came, by twos and threes and by the dozens. Through the passing years many of the details of these battles have faded, despite the help of a religiously kept diary. But several episodes stand out clearly.

Unforgettable was the slaughter of May 24 when an alarm of incoming planes threw Lae into an uproar. Six stand-by planes were already off the ground when the rest of us, clutching the sideboards of the swaying truck which brought us from our billet to the runway, reached the field. We were airborne without a moment to spare; my own fighter cleared the ground even as a stick of bombs tore the runway apart directly behind me. At least eleven Zeros were airborne by the time six B-25s completed their runs and turned to flee for Moresby. Nishizawa and Ota were the first to reach the enemy planes, and they each hit one bomber, raking the Mitchells with cannon fire. In a few seconds both B-25s were enveloped in flames. They crashed just beyond our airstrip. The rest of us jumped the four remaining bombers which, by excellent evasive flying, dodged our firing passes and reached the open sea. All eleven fighters winged in hot pursuit of the enemy.

Off Salamaua, we pressed home the attack. Again it was a case of poor formation flying on the part of our pilots. Every man seemed to think the battle was his own, and raced in against the bombers without regard for his fellow pilots. Zeros banked sharply to evade ramming other fighters, and more than one pilot rolled desperately to evade the fire of another Zero shooting blindly at the bombers! Once they were over the water, the B-25s dropped to the deck, skimming not more than ten yards over the waves. Their tactics were sound; we could not dive too steeply and we were denied climbing passes. One Zero, screaming down in a dive at the lead bomber, misjudged his distance and plunged at full speed into the ocean.

I caught the last bomber in a firing pass from above its tail. The B-25 held a straight course, and it was not difficult to concentrate my fire into the fuselage. In moments the air was filled with fire and smoke as the bomber reeled to the left and exploded as it hit the ocean.

At sea-level height the B-25s were almost as fast as the Zero fighter, and we were hard pressed to keep up with the bombers and also go into our firing passes. Three enemy planes were still in the air, when the six stand-by fighters turned for home, out of ammunition.

Lieutenant Sasai chalked up the fourth bomber, and we kept hammering at the two surviving planes. I got the fifth when, with its gunners apparently out of ammunition, the B-25 made a run for home after breaking away from the other remaining plane. The Mitchell took 1,000 rounds of machine-gun bullets in its fuselage tank and exploded flame from the right wing; it skidded wildly and hit the water, where it exploded. It was a good day. Five out of six planes definitely destroyed.

Several days later I was involved in a new aspect of air combat, and one which proved—even after all our battles—sickening. I caught a lone B-26 over Lae, and pursued the enemy plane over the sea, shooting up the fuselage and right wing. The Marauder burst into flames over the water, but before it crashed four men bailed out. Each landed safely on the sea, and the next moment a small bright life raft popped up. As I circled the raft, I saw that the men clung to its sides. Since they were only two miles from the Lae air base, it was only a matter of time before a boat would pick them up and make them prisoner.

Suddenly one of the men thrust his hands high above his head and disappeared. The others were beating fiercely at the water, and trying to get into the raft. Sharks! It seemed that there were thirty or forty of them; the fins cut the water in erratic movements all about the raft. Then the second man disappeared. I circled lower and lower, and nearly gagged as I saw the flash of teeth which closed on the arm of the third man. The lone survivor, a big, bald-headed man, was clinging to the raft with one hand and swinging wildly with a knife in the other. Then he, too, was gone.

When the men on the speedboat returned to Lae, they reported that they had found the raft empty and blood-stained. Not even a shred of the men was visible.

CHAPTER EIGHTEEN

ON May 20 we fought the highest air battle in our history, when Commander Nakajima led fifteen Zeros into the enemy zone at Moresby at a height of 30,000 feet. It took us an hour and twenty minutes, fighting for altitude all the way, to reach Moresby from Lae. We relied on our height to give us the advantage of surprise, and were astonished to encounter an enemy formation several miles ahead of us at the same altitude.

I was doubtful of the Zero's ability to perform aerobatics at this height. My personal record height with the Zero was 37,720 feet, achieved with an oxygen mask and an electrically heated jacket. At that height the plane was extremely sluggish at the controls and refused to climb another foot. Consequently, it seemed unwise to fight with the Zero at a height of 30,000 feet.

There were ten enemy fighters, apparently P-39s of a new design. I led the attack and was engaged at once. The fourteen other Zeros met the head-on attack of the remaining planes.

The controls were sluggish in the thin air. As the other plane came at me, I tried for an advantageous position from which to fire. We seemed almost to be moving in slow motion. I kept edging closer to the other fighter in a tight spiral, and maneuvered in for a quick burst. I yanked the stick over hard—too hard! Something seemed to crash into my chest, and the oxygen mask slipped down to my chin. Afraid to release the controls because I might spin out of control, I fumbled helplessly in the cockpit, and then everything faded into darkness. I had blacked out.

It seems that when a man is concentrating with all his power on a certain action, even a loss of oxygen fails to prevent him from carrying out to some extent what he had originally planned to do. I felt, even when I seemed to fall into unconsciousness, that my hands had frozen on the controls and kept the plane descending in its spiral maneuver. For when my head cleared and vision returned, I was at 20,000 feet, the plane still under control.

I snapped out of the turn instantly, for it was likely that the Airacobra had followed me down and was setting me up for the kill. But the other plane was also in trouble! Possibly the pilot had turned too sharply at that height and had spun out, or, perhaps he, too, suffered from lack of oxygen. Whatever the cause, there he was at 20,000 feet with me, spiraling around slowly. I shoved the throttle forward and headed for him, even as he came out of his seeming stupor. The next instant his wing was up and around and the P-39 came at me with all guns blazing. But the Zero was back in its element. I came out of a turn with the Airacobra above and to my right. One quick burst with my cannon and the plane broke in two. Only one other pilot registered a victory that day. Ota managed to bring down another P-39.

The following day I got my first enemy fighter without firing a shot, in a battle which was exactly the opposite of the maximum-height encounter. This time, on May 26, we fought a wild running duel at treetop level. We were in a group of sixteen Zeros when we encountered a strange enemy formation, four B-17s flying in a column, with about twenty fighters flying in echelons of two and three planes grouped around the Fortresses. We were below the enemy planes, and were able to catch them almost unawares in a steep climbing attack. I flamed one P-39, and then the sky erupted into a swirling mixture of fighter planes clawing at each other in individual dogfights.

Most of the enemy fighters broke for the deck, pulling away from our own planes. A few, however, were forced to pull out of their dives by higher peaks and went into evasive maneuvers, as we hoped they would. I dropped to the tail of one P-39 directly over the jungle. The pilot was fearless; he seemed to brush trees and rock outcroppings as he turned and dove, banked and climbed with me on his tail. Every time he climbed, turned, or rolled, I cut down the distance between our planes. I snapped out a burst, which the Airacobra evaded by rolling violently to the left. The next moment the pilot dove again, directly into a tortuous valley, flanked closely by towering crags.

Before I knew it, I was within the dangerous mountain pass, hot on the tail of the P-39. There was no time to concentrate on firing; I had all I could do to stick to the enemy fighter, which banked and wheeled in its hair-raising escape between the peaks. In no time at all I had forgotten my original purpose. I was drenched in my own sweat. The motor seemed to thunder louder and louder in my ears, and the peaks and rocks swept perilously close to the Zero as I rushed by at several hundred miles an hour.

Then the mountain caught up with the enemy plane. The P-39 came out of a tight turn and without warning faced a tremendous overhanging rock cliff which blocked our path. Instantly the pilot jerked the Airacobra upward and rolled to get his wings out of the way. It was not enough. The wing hit and the fighter snapped around, then exploded with a terrifying roar in the canyon.

I saw the pieces hurtling by me only vaguely; no sooner did I see that rock than I hauled the stick back with every ounce of strength in my arms and kept it back. The Zero whipped upward in a violent loop, and for an eternity of a split second it seemed that I would meet the wall just as the Airacobra had. But the Zero responded perfectly and I cleared the cliff by what appeared to be a matter of inches.

It took me a few minutes to calm down and to wipe away the perspiration that drenched my face. I eased off on the throttle and climbed slowly, trying to relax, to shake off the tension. That was my thirty-seventh conquest and, although I had not personally destroyed the plane, this was one of the most harrowing air battles I'd known! I found out later that day that Nishizawa and Ota had both done almost exactly the same thing, chasing two P-39s down a mountainside and whipping away in almost impossible rolling turns as the fighters in front of them smashed and exploded. That night the billet roared in jubilation over the day's events.

CHAPTER NINETEEN

DURING the last week of May the Lae Wing carried out maximum-effort fighter sweeps of the Moresby area, and in three days of wild air fighting scored tremendous successes against the Allied planes. Accordingly, Moresby was judged ripe for a knockout blow. On June 1, eighteen bombers from Rabaul, escorted by thirteen fighters from Lae and eleven others from Rabaul, tried for the finishing stroke against the vital enemy bastion.

We did not consider it possible for the Allies to mount any strong fighter opposition after the preceding battles, but we were wrong in this estimate. Twenty fighters roared into the big Japanese formation; once more it was a one-sided fighter-versus-fighter battle. Seven enemy fighters fell in flames, one from my guns. But they accomplished their purpose, scattering our bombers and destroying the accuracy of their aim.

On the return to Lae one of our bombers dropped out of formation, weaving erratically in the air. I dropped down with five other fighters to fly cover. The bomber was a flying shambles. Bullet holes and gaping openings from cannon shells riddled the wings and the fuselage and gave it the appearance of a sieve. I pulled up close to the nose and stared into the cockpit. Even at that distance I could see the blood on the instrument panel and on the seats. It was a miracle that the plane flew at all.

The pilot and copilot lay sprawled on the deck in pools of blood. The flight engineer struggled with the unfamiliar controls. I could not see the other four crewmen. Two turrets were smashed, and the men who had manned them were either dead or wounded. Only the flight engineer, fighting to keep the plane aloft, appeared unhurt.

Somehow, he kept the plane flying, rolling and weaving drunkenly until he reached our Lae airstrip. The man was doing a magnificent job. Apparently he was flying from his memory of watching the pilots in the air. That is difficult enough, impossible for most men without pilot training, but with a badly damaged bomber it was virtually impossible. Now that he had reached Lae, the engineer was at a loss as to what to do. He could keep the bomber flying, but landing, with its long, steady approach and lowering air speed, was another matter entirely.

The crippled airplane circled slowly over the airstrip, going around and around, as the engineer studied the narrow runway below him. There was no way to help the unhappy man in the cockpit. We closed in and tried to guide him down, but whenever he took his eyes off the controls the plane lurched dangerously. Gradually he lost speed as he descended. There was no use in remaining aloft until his fuel ran out. The bomber circled over the water, skidded badly as it turned, and then approached the runway. I held my breath. He couldn't make it. With speed down, the plane rocked badly in the air and began to slide into a stall. It would crash at any moment.

Then a miracle occurred. The pilot staggered to his feet. His face was white and caked with blood. He leaned heavily on the shoulders of the engineer. For those brief vital seconds of the approach he shoved the wheel forward and regained speed. With its wheels and flaps up the cripple soared down and touched the runway. A flurry of dust burst upward as the airplane skidded wildly. In a moment it smashed two fighters into wreckage, then lurched to a halt and broke in two.

We landed immediately afterward, taxiing up to the wreckage, which miraculously failed to bum. The pilot who had forced himself to his feet only a minute before was unconscious. The copilot was dead. The engineer who had flown the cripple home was so badly wounded in the legs that he had to be carried from the airplane. Both bombardiers were badly shot up. The bone of one man's arm jutted through broken skin, and both were caked with their own blood. The two gunners were semiconscious, also blood-soaked and seriously wounded, but were clinging to their guns with iron grips.

It was the first time we had ever seen with such intimacy the terrible power of fighters' weapons. Death in the air had never been close. Even those men who died in burning planes were remote and distant. A man either came home, or he didn't. But now we saw it for what it really was.

The fighter sweeps continued, and during the next two days we shot down three more fighters. But no one at Lae realized that our steady victories paled by contrast with the catastrophic defeat of a major Japanese task force at Midway on June 5. We knew of the battle, since Tokyo had announced a major victory for our fleet forces. Imperial Headquarters minimized our losses as insignificant. For the first time, however, we had doubts as to the accuracy of the reports. Our reasoning was simple enough; we knew Midway was to be invaded and occupied. If our fleet had withdrawn without carrying out that occupation, then something unforeseen had happened.

We did not learn for a long time to come that four of our largest and most powerful aircraft carriers, along with 280 planes and most of their pilots, as well as thousands of men who formed the warships' complements, were lost.

From June 5 through 15 a strange lull settled over the New Guinea front, broken only by a single raid against Lae on the ninth. I added two B-26 bombers to my score. On the sixteenth the air war exploded with renewed fury. It was a field day for our fighters, when twenty-one Zeros caught three enemy fighter formations napping.

We hit the first group of twelve fighters in a massed formation dive which shattered the enemy ranks. I shot down one plane, and five other pilots each scored a victory. The remaining six enemy fighters escaped by diving.

Back at high altitude, we dove from out of the sun at a second enemy formation of twelve planes. Again we struck without warning, and our plunging pass knocked three fighters out of the air. I scored my second victory in this firing run.

A third wave of enemy planes approached even as we pulled out from the second diving attack. Some two dozen fighters came at us as we split up into two groups. Eleven Zeros dove to hit a climbing formation, and the others met us at the same height. The formations disintegrated into a tremendous free-for-all directly above the Moresby air base. The enemy planes were new P-39s, faster and more maneuverable than the older models; I jumped one fighter, which amazed me by flicking out of the way every time I fired a burst. We went around in the sky in a wild dogfight, the Airacobra pilot running through spins, loops, Immelmanns, dives, snap rolls, spirals, and other maneuvers. The pilot was superb, and with a better airplane he might well have emerged the victor. But I kept narrowing the distance between our two planes with snap rolls to the left, and clung grimly to his tail at less than twenty yards. Two short cannon bursts and the fighter exploded in flames.

That was my third victory of the day. The fourth, which followed almost immediately after, was ridiculously simple. A P-39 flashed by in front of me, paying attention only to the pursuing Zero which zoomed upward in a desperate climb, firing as he went. The Airacobra ran directly into my fire, and I poured 200 rounds of machine-gun bullets into the nose. The fighter snapped into an evading roll. I was out of cannon shells, and fired a second burst into the belly. Still it would not fall until a third burst caught the still-rolling plane in the cockpit. The glass erupted and I saw the pilot slam forward. The P-39 fell off into a spin, then dove at great speed to explode in the jungle below.

Four enemy fighters in one day! That was my record to date, and it contributed to the greatest defeat ever inflicted on the enemy in a single day's action by the Lae Wing. Our pilots claimed a total of nineteen enemy fighters definitely destroyed in the air.

On our way back to the field Yonekawa kept breaking formation. He went into wild rolls, climbed, dove, dropped in falling leaves. He cavorted all over the sky, flying circles around my fighter. I understood why when he pulled alongside my own plane and held up two fingers, grinning broadly. Yonekawa was no longer the untried fledgling; now he had three planes to his credit. He bubbled with exuberance. He flew upside down, waving both hands around in the cockpit. Then he flew directly over me, under me, and went through a wide hesitation roll around my fighter. He was like a kid showing off. He finally flew on my wing and held the stick between his knees. Still grinning, he waved his lunchbox at me and started to eat. His exuberance was infectious. I waved four fingers at him, and then opened a soda bottle. He pulled his out from his lunchbox and we drank a happy toast to one another.

The day of victory was not over yet. Hardly had our planes been refueled and our ammunition belts replaced than a spotter report came in. Ten B-26s were on their way to the base. They could not have chosen a worse time, for nineteen fighters were off the ground before the Marauders reached Lae. We failed to shoot any down, but damaged most of the planes, and caused them to scatter their bombs wildly. During the pursuit away from Lae, ten P-39s came after us over Cape Ward Hunt, apparently in reply to the bombers' distress calls. One Airacobra went down in flames.

Lae went wild with the victory that night. All the pilots were given extra rations of cigarettes, and the mechanics swarmed over us to share our jubilation. Even better news was the word that we were to receive five days' leave at Rabaul. The cheers of the pilots shook the surrounding jungle. I was particularly relieved at the news of the five days' rest. Not only was I tired from the almost daily fights, but my mechanics wanted several days in which to work on my fighter. They called me over to show me the bullet holes in the wings and fuselage, and my stomach dropped when I saw a row of holes running directly behind the cockpit. They had missed me by no more than six inches.

In 1942 none of our fighter planes carried pilot armor, nor did the Zeros have self-sealing tanks, as did the American planes. As the enemy pilots soon discovered, a burst of their 50-caliber bullets into the fuel tanks of a Zero caused it to explode violently in flames. Despite this, in those days not one of our pilots flew with parachutes. This has been misinterpreted in the West as proof that our leaders were disdainful of our lives, that all Japanese pilots were expendable and regarded as pawns instead of human beings. This was far from the truth. Every man was assigned a parachute; the decision to fly without them was our own and not the result of orders from any higher headquarters. Actually, we were urged, although not ordered, to wear the parachutes in combat. At some fields the base commander insisted that chutes be worn, and those men had no choice but to place the bulky seat packs in their planes. Often, however, they never fastened the straps, and used the chutes only as seat cushions.

We had little use for these parachutes, for the only purpose they served for us was to hamstring our cockpit movements in a battle. It was difficult to move our arms and legs quickly when encumbered by chute straps. There was another, and equally compelling, reason for not carrying the chutes into combat. The majority of our battles were fought with enemy fighters over their own fields. It was out of the question to bail out over enemy-held territory, for such a move meant a willingness to be captured, and nowhere in the Japanese military code or in the traditional *Bushido* (Samurai code) could one find the distasteful words, "Prisoner of War." *There were no prisoners.* A man who did not return from a flight was dead. No fighter pilot of any courage would ever permit himself to be captured by the enemy. It was completely unthinkable. Nevertheless, it was acutely discomforting to discover a row of bullet holes only inches from where I sat.

That night I received confirmation of my four kills for the day's fighting. This was by no means unique in the Imperial Navy, and I know of a score of other naval fliers who matched or exceeded this number of planes shot down in a single day. This gave me a total of forty-three victories.

Nishizawa, who went on to become Japan's greatest ace with a final toll of just over 100 enemy planes shot down in combat, hit his record on August 7 over Guadalcanal, when he gunned six American Navy fighters out of the air. A year later Naval Air Pilot 1/C Kenji Okabe shot down a total of seven F4F Wildcats, TBF Avengers, and SBD Dauntlesses in a single day in a series of actions over Rabaul. Okabe landed his plane three times to refuel and rearm during the day's fighting, to set an all-time record for the Navy.

Almost every pilot who accomplished this feat was, however, killed shortly afterward in combat. The two exceptions of whom I personally know are myself and Nishizawa, and the Devil never lived out the war. Ironically, Nishizawa was killed in October of 1944 over Cebu in the Philippines, unable to fire a single shot in defense of his life. Several Hellcat fighters caught him in an unarmed, unescorted DC-3 transport and shot down the plane in flames, an ignominious end for Japan's greatest pilot.

That night I received orders to report to the base commander, an event of rare occurrence. At Captain Saito's billet I found that Lieutenant Sasai also had been summoned, and that Deputy Commander Nakajima was with Saito. Both officers appeared glum.

Captain Saito spoke: "I have been questioning the wisdom of telling you this news, and am doing so at the direct recommendation of Commander Nakajima. It is an unpleasant task for me.

"Earlier this month I requested Tokyo Headquarters to reward Lieutenant Sasai for his extraordinarily fine leadership of his squadron in combat. At the same time I also asked for recognition of Sakai's outstanding accomplishments in battle, which make him, so far as we know, the leading ace of the entire Imperial Navy.

"However, these requests were not granted. Tokyo did not see fit to break with established precedent. There has never in all our history been a living hero," Saito emphasized, "and apparently Tokyo is adamant about making any changes at this time. They have refused," he added with regret, "even to award a medal or to promote you in rank.

"I was undecided about revealing these details to you," he concluded, "lest it lead you falsely to criticize the actions of our high command. But it is equally important to me that you both be aware that I, as your commanding officer, am fully cognizant of your devotion and your unflagging effort."

Commander Nakajima spoke up. "It has always been the Navy's tradition—right or wrong—to award decorations and grant special promotions only on a posthumous basis. This tradition, of course, is of little comfort to you at the moment. I feel you should know that Captain Saito requested for Lieutenant Sasai the rank of commander, for Sakai his ensign's bar."

Sasai answered at once. "I cannot tell you how grateful I am for your consideration, and your efforts on my behalf. I must add, however, that neither Sakai nor I are dissatisfied with Tokyo's decision. I do not see any reason for us to hold any malice. It is my opinion, and I am sure that I speak for Sakai as well, that our accomplishments and air victories are not ours alone. Without our wingmen flying cover for us, without the devotion of our ground crews, we would be able to do nothing. I am satisfied that our team functions so well, and I do not feel that individual recognition is necessary as a reward, although I am most honored that you should have acted for us the way you did." Sasai expressed perfectly everything I could have hoped to say, and I nodded my agreement.

The naval policy of abstaining from recognition of individual exploits was carried out steadfastly to the end of the war. There was but one exception to this rule, and it was made as late as March of 1945, when Admiral Soemu Toyoda, Commander of the Combined Fleet, commended NAP 1/C Shoichi Sugita and me, then an ensign, for our outstanding number of victories in the air. By then the commendation was meaningless. The great pilots of our Navy—Nishizawa, Ota, Sasai, and others—were dead.

CHAPTER TWENTY

DURING the month of June we encountered an ever-increasing number of enemy fighters and bombers. We were told that the enemy was staging a major build-up of air power in the area, and that from now on we would carry out stronger fighter sweeps. It was clear to all that we would need every Zero we could lay our hands on. The enemy was hacking more airstrips out of the jungle growth in the general area of Moresby.

Our bomber attacks also increased in weight and frequency, and enemy fighters met every raid with determined aggressiveness. On June 17, twelve Zeros escorted eighteen bombers against Port Moresby, and held seven intercepting fighters away from the bombers, which hit the pier area and sank an 8,000-ton freighter docked in the harbor. The seven American fighters harried our force of thirty planes all the way from Moresby to Cape Ward Hunt, but without success. The following day nine bombers and an equal number of fighters raided Kido in Rescar Bay, a new enemy base north of Moresby which was rapidly being stocked with fighters. Ten enemy fighters hit the eighteen Japanese planes, again without causing any losses, and lost two of their own number.

On June 24 I returned to Lae from my leave at Rabaul, and took off the next morning as part of a sweep of twenty-one fighters against Moresby. Action was brisk, and I shot down one of the eleven enemy planes claimed for the day's action.

The next morning Rabaul sent nineteen bombers back to Moresby, with eleven fighters escorting. Twelve enemy planes intercepted them, and the Zeros shot down three.

That was the last raid during June. The next day a torrential downpour engulfed the New Guinea area. The rain continued to beat down not only against our fields but against those of the Allies as well. Our successes in April, May, and June had been due in part to the excellent flying weather we enjoyed during the day. Clouds gathered almost every afternoon, but not until 3:00 or 4:00 p.m., by which time we were back on the ground. Violent squalls swept over the area in the evening and continued intermittently during the night. These were more of a blessing than an inconvenience, because they prevented the enemy from conducting his nocturnal assaults with any regularity, and we were able to sleep through most of the nights.

July brought an abrupt change in the weather. No longer did the evening squalls permit uninterrupted slumber, and for days on end the night skies were clear and starlit. The bombers came; almost every night their thunder shattered the darkness, and then the bombs rained down ceaselessly. The Mitchells and Marauders swept up and down the field, bombing and strafing at will. We were helpless against the attacks. Even had the runway been large enough to accommodate night operations, it is doubtful that we could have done much damage with the Zero. So we remained on the ground, cowering in shelters and cursing the Americans. Those who suffered the most were the maintenance crews. They were denied even the satisfaction of going out on missions and seeing the enemy planes falling in flames. Instead, their lot was almost round-the-clock labor to keep our relatively low number of fighters in operational condition. In addition, they were now deprived of even their snatches of sleep as the nightly bombing attacks increased in fury.

We were hit with a particularly heavy raid on the early morning of July 2. The clamor of the air-raid alarms roused us out of our sleep before daybreak. We threw on our flying suits and ran to the field. Hardly had we reached the runway when the thunder of motors, accompanied by the shattering roar of the first bombs, burst out of the night. Every pilot ran frantically for the nearest shelter. There was no time to reach the dugouts. Instead we hurled ourselves into the nearest craters.

We could see the bombers against the stars. They were Mitchells and Marauders, no higher than 600 feet, the bluish flames from their exhaust pipes flickering in the night sky with an eerie radiance. But they seemed anything but beautiful to us as we cowered at the bottom of our craters.

With their bombs expended, the planes came back at tree-top level, strafing across the runway and pouring their slugs into every building within sight. We dashed back for the craters and huddled miserably. The enemy bullets sprayed the field like bursts of hail. Somehow none of the pilots was hit. Then the planes were gone, working over the other end of the field. I crawled from the crater and dashed for the Command Post. There was little time to lose in crossing the field. With all our planes held down, it seemed only a matter of seconds or minutes before another wave would hit us. The open crater was no place to linger during a strafing attack.

The Command Post was still intact. But now the bombers had swung around and were spraying the tower and the shack with machine-gun bullets. Sailors entrenched in the barricades around the CP threw a storm of bullets into the air from their guns, but succeeded only in wasting ammunition. The men knew nothing about leading a plane, and the tracers arced away in the night behind the speeding bombers.

Their lack of accuracy astounded me. I forgot about the shelters and ran for the gun positions. I shoved one man away from his gun, telling him that I would take over. The man clung grimly to his weapon, refusing to abandon his post, shouting he had no authority to leave. I wasted no time arguing with him, but knocked him out of his seat. He rose to his feet, muttering curses, but another pilot who had come up behind me shoved him out of the way and picked up the ammunition belts. The sailor departed in a hurry.

The second wave of six B-26s hit the field at that moment. I jerked back on the trigger and held it down, watching the tracers flaring into the air. A Marauder passed almost overhead, and I walked the flaming shells from the nose back to the tail. But the bomber never wavered, and came roaring down at the gun position in a shallow dive, the nose gunner answering my fire.

This was my first experience on the ground with a plane coming straight at me, and fear of the ripping shells engulfed me. The vision of the bombs hurtling down and exploding directly on the gun position was both startling and fearsome. Fright overcame every other emotion and I abandoned the gun, running as quickly as I could for the sandbag shelter behind me. I didn't even run all the way, but I leaped in a flying tackle for the shelter. For a few seconds I sat there, feeling like an idiot and an unreasonable coward. The B-26 roared overhead, passing by without bombing. I cursed my own quaking body and returned to the gun I had deserted. Slowly I stopped shaking and regained my presence of mind. This time, as I squatted behind the gun, I swore I would not run like a rabbit.

The bombers were back, the sound of their motors from only 150 feet overhead a thundering, pounding crescendo which smashed against my eardrums. They were great black shapes darting out of the darkness, spitting flame from their turrets, their exhausts piercing the gloom in flickering blue fire. I caught the trailing bomber with a burst, holding the gun steady as the plane flew into my line of fire. A thin streamer of smoke appeared, but the plane flew on steadily and then disappeared in the distance, still in formation.

Dawn broke after more than one full hour of continuous bombing and strafing attack by the enemy planes, which had swept over Lae with impunity. Not a single plane was shot down, although many thousands of rounds of ammunition were fired by the antiaircraft weapons. The pilots were so demoralized by the attack that even after the last bombs had fallen no one ran out to the fighters to take off in pursuit, as we had always done before.

Most of the installations on the field were burning. Deep craters had turned the runway into a shambles which would have prevented any flying, even had we attempted it. It seemed impossible, but the twenty fighter planes parked on both sides of the runway were safe, holed only with stray bullets and bomb fragments. We assembled at the Command Post for further orders. The pilots were bewildered and enraged by the pounding we had suffered. One flier in particular, NAP 2/C Mitsuo Suitsu, recently assigned to Lae, fairly choked with anger. He swore he would get a bomber on the next raid, even if he had to ram the plane. However, few paid much attention to him.

Before the enemy planes were out of sight, nearly 200 men were on the field, working furiously with shovels and wheelbarrows to fill in the many craters, and to clear the stones and pieces of steel from the runway.

Suddenly several orderlies came running from the Command Post, shouting hysterically: "Another attack is on the way! More than one hundred enemy planes are approaching the field!" One hundred planes! That was an incredible number; we had never heard of an attack of such magnitude. There was a flurry among the staff officers, and then shouted orders for every plane to get into the air at once. We ran to our fighters and as soon as the engines were warmed up started to taxi to the runway, which had now been prepared sufficiently for safe take-off.

The Zeros were moving into take-off position when the staff officers dashed out of the Command Post, waving their arms wildly in the air, shouting and running down to the strip. They crossed their arms in the air, the signal to cut our engines. When they came up to the fighters they explained. "The alert is called off. Our spotters made a mistake." One officer even laughed. "The one hundred enemy planes turned out to be a formation of migrating birds! " Everyone burst into laughter. The entire episode seemed ludicrous after the tension under which we had labored.

We ate lunch as we sat around the Command Post, ready to take off in event of any further attacks. The enemy was busy today; we were still eating when the orderlies ran to us with news that Salamaua had reported six B-17s on their way to our base. No one wasted a moment. Our mess kits went flying in all directions as we raced for the fighters. Salamaua was only several minutes by air from Lae, and the bombers would soon be upon us. I never got off the ground. The other fighters were racing down the runway while I cursed an engine which refused to turn over. I tried again and again, kicking the starter. The engine was dead, and by the time I climbed in disgust from the airplane all the other fighters were in the air.

I ran across the strip for the shelters. Commander Nakajima was waving his arms furiously, shouting for me to hurry. He kept pointing to the sky. I was twenty yards from the shelter when the shriek of a falling bomb split the air like a great knife. I flung myself the last few feet through the air and crashed onto the back of men already huddled on the ground in the dugout.

In that same second the world seemed to blow up. There was a deafening roar, and the earth heaved wildly below me.

I felt something heavy pressing on my body from all directions, a terrible pressure, and then absolute blackness. I saw nothing and heard nothing. It was as though I had been cut off from the world around me. I tried to move my arms and legs, but without success. I was gripped solidly.

It may have been seconds or minutes, it was impossible to tell, when I heard a voice calling from far off. It was Commander Nakajima. "Sakai! Sakai! Where are you?" Silence for a while. Then the shouting again. "Where is he? Did Sakai make it? Look for him, damn it!"

I tried to shout back in reply. I thought I had shouted but, strangely, I could not hear my own voice. My mouth, my lips had not even moved. Something heavy was pressing against my chin.

Again Nakajima's voice came, dimly, far away. "He must be buried. Start looking for him. Don't waste a second. Dig!"

Buried? Of course! I was beneath rocks and sand. I opened my eyes slightly. Blackness. Then fear swept over me. I felt I was choking, that the sand was suffocating me. I tried to writhe, but I could not move an inch. The terror was choking.

Nakajima's voice came again, a little louder this time. "Dig with anything you can get your hands on. Come on; use sticks. Use your hands and your fingernails if you have nothing else! Hurry!"

Then the sounds of scratching, of shovels digging in the sand. I waited, trying to keep from squirming. Then they were through. A hand brushed my face, felt for my skin, then brushed the sand away from my mouth and nose. Sunlight burst about me suddenly as my rescuers broke through and pulled me out.

I was not the only one buried. At least a dozen men were caught in the sudden collapse of the dugout when a bomb exploded nearby. But not a single man was injured! We were covered from head to foot with sand and mud which had, fortunately for us, cushioned the shock of the shelter's collapse.

The Command Post was scattered wreckage, and a gaping crater nearby attested to our good fortune in escaping a direct hit. Most of the planes still on the runway had been smashed into small pieces, and the fuel tanks of several were flaming. Nearly an hour later, the fighters which had taken off returned to the base. The men were glum. The six Fortresses had fought off their attacks with apparent ease.

It took us two days to restore the air base after the July 2 attacks. By the fourth we were ready for a retaliation raid against Moresby. It was still July 3 by the Americans' calendar, but we felt we could add to their celebration of their Independence Day with a few fireworks of our own. Twenty-one Zero fighters hit Moresby to find a welcome committee of twenty enemy fighters waiting for us. We attacked while the Allied planes were still diving. Our pilots claimed nine fighters definitely destroyed, and three others as probables.

We were still many miles from Lae on our return flight when I noticed a haze of black smoke drifting before the wind. As the air base came into sight, we saw that the smoke came from flaming installations directly on the field. Sheets of fire soared into the air, spilling boiling clouds of black smoke over the jungle and the beach. What had happened was obvious; in our absence enemy bombers had struck our fuel dumps.

We were still gliding in on our landing approach when seven Marauders roared in low over the jungle. We failed to see the bombers before they were over the field, their black bombs tumbling through the air to send geysers of flame and dirt high above the runway. Even as we wheeled in pursuit several fighters shot into the air from the field, and more than twenty-six Zeros in all went racing madly after the seven fleeing B-26s. For several moments there was near chaos in the sky as everyone rolled madly to get away from the other pursuing planes. Collisions were averted by only a few feet.

One fighter which had taken off from Lae pulled away from the main group. The Zero passed the bombers and then swung up and around in a sharp 180-degree turn, and plunged with terrifying speed toward the lead bomber. What appeared to be a fearless head-on attack exploded into a terrifying moment of carnage. The Japanese pilot was not firing his guns; he was going to ram! In a blur of movement, with a closing speed of nearly 600 miles an hour between the two planes, the Zero barely missed the Marauder's right propeller, slipped along the fuselage and with its wing razored off the bomber's vertical fin and rudder.

The Zero continued flying straight and level, apparently unharmed. Then it began a series of slow rolls, gradually losing altitude. It plunged into the sea at full speed. Seconds afterward the B-26, without its vertical fin, yawed and rolled crazily, flipped over on its back, and plunged into the water with a blinding explosion. Less than five minutes later, with at least six fighters pouring a torrent of cannon shells and bullets into its fuselage and wings, another B-26 plummeted into the waves. The five other bombers escaped.

Back at Lae, I found that the pilot who had rammed the Marauder was the same man who, on July 2, had sworn he would take an enemy bomber down with him. Suitsu had made good his threat.

We hit Moresby again on the sixth. Fifteen fighters escorted twenty-one bombers, and our planes claimed three fighters destroyed.

From July 7 through the 10 it was the enemy's turn. For three successive nights we cowered like rats in our shelters. Lae became a nightmare of exploding bombs, of tracers raking the air base from one end to the other, of geysers of flame and smoke, burning planes, wrecked buildings, and hundreds of bomb craters. There was no doubt that the enemy intended to try to blast the Lae installation into a smoking ruin. But despite his attacks, he never achieved his main purpose—we always had fighters available to fly.

On the eleventh we made another maximum bomber effort against Moresby, with twelve fighters escorting twenty-one bombers from Rabaul. We were en route to the enemy base when Lieutenant Sasai discovered six B-17s on their way to hit our field; he broke off from the escort formation, taking five other fighters with him. It was poor judgment on Sasai's part. He signaled Nishizawa, Ota, and me to join his flight, and the six of us attacked the big bombers in a long series of firing passes. But the Flying Fortresses proved as formidable as their name implied. We damaged three bombers, but failed to down any of the enemy planes. Their gunners were improving; one Zero went down in flames, and the other fighters, including my own, were holed with enemy bullets.

With only six Zeros flying escort, the formation which hit Moresby was scattered by enemy fighters; consequently, their bombs fell over a wide area and caused little damage to the enemy installations.

Sasai received a severe reprimand for leaving the bombers with such slight protection. He made no attempt to vindicate his action and accepted his rebuke silently. There was no doubt that he had violated the cardinal rule of escort fighters: never leave the bombers unprotected. His pilots, however, sympathized with Sasai. The B-17s were a painful thorn in our side. Their ability to ward off our attacks with such success both baffled and enraged us.

We entered a new phase of fighter operations on July 21 when a Japanese army division landed at Buna, 110 miles south of Lae. The troops at once worked their way inland on a frantic march through wild jungle toward Port Moresby. On a map the proposed maneuver appeared simple to execute. Buna seemed but a stone's throw away from Moresby, across the neck of the Papuan Peninsula.

But the maps of the jungle islands are altogether different from the fierce conditions below in the dense foliage. The Japanese high command made a terrible and fatal error in committing our troops to the Moresby attack. Before the battle was ended, Japan had suffered one of her most tragic and humiliating disasters.

The Owen Stanley Mountains are nearly as high as the fearsome Alps. To describe the wild jungle on the mountain slope merely as dense growth is to indulge in understatement. The profusion of plant life is unbelievable. If there were no swamps underfoot, nor bogs, nor mud, nor soft, yielding dead plant growth, then there were razor-sharp rocks, precipitous slopes, all manner of vines and insects, oppressive heat, and diseases which struck men down mysteriously.

Crossing the Alpine glaciers is a simple task in comparison to the heartbreaking and brutal struggle of breaking through the Owen Stanley Mountain jungles. It was virtually impossible to supply the troops once they were swallowed up by the jungle morass. The injured and wounded found their wounds festering in the sweltering heat and sodden humidity. Water drained from men's bodies from every pore. Equipment rotted away, clothes fell off in tatters, feet were cut to pulp by rocks and razor-sharp jungle grass and leaves.

For several months our troops struggled doggedly through the worst enemy they had ever faced, an enemy which did not fire guns or sow land mines or strafe, but which swallowed up hundreds of men with a single gulp, and never again released their captives. Through superhuman feats, several elements actually managed to close within a few miles of their coveted goal, the Moresby bastion. But even these successful troops met only heartbreaking failure. Almost is not enough, and before the operation was over—or, more properly, before it simply dissolved—every man perished, the majority from starvation deep within jungles from which they could find no escape.

The overland attack was a move of desperation. Originally our high command scheduled a massive amphibious assault against Moresby, but this move was eliminated on May 7 and 8 during the Coral Sea Battle, when two Japanese carriers encountered two enemy carriers in the first sea duel in which no surface ship fired at an opponent. Each force used its planes to pound the other with constant aerial bombing. We won the battle, but the enemy achieved his objective; the amphibious assault was canceled.

With our troops ashore at Buna, Rabaul headquarters ordered our attacks against Moresby discontinued, and called for constant air support of the beachhead. The Buna landings were but a part of a larger operation, which was doomed to defeat even as it got under way. Not only did the jungle pose a threat of enormous magnitude, but our men were hobbled by a thorough lack of understanding of the problems of logistics on the part of their leaders. These weaknesses, combined with brilliant moves on the part of the enemy, assured a disaster from the very first.

Simultaneously with the Buna landings, a commando unit raced ashore at the easternmost tip of New Guinea. Working day and night, the men hacked a new airstrip out of the jungle at Rabi, which was intended to safeguard the flow of overland supplies to the men moving across New Guinea from the Buna beachhead. Strangely, the enemy failed to bomb the construction work at Rabi, but remained satisfied with photographs taken from reconnaissance planes. However, almost as soon as the men completed the new Rabi field, enemy troops burst onto their unsuspecting ranks in a surprise attack and overwhelmed the Japanese garrison. It was a brilliant stroke. We built the field, the Americans and Australians used it for their own planes!

They were not content with merely this one new field. It was evident to all of us that the Allies were building up their air strength for an all-out interdiction of Lae and Rabaul. Their engineers hacked out new airstrips from the jungle with amazing speed. Medium bombers and fighters moved onto the new runways even as their construction equipment kept working. And the attacks against Lae continued to increase in weight of aircraft and bombs. Rarely did a night pass when their Mitchells and Marauders failed to appear, bombing and strafing at will.

During the day Lae juggled its twenty to thirty operational fighters to keep six to nine Zeros always in the air over Buna, as well as a standby force to protect the field. The air cover at Buna was far below our needs, but the fighters managed to prevent any large-scale attacks from destroying the beachhead facilities.

Buna was a shock to me on my first patrol. I had seen many landing operations before from the air, but never had I witnessed such a pathetic attempt to supply a full infantry division. Soldiers milled around on the beach, carrying cases of supplies into the jungle by hand. Only two small transports with a single small sub chaser as their escort stood off the beach unloading new supplies!

Flying cover for the beachhead proved eventually more difficult than anticipated. No longer did heavy cloud layers mean a day of comparative rest. On July 22, in a group of six Zeros, we flew wide circles in what appeared to be an otherwise empty sky. A thick overcast hung at 7,000 feet above the ground. Without warning a series of tremendous explosions rocked the beach area, and columns of flame and smoke erupted into the sky. Seconds later thick, greasy smoke boiled out of the critical supply dumps several hundred yards off the shore. No other planes could be seen. Either they had dropped their bombs through the overcast with spectacular accuracy—which seemed highly unreasonable—or one or more planes had dropped be low the clouds, released their bombs, and slipped back into the protection of the gray mass without being seen.

The latter proved to be the case, for several minutes later I caught sight of a tiny speck moving out of the edge of the overcast, far to the southeast. We turned and pursued the fleeing plane which, as we drew closer, was identifiable as our old friend, the twin-engined Lockheed Hudson. We were about a mile away when we were sighted. The bomber nosed down and fled along the coast, trying to make Rabi. Its speed was high, almost as great as that of our own fighters. I jettisoned the fuel tank and pushed the throttle to maximum over-boost.

From a distance of 600 yards and to the rear left, I fired a burst from all four guns at the plane, hoping the Hudson would turn and allow me to lessen the distance between our two planes. What happened next was startling. No sooner had I fired than the Hudson went up in a steep climbing turn to the right, rolled quickly, and roared back with full speed directly at me. I was so surprised that for several moments I sat motionless in the cockpit. The next second every forward-firing gun in the Hudson opened up in a withering barrage.

Our Zeros scattered wildly, rolling or diving in different directions. Nothing like this had ever happened before! I caught a glimpse of Lieutenant Sasai; his jaw hung open in astonishment at the audacity of the enemy pilot. One Zero—piloted by Nishizawa, who refused to be impressed by anything—rolled out of his sudden breakaway and came down behind the bomber, his guns spitting flame. Again we were astounded. The Hudson heeled over in a snap roll, the fastest I had ever seen for a twin-engined plane. Nishizawa's guns sprayed only empty air.

The remaining pilots, myself included, hurled our planes at the Hudson. All of us failed to score a single hit. The bomber rolled and sawed up and down in violent maneuvers, with the top gunner firing steadily at our planes.

The Zero pilots went wild with fury. Our formation disintegrated and every man went at the Hudson with everything he had. I made at least four firing passes, and was forced to break off my attack by other pilots who screamed in without regard for their wingmates. For nearly ten minutes we pursued the Hudson, pouring a hail of lead and explosive shells at the amazing plane. Finally a heavy burst caught the rear turret; I saw the gunner throw his hands up and collapse. Without the interfering stream of bullets from the turret, I closed in to twenty yards and held the gun trigger down, aiming for the right wing. Seconds later flame streamed out, then spread to the left wing. The pilot stayed with the ship; it was too low for him or the crew to bail out. The Hudson lost speed rapidly and glided in toward the jungle. Trees sheared off the two flaming wings and the fuselage, also trailing great sheets of flame, burst into the dense growth like a giant sliver of burning steel. There was a sudden explosion, and smoke boiled upward.

The day was full of surprises. We were on our way back to Lae to resume the beachhead patrol when five Airacobras attempted a surprise attack against our formation. The enemy planes flew in a long column low over the water, attempting to climb rapidly and catch us unawares. I was the first to sight the enemy group. I went into a steep turn and dove for the Airacobras, heading directly at the lead plane. Abruptly the five P-39's scattered in all directions, turned, and raced away. With their advantage of surprise gone, and five other Zeros directly behind me, they wanted no part of a battle in which they were at a height disadvantage.

With the speed from my dive, I was soon among the enemy group. Two fighters zoomed wildly and disappeared into low-hanging clouds. Another disappeared within a shower of rain, and yet another seemed to have vanished into thin air. One Airacobra was still in the clear, and I went after the fighter at maximum speed. He was heading for clouds, but a burst across his nose changed his mind. The P-39 flicked over in a left roll and dove for the sea with me 200 yards behind.

It was the new model Airacobra which, at sea level, was equal in speed to my own fighter. But the pilot had made a fatal error—he was flying in the wrong direction! Instead of fleeing to Moresby, he was headed in exactly the opposite direction. I still had plenty of fuel, and was content to maintain the distance between our planes—all the way to Rabaul, if necessary. Several minutes later the American pilot came to his senses, and realized his error. He had no choice but to reverse his course, and the fighter winged over in a sharp left bank and turn.

This had happened many times before. I cut inside his turn, moving in slightly below and to the left of the fighter. A short burst sent the Airacobra rolling violently to escape my fire. I clung to his tail as he whipsawed back and forth, heading for the coastline. For precious seconds I lost the fighter when he went through some unusually wild maneuvers, and the P-39 raced away for his home base, with several hundred yards' distance between our two planes. Even with the engine on over-boost I could not close the distance between us. I was almost ready to turn away; so long as the P-39 kept a straight and true course it was impossible for me to reach firing position.

The enemy pilot chose otherwise. Instead of staying over the sea, he headed directly for the Owen Stanley Mountains, which forced him into a climb. And no P-39 could outclimb a Zero. Slowly but steadily I closed the distance between us. I held my fire for a burst at the closest possible range. With my ammunition low after the battle with the Hudson, I would have enough for only one or two quick bursts.

Fifty yards. Then it shrunk to forty, then thirty. I gripped the gun trigger, aiming carefully.

I had not fired a single shot when the pilot bailed out of the fighter! The Airacobra was less than 150 feet above the ground when his form tumbled into the air, in a drop which seemed to be certain death. I knew of no instance where a pilot had survived a bailout from less than 300 feet.

Miraculously, the chute snapped open a split second before the pilot struck the ground. He dropped into a small clearing while his fighter exploded a scant few yards in front of him. I still could not believe that the enemy pilot had lived through his incredible descent. I turned steeply and flew back over the jungle clearing. Only the parachute was visible. The pilot had lived, and was in good enough condition to flee from sight. It was my second victory without firing a shot, and raised my total to forty-nine planes.

The next few weeks were spent in maintaining cover over the Buna beach area, but the latter half of July meant a new and strange phase of the war for us. No longer did we fly without parachutes. Orders had come down from higher headquarters, and Captain Saito directed every pilot to wear his chute into combat. It was a strange sensation to feel the chute packed on my seat below me, and the straps around my body. I had never flown with one before.

Equally disturbing to us were further orders which carried unspoken but ominous implications. We were taken off the offensive. Captain Saito issued orders that from now on no fighters would cross the Owen Stanley Range, no matter how compelling the reason.

Only on one occasion—July 26—did I see Port Moresby again. We had intercepted five Marauders over Buna, and during the running fight as the bombers fled for home I shot two B-26s out of the air, kills confirmed by the other pilots. With Sasai and Endo behind me, I pursued the remaining bombers, crossing the mountain range against orders. I shot up one bomber, but failed to see it crash, and received only a probable.

That was the last time I ever flew over the enemy base. Our situation was changing rapidly. By the end of the first week in August, we began to fight under conditions we had never before known. The Americans had launched a tremendous invasion of Guadalcanal Island.

CHAPTER TWENTY-ONE

ON JULY 29 Lieutenant Joji Yamashita returned to Lae from his Buna patrol with news which electrified the entire base. His planes had been attacked for the first time by American naval aircraft. He reported to Commander Nakajima and Captain Saito that his nine Zeros had encountered a mixed force of American SBD Dauntless dive bombers and F4F Wildcat fighters, led to the Buna area by P-39 pathfinders which, he estimated, had come from Rabi. The Navy warplanes were the first to appear in our theater.

The news that an American aircraft carrier had moved into New Guinea waters was ominous, and our staff officers appeared upset. If the Americans had carriers to spare for operations against our forces at Lae, Buna, and Rabaul, then there appeared to be some truth in their claims of victory at Midway and their denials of major losses during the Coral Sea Battle. If what Tokyo had claimed was true, that our fleet had destroyed the enemy carriers encountered in the Coral Sea and off Midway, how could there be a carrier in our vicinity? Something was wrong, and for the first time we felt doubts regarding the authenticity of Tokyo's repeated claims of victory.

The majority of fighter pilots at Lae, however, greeted the news in an entirely different fashion. Late into the night we threw questions at Yamashita's pilots. How many Navy planes were there? Were the Wildcats better than the P-39s and the P-40s? How good were the American Navy pilots?

Their answers were encouraging, for Yamashita's squadron put in claims for three dive bombers, five fighters, and one P-39 definitely shot down, without the loss of a single Zero. This made unimportant what might have happened at Midway, or at the Coral Sea, or anywhere else! All we cared about was that for four successive months we had whipped the enemy's fighters and bombers time and time again, and that the appearance of his Navy planes meant that much greater an opportunity for gaining even more victories.

But for the next three days the new enemy planes failed to appear over Buna. On the thirtieth nine B-17s attacked the beachhead area with considerable success, and our nine fighters managed to shoot down only one bomber of the enemy formation. I received credit for the victory when I caught the fourth Fortress over Cape Nelson and managed to concentrate my fire into its nose. Apparently the pilot and copilot were killed, for the big airplane plunged into the ocean out of control. It was one of my hardest air battles, for I returned to Lae with several inches of skin scraped off my right arm from the bomber's guns. I had missed death by no more than the thickness of a hair, and my mechanics worked all night to patch up the dozens of bullet holes in the fuselage and wings.

On August 2, all thought of Navy planes fled from our minds. Before the day was over, we had behind us a tremendous occasion to remember—the dream of all Japanese fighter pilots come true. We were circling over Buna at 12,000 feet when we sighted five tiny specks against the clouds several miles away from the beachhead. They were at our height, and they appeared to be Fortresses. I flew alongside Sasai's plane and indicated the oncoming bombers. He nodded and we both pointed out the B-17s to the other pilots. We kept our formation, circling slowly, until the four engines of each bomber became clearly visible. Sasai signaled us to follow him. He raised his right hand, rocked his wings to give the order to break up our V formations into a single column for a head-on attack. Our fuel tanks tumbled through the air.

Now was our chance to put to the acid test the theories we had worked out in our billets at night. In a few moments we would know whether or not the Fortresses were vulnerable to the head-on attack. The situation was perfect. Nine Zero fighters against five of the great B-17s, and among that nine we had the leading aces of all Japan. Sasai led the attack. Ota dropped 500 yards behind his plane, followed by Endo. I slipped into fourth position, also at a 500-yard distance, and my wingmen, Yonekawa and Hatori, followed me as numbers five and six in the column. Nishizawa took seventh place, then Takatsuka, and finally NAP 3/C Yoshio Sueyoshi in the rear slot. Nine Zeros, spread out over a distance of 4,000 yards, and carrying the best pilots Japan had produced.

The Fortresses tightened their formation as we closed in. Sasai's fighter dropped below the lead bomber, then climbed at a shallow angle, rolling slowly as he aimed at the lower nose section of the plane. The next second he flashed up and over as he completed his firing run. Smoke trailed from all five bombers but it was the smoke of their 50-caliber guns. The enemy formation continued on.

Then Ota made his bid, following exactly the same maneuver as Sasai. I watched the flashes of his tracers as they bit into the lead bomber, then Ota's wing lift up as he began his breakaway turn. The next instant a violent explosion hid every plane from view. A flash of intense light appeared in the sky, followed by a tremendous smoke cloud. Even from a half-mile distance, the shock wave jolted my own fighter. The B-17 was no longer in the sky. It had disappeared, shattered into small pieces of wreckage when its full bomb load went off under the impact of Ota's cannon shells. It was the most spectacular air kill I had ever seen, and I cheered loudly as Ota's Zero rocketed upward through the smoke.

By now Endo was in his firing run, diving and climbing upward at a shallow angle. The Zero rolled slowly as it raced against the bombers, both cannon and machine guns spitting out flame as he closed in. His tracers went wild and Endo went for altitude as the bomber guns bracketed him in a heavy crossfire.

My turn now! I pulled back gently on the stick and the third Fortress in the formation expanded slowly in my range finder. Closer and closer he came, and I squeezed the trigger. Nothing happened! The bomber seemed to fill the entire sky before me before I found out what was wrong. *Stupid!* I had failed to release the safety lock on the trigger; an error not even the greenest pilot would make. It was almost my undoing, and I rolled violently to clear the B-17 at a distance of only twenty yards.

Their gunners had me in a crossfire. The Zero lurched as bullets slammed into the fuselage, and I felt the shock of the heavy slugs ripping through metal. I was frantic now, and, with my fighter's belly up, I held the stick over hard to the left, rolling wildly. I was through, but not without damage. I raged at my own stupidity, but it was too late. I had wasted a perfect firing pass. I dropped below the enemy formation and gunned the engine to over-boost to race ahead of the bombers for another run.

Nishizawa was already climbing against his B-17. He went in beautifully, his fighter arcing up slowly in its gradual climb, rolling steadily as the distance narrowed between his fighter and the enemy plane. His attack was perfect, as he kept pouring cannon shells into the wing fuel tanks. Abruptly a splash of flame burst through the wing, spread rapidly, and in a few seconds the Fortress seemed to turn into a gigantic flame thrower. Brilliant fire streamed into the wind from the wing and along the fuselage. The plane skidded wildly and its nose dropped. Then it was gone. Another mighty explosion flipped Nishizawa's fighter over on its back like a toy and rocked my own Zero sharply. The other bombers reeled under the shock wave even as the remaining fighters screamed by on their firing passes.

Now Sasai went in again, raking a third bomber from nose to tail. He started firing from a distance of almost 150 yards, and his shells slowly moved back along the fuselage. Pieces of metal erupted from the plane and flipped away in the slipstream. The airplane rolled wildly to the right, out of control. I saw flames within the fuselage, licking out of the cockpit and the second gun turret. The B-17 dropped in a long sweeping turn, rolling and skidding as it descended, the sure sign of a dead pilot and copilot. The flames increased and, for the third time in two minutes, another roaring explosion marked the finish of the third B-17.

I could hardly believe my eyes. These were the planes which had been driving our fighter pilots frantic wherever they appeared. And now, one, two, three! Three blasting detonations and as many Fortresses just so many small pieces of charred wreckage falling from the sky.

The two surviving bombers split up as I came in for my second pass, and I found only empty space in my range finder. I went up and over in a high loop, coming out to see the two B-17s racing away in different directions. One headed for the mountains and the other turned for the open sea. I went after the plane racing for the water. The B-17 rolled and turned continuously as I tried for a long burst at the cockpit or fuel tanks. For some strange reason the bombardier failed to jettison his lethal load, and the plane fled under the weight penalty of all its bombs. I dove to gain speed, and came up beneath the bomber, closing in toward the left wing. The B-17 grew larger and larger in my sight, and I opened up, watching the shells exploding along the left wing by the fuselage and chewing up the metal skin as they moved toward the bomb bay.

The world was blotted out in the next instant. A bolt of light, searing and intense, filled the sky, blinding me. A great fist gripped the Zero and flipped it wildly through the air. My ears rang and I tasted blood trickling down from my nose. The fourth Fortress was gone! Every one had been destroyed by its own bombs. Now only one remained. The bomber fled for the mountains, eight Zeros clawing at the great plane like hunting dogs after a massive wild boar. They were hard pressed to keep up with the B-17, which evidently had jettisoned its bombs and had gained speed. The B-17's course, cutting across my nose, gave me a chance to intercept the airplane before it reached land.

My decision was fortunate, indeed. No sooner had I turned and pushed the throttle all the way forward than I sighted three Airacobras rushing down from the east, skimming over the water, obviously answering the distress calls of the Fortresses. They closed in on the eight pursuing Zeros, which had no warning of their approach. It was a unique situation. The three P-39s began climbing after eight unsuspecting Zero fighters, and I came around in a wide sweeping turn on the three unsuspecting enemy planes.

The first P-39 moved into firing position against the last Zero when I hit him in a shallow dive. The enemy pilot never knew what happened; bullets and cannon shells smashed into his fuselage at the wing roots and the airplane disintegrated, one wing flipping wildly through the air. My gun reports carried to the other Zeros, and at once two fighters clawed around in a tight spiral and fell upon the other two P-39s. It was over in seconds. I recognized the planes of our two peerless aces, Nishizawa and Ota. Each pilot fired but one heavy burst, and the Airacobras fell in flames. The three enemy pilots had attacked three times their number in Zero fighters; regrettably, their skill failed to match their courage.

But there was still unfinished business in the air: the lone surviving Fortress, which now turned from the land and headed back for the sea. Its speed was visibly reduced, and with its crippled engines it was only a matter of time before we cut the bomber out of the air. I had barely come out of a long climb after pulling out of my dive against the Airacobra when the B-17 moved before my nose. It happened too suddenly to enable me to aim properly, but I snapped out a heavy burst. The shells went wild, and I rolled up and turned to come back for another attack.

The crippled Fortress was still full of fight. I was climbing past the bomber, watching the tracers arcing through the air after me, when suddenly the Zero shuddered violently. The sounds of hammers beating against metal startled me, and something shook me wildly in the cockpit. My right hand went numb. The Zero skidded crazily, its belly up, and flipped downward out of control. I searched the instruments with fear, but the engine kept up its powerful drone. No flame or smoke; relief swept over me, for I was prepared to go over the side if necessary. A burning Zero doesn't stay in one piece for very long.

I was less than 1,000 feet over the water when I brought the fighter out of its careening plunge. The plane had been hit badly, but its vital parts had not been damaged. Back in normal flying position, I looked at my right hand. A piece of metal was sticking through the glove where it had penetrated the palm. Good fortune was certainly with me today; the jagged piece of metal had been ripped loose by a passing bullet, but without enough energy to cause any serious injury.

The Fortress lost altitude steadily, trailing a long streamer of white smoke. The Zeros kept at the bomber in their long column, each one snapping out a burst as the pilot dove against the crippled bomber. One fighter broke away from the pack harassing the B-17. It went into a wide, lazy turn and began a gradual descent across the island coastline. A thin white film trailed in the air behind it. The plane did not seem to be seriously damaged; its wings were level. But it lost altitude and speed steadily. I turned and glanced at the bomber, which now plunged toward the sea, obviously out of control. By the time I looked again for the lone Zero, the airplane was gone.

A wild ovation greeted us at Lae as we told the mechanics of our destruction of five Flying Fortresses. The men leaped and shouted in glee as they heard the details. Five Fortresses and three Airacobras—an excellent day!

Nishizawa was the seventh pilot to land. He climbed out of his cockpit and ignored the hilarious cheers of his ground crew. He asked one question. "Where's Sueyoshi?" Silence fell on the crowd.

"Where is my wingman?" Nishizawa demanded. Takatsuka climbed from his fighter and walked silently up to Nishizawa.

"Hasn't Salamaua radioed in?" Nishizawa cried. "What's the matter with all of you? Hasn't there been any word?"

Nishizawa went wild. There had been no news from Salamaua, and no one had seen Sueyoshi's fighter after it dropped toward the coast.

"Refuel my plane and load my guns! " Nishizawa ordered. We tried to dissuade him from going out on what seemed to be a hopeless search, but Nishizawa would not be dissuaded.

Two hours later he returned, misery written on his face. Sueyoshi, one of the most popular young fliers at Lae, was never found. The day's victory turned bitter in our mouths.

CHAPTER TWENTY-TWO

ON AUGUST 3 Rabaul called back most of the Zero fighters assigned to Lae. We welcomed the transfer, for it promised relief from the daily patrols over Buna and an escape from the nightly bombings. We left behind us at Lae our personal belongings, fully believing we would soon return. We were wrong. Our first four days at Rabaul we flew reconnaissance and fighter sweep flights to Rabi, which rapidly had been built up into a major enemy fighter nest comparable to Moresby.

On August 8, after receiving our patrol orders from the Command Post, we started walking across the airfield to our fighters. Most of the eighteen pilots were in their cockpits when orderlies ran after us shouting that the flight had been canceled. We were to report back at once to the Command Post. The CP was in a wild turmoil. Orderlies and messengers ran to and fro, and the officers who passed us wore worried expressions on their faces. Commander Nakajima, who was to lead today's mission, came out of the admiral's room, obviously angry, and shouted to us, "Today's mission has been called off. We're going somewhere else." He looked around the room. "Where the hell is that orderly? You," pointing to a startled messenger, "get me a chart, quick!"

He spread the map on a large desk and began plotting a course with a compass. He paid no attention to any of the pilots as he pored over the map. I asked Lieutenant Sasai if he knew what had happened; Sasai questioned Nakajima, received a curt explanation, and rushed into the admiral's rooms without speaking to any of us. Several minutes later he returned, and signaled the pilots to gather about him. His words were like a bombshell. "At 0520 hours this morning a powerful enemy amphibious force began an invasion at Lunga, on the southern end of Guadalcanal Island. Our first reports indicate that the Americans are throwing a tremendous amount of men and equipment onto the island. They also have struck in simultaneous attacks at Tulagi on Florida Island. Our entire flying-boat flotilla has been destroyed. As soon as the commander has worked out our new routes, we will take off at once for Guadalcanal to attack the enemy forces on the beaches."

Orderlies passed out charts of the islands to each pilot. We studied the maps, searching for the unfamiliar island which had so suddenly become important. The men murmured among themselves. "Where is that damned island anyway?" cried one exasperated pilot. "Who ever heard of such a crazy place?"

We checked the distance from Rabaul to Guadalcanal. There were low whistles of disbelief. Five hundred and sixty miles! We would have to fly that distance to the enemy beachhead, engage his fighters, and then fly the same mileage back to Rabaul. The distance was unheard of. It meant a round-trip flight of more than 1,100 miles, without allowance for combat or storms, which would consume fuel in prodigious quantities.

That was enough to stop all speculation. We waited silently for the commander to lift his head and give us our new orders. In the meantime one orderly after the other rushed into the admiral's office with fresh reports from the battlefront. We heard one messenger tell Nakajima that all contact had been lost with Tulagi, that the garrison had died to the last man.

Sasai turned pale at the news. I had to ask him several times if anything was wrong. Finally, staring straight ahead, he spoke quietly. "My brother-in-law was assigned to Tulagi." There was no denying the certainty of his words. He referred to his sister's husband in the past tense. If Tulagi was now occupied by the enemy, then his brother-in-law, Lieutenant Commander Yoshio Tashiro, a flying-boat commander, could no longer be among the living. He would fight to the last. (His death was confirmed later.)

Nakajima called for order. "You are going to fly the longest fighter operation in history," he warned us. "Don't take any unnecessary chances today. Stick to your orders, and, above all, don't fly recklessly and waste your fuel. Any pilot who runs short of fuel on the return from Guadalcanal is to make a forced landing at Buka Island. Our troops there have been instructed to be on the lookout for our planes.

"Now, to fly to Guadalcanal and return to Buka means covering roughly the same distance as we flew from Tainan to Clark Field in the Philippines, and return. I am positive that we can fly that distance without trouble. Returning to Rabaul is another matter. You should be able to make it, but there may be trouble. So I repeat my warning: don't waste fuel."

(Commander Nakajima told me in Tokyo after the war that the admiral wished him to take to Guadalcanal on August 7 every Zero fighter at Rabaul which could fly. Nakajima protested, and offered instead to take the twelve best pilots in his wing, because he expected to lose at least half of his men during a mission of such extreme range. A bitter argument raged between the two men until they reached a compromise on the figure of eighteen fighter planes, with the understanding that the stragglers who landed on Buka were to be picked up later.)

As soon as we had our orders, the pilots broke up into trios. I told Yonekawa and Hatori, my two wingmen, "You'll meet the American Navy fliers for the first time today. They are going to have us at a distinct advantage because of the distance we have to fly. I want you both to exercise the greatest caution in every move you make. Above all, never break away from me. No matter what happens, no matter what goes on around us, stick as close to my plane as you can. Remember that—don't break away."

We ran out to our planes and waited for the runways to be cleared. Twenty-seven Betty bombers thundered down the airstrip before us. Commander Nakajima waved his hand over his cockpit. By 8:30 a.m. all the fighters were airborne. The maintenance crews and the pilots who were not flying that day lined both sides of the runway, waving their caps and shouting good luck to us. The weather was perfect, especially for Rabaul. Even the volcano was quiet; its eruptions had ended in June, and only a thin streamer of smoke drifted to the west.

We took up our escort positions behind the bombers. I was surprised to see that the Bettys carried bombs instead of torpedoes, the usual armament for attacking shipping. The bombs disturbed me; I knew the problems of hitting moving targets on the sea from high altitude. Even the B-17s, despite their vaunted accuracy, wasted most of their bombs when attacking the shipping off Buna.

We gained height slowly, then flew to the east at 13,000 feet for Buka Island. About sixty miles south of Rabaul, I noticed a particularly beautiful island on the water. Brilliantly green and in the shape of a horseshoe, the atoll was listed on the map as Green Island. I had no idea that the eye-catching qualities of the colorful atoll would later prove the key to saving my life.

Over Buka the formations turned and flew south along Bougainvillea's west coast. The sun beat down warmly through the canopy. The heat made me thirsty, and, since we still had some time before reaching the enemy area, I took out a bottle of soda from my lunchbox. Without thinking I opened the bottle; I had forgotten the altitude. No sooner had I made a slit in the cork than the soda water geysered violently, the pressure escaping in the rarefied air. In seconds the sticky soda water was over everything in front of me; fortunately, the strong cockpit draft dried it almost immediately. But the sugar in the soda water dried on my glasses and I was unable to see! Disgusted with my own stupidity, I rubbed the goggles. I could see dimly.

For the next forty minutes I struggled to clean not only my goggles but the windscreen and the controls as well. I had never felt more ridiculous. My fighter wandered all over the formation as I scrubbed with increasing irritation. By the time I could see clearly in all directions we were already over Vella Lavella, about midway between Rabaul and Guadalcanal.

Over New Georgia we went for higher altitude and crossed Russell at 20,000 feet. Fifty miles ahead of us Guadalcanal loomed out of the water. Even at this distance I saw flashes of yellow flame against the blue sky over the disputed island. Apparently battles were already under way between Zero fighters from bases other than Rabaul and the defending enemy planes. I looked down at Guadalcanal's northern coastline. In the channel between Guadalcanal and Florida hundreds of white lines, the wakes of enemy ships, crisscrossed the water. Everywhere I looked there were ships. I had never seen so many warships and transports at one time.

This was my first look at an American amphibious operation. It was almost unbelievable. I saw at least seventy ships pushing toward the beaches, a dozen destroyers cutting white swaths through the water around them. And there were other ships on the horizon, too far distant to make out in detail or to count.

Meanwhile the bombers swung slowly for their runs. Dead ahead of them small clouds drifted at 13,000 feet. To our right and above was the sun, its blinding glare blotting everything from view. I was uncomfortable; we would be unable to see any fighters dropping from that angle. My fear was soon realized. Without warning six fighter planes emerged from that glare, almost as if they had suddenly appeared in the sky. A snap glance revealed that they were chubbier than the other American planes we had fought. They were painted olive green, and only the lower sides of the wings were white. Wildcats; the first Grumman F4F fighters I had seen.

The Wildcats ignored the Zeros, swooping down against the bombers. Our fighters raced ahead, many of them firing from beyond effective range, hoping to distract the enemy planes. The Wildcats plunged into the bomber formation, rolling together, and then disappeared in dives. Over the water just off Savo Island, the bombers released their missiles against a large convoy. I watched the bombs curving in their long drop. Abruptly geysers of water erupted from the sea, but the enemy shipping sailed on undisturbed.

It was obviously stupid to try to hit moving ships from four miles up! I could not understand the failure to use torpedoes, which had proven so effective in the past. Our entire mission had been wasted, thrown away in a few seconds of miserable bombing inaccuracy.

(The following day the bombers returned, this time carrying torpedoes for low-level attacks. But by then it was too late. Enemy fighters swarmed all over the bombers, and many fell blazing into the ocean even before they could reach their targets.)

The bomber formation banked to the left and picked up speed for the return to Rabaul. We escorted them as far as Russell, beyond the enemy fighter patrols, and turned back for Guadalcanal. It was about 1:30 p.m. We swept over Lunga, the eighteen Zeros poised for combat. Again bursting out of the blinding sun, Wildcats plunged against our planes. I was the only pilot who spotted the diving attack, and at once I hauled the fighter up in a steep climb, and the other planes followed me. Again the Wildcats scattered and dove in different directions. Their evasive tactics were puzzling, for nothing had been gained by either side. Apparently the Americans were not going to pick any fights today.

I turned back to check the positions of my wingmen. They were gone! Things weren't as obvious as they seemed; the enemy would fight, after all. I looked everywhere for Yonekawa and Hatori, but could not find them. Sasai's plane, the two blue stripes across its fuselage, regained formation, several other fighters moving up to position behind him. But not my wingmen.

Finally I saw them, about 1,500 feet below me. I gaped. A single Wildcat pursued three Zero fighters, firing in short bursts at the frantic Japanese planes. All four planes were in a wild dogfight, flying tight left spirals. The Zeros should have been able to take the lone Grumman without any trouble, but every time a Zero caught the Wildcat before its guns the enemy plane flipped away wildly and came out again on the tail of a Zero. I had never seen such flying before.

I banked my wings to signal Sasai and dove. The Wildcat was clinging grimly to the tail of a Zero, its tracers chewing up the wings and tail. In desperation I snapped out a burst. At once the Grumman snapped away in a roll to the right, clawed around in a tight turn, and ended up in a climb straight at my own plane. Never had I seen an enemy plane move so quickly or so gracefully before; and every second his guns were moving closer to the belly of my fighter. I snap-rolled in an effort to throw him off. He would not be shaken. He was using my own favorite tactics, coming up from under.

I chopped the throttle back and the Zero shuddered as its speed fell. It worked; his timing off, the enemy pilot pulled back in a turn. I slammed the throttle forward again, rolling to the left. Three times I rolled the Zero, then dropped in a spin, and came out in a left vertical spiral. The Wildcat matched me turn for turn. Our left wings both pointed at a right angle to the sea below us, the right wings at the sky.

Neither of us could gain an advantage. We held to the spiral, tremendous G pressures pushing us down in our seats with every passing second. My heart pounded wildly, and my head felt as if it weighed a ton. A gray film seemed to be clouding over my eyes. I gritted my teeth; if the enemy pilot could take the punishment, so could I. The man who failed first and turned in any other direction to ease the pressure would be finished.

On the fifth spiral, the Wildcat skidded slightly. I had him, I thought. But the Grumman dropped its nose, gained speed, and the pilot again had his plane in full control. There was a terrific man behind that stick.

He made his error, however, in the next moment. Instead of swinging back to go into a sixth spiral, he fed power to his engine, broke away at an angle, and looped. That was the decisive split second. I went right after him, cutting inside the Grumman's arc, and came out on his tail. I had him. He kept flying loops, trying to narrow down the distance of each arc. Every time he went up and around I cut inside his arc and lessened the distance between our two planes. The Zero could outfly any fighter in the world in this kind of maneuver.

When I was only fifty yards away, the Wildcat broke out of his loop and astonished me by flying straight and level. At this distance I would not need the cannon; I pumped 200 rounds into the Grumman's cockpit, watching the bullets chewing up the thin metal skin and shattering the glass.

I could not believe what I saw; the Wildcat continued flying almost as if nothing had happened. A Zero which had taken that many bullets into its vital cockpit would have been a ball of fire by now. I could not understand it. I slammed the throttle forward and closed in to the American plane, just as the enemy fighter lost speed. In a moment I was ten yards ahead of the Wildcat, trying to slow down. I hunched my shoulders, prepared for the onslaught of his guns. I was trapped.

No bullets came. The Wildcat's guns remained silent. The entire situation was unbelievable. I dropped my speed until our planes were flying wing-to-wing formation. I opened my cockpit window and stared out. The Wildcat's cockpit canopy was already back, and I could see the pilot clearly. He was a big man, with a round face. He wore a light khaki uniform. He appeared to be middle-aged, not as young as I had expected.

For several seconds we flew along in our bizarre formation, our eyes meeting across the narrow space between the two planes. The Wildcat was a shambles. Bullet holes had cut the fuselage and wings up from one end to the other. The skin of the rudder was gone, and the metal ribs stuck out like a skeleton. Now I could understand his horizontal flight, and also why the pilot had not fired. Blood stained his right shoulder, and I saw the dark patch moving downward over his chest. It was incredible that his plane was still in the air.

But this was no way to kill a man! Not with him flying helplessly, wounded, his plane a wreck. I raised my left hand and shook my fist at him, shouting, uselessly, I knew, for him to fight instead of just flying along like a clay pigeon. The American looked startled; he raised his right hand weakly and waved.

I had never felt so strange before. I had killed many Americans in the air, but this was the first time a man had weakened in such a fashion directly before my eyes, and from wounds I had inflicted upon him. I honestly didn't know whether or not I should try and finish him off. Such thoughts were stupid, of course. Wounded or not, he was an enemy, and he had almost taken three of my own men a few minutes before. However, there was no reason to aim for the pilot again. I wanted the airplane, not the man.

I dropped back and came in again on his tail. Somehow the American called upon a reserve of strength and the Wildcat jerked upward into a loop. That was it. His nose started up. I aimed carefully at the engine, and barely touched the cannon trigger. A burst of flame and smoke exploded outward from his engine. The Wildcat rolled and the pilot bailed out. Far below me, almost directly over the Guadalcanal coast, his parachute snapped open. The pilot did not grasp his shroud lines, but hung limply in his chute. The last I saw of him he was drifting in toward the beach.

The other three Zero fighters quickly reformed on my wings. Yonekawa grinned broadly at me as he slid into position. We climbed and headed back for the island in search of other enemy planes. Antiaircraft shells began to burst around us. Their aim was sporadic, but the fact that heavy flak guns were already on shore, only hours after the invasion, was upsetting. I knew that our own forces required at least three days following a beach landing to set up their antiaircraft weapons. The speed at which the Americans moved their equipment ashore was astounding.

(Long after the day's flight was over, Commander Nakajima filled me in on what had happened to the other fourteen Zeros. The enemy Navy fighters held a constant advantage over Guadalcanal. They kept diving in groups of six and twelve planes, always from out of the sun, raising havoc with the Zero formations. Never before had Nakajima and his men encountered such determined opposition or faced an enemy who would not yield. Again and again the plunging Wildcats shredded the Zero formation.

(Every time the Wildcats dove, they fired, rolled back, and disappeared far below, refusing to allow the Zeros to use to their own advantage their unexcelled maneuverability. The tactics were wise, but the Americans' gunnery was sadly deficient. Only one Zero fighter fell before these attacks.

(It was Nishizawa's day to shine. Before his ammunition ran out, the astounding ace in incredible maneuvers which left his wingmen hopelessly far behind him had shot six Grumman fighters out of the sky.

(For the first time Nakajima encountered what was to become a famous double-team maneuver on the part of the enemy. Two

Wildcats jumped the commander's plane. He had no trouble in getting on the tail of an enemy fighter, but never had a chance to fire before the Grumman's teammate roared at him from the side. Nakajima was raging when he got back to Rabaul; he had been forced to dive and run for safety. And Nishizawa and I were the only two pilots in the entire group to down any enemy planes during the day's fighting.)

Meanwhile I returned to 7,000 feet with my three fighters behind me. We flew through broken clouds, unable to find any hostile planes. No sooner had we emerged from one cloud than, for the first time in all my years of combat, an enemy plane caught me unawares. I felt a heavy thud, the scream of a bullet, and a hole two inches across appeared through the cockpit glass to my left, only inches away from my face.

I still had not seen any other planes in the air. It might have been ground fire which hit me. Then I caught a glimpse of an enemy bomber—not a fighter!—which had caught me napping. The Dauntless hung on its wing, racing for cloud cover. The audacity of the enemy pilot was amazing; he had deliberately jumped four Zero fighters in a slow and lightly armed dive bomber.

In a moment I was on his tail. The Dauntless jerked up and down several times, then dove suddenly into a cloud. I wasn't giving up that easily; I went right in after him. For a few seconds I saw only white as we raced through the billowing mass. Then we were through, in the clear. I closed in rapidly and fired. The rear gunner flung up his hands and collapsed over his gun. I pulled back easily on the stick and the shells walked up to the engine. The SBD rolled repeatedly to the left, then dropped into a wild dive. Yonekawa saw the pilot bail out. It was my sixtieth kill.

Back at 13,000 feet, we searched for but failed to find the remainder of our group. A few minutes later, over the Guadalcanal coast, I spotted a cluster of planes several miles ahead of our own. I signaled the other fighters and gunned the engine.

Soon I made out eight planes in all, flying a formation of two flights. Enemy. Our own planes did not form up into flights in their formations. I was well ahead of the other fighters and kept closing in against the enemy group. I would take the planes on the right and leave the others for the three Zeros following. The enemy group tightened formation; perfect! They appeared to be Wildcats, and tightening their formation meant that I had not been sighted.

If they kept their positions I would be able to hit them without warning, coming up from their rear and below. Just another few seconds... I'd be able to get at least two on the first firing pass. I closed in as close as possible. The distance in the range finder shrank to 200 yards—then 100—70—60 ...

I was in a trap! The enemy planes were not fighters, but bombers, the new Avenger torpedo planes, types I had never seen before. From the rear they looked exactly like Wildcats, but now their extra size was visible, as were the top turret with its single gun and the belly turret with another 50 caliber gun.

No wonder they had tightened their formation! They were waiting for me, and now I was caught with eight guns aiming at me from the right, and an equal number from the left. I was on engine over-boost, and it was impossible to slow down quickly.

There was no turning back now. If I turned or looped, the enemy gunners would have a clear shot at the exposed belly of the Zero. I wouldn't stand a chance of evading their fire. There was only one thing to do—keep going, and open up with everything I had. I jammed down on the firing button. Almost at the same moment every gun in the Avenger formation opened up. The chattering roar of the guns and the cough of the cannon drowned out all other sound. The enemy planes were only twenty yards in front of me when flames spurted from two bombers. That was all I saw. A violent explosion smashed at my body. I felt as though knives had been thrust savagely into my ears; the world burst into flaming red and I went blind.

(The three pilots following me reported to our commander that they saw both Avengers falling from the sky, along with my plane. They stated further that the enemy planes were trailing fire and smoke; these were officially credited to me as my sixty-first and sixty-second air victories. But an official American report of the battle denied any losses of Grumman TBF Avengers operating from the three aircraft carriers southwest of Guadalcanal. Perhaps the two planes made it back to their ships. As my own plane dove, with me unconscious in the cockpit, the three Zeros followed me down. They abandoned their chase when my fighter disappeared into a low overcast.)

Several seconds must have passed before I regained consciousness. A strong, cold wind blowing in through the shattered windshield brought me to. But I was still not in control of my senses. Everything seemed blurred. I kept lapsing back into waves of darkness. These swept over me every time I tried to sit up straight. My head was far back, leaning against the headrest. I struggled to see, but the cockpit wavered and danced before my eyes. The cockpit seemed to be open; actually, the glass had been shattered, and the wind streamed in to jar me back to semi-consciousness. It struck my face; my goggles were smashed.

I felt . . . nothing but a soothing, pleasant drowsiness. I wanted to go to sleep. I tried to realize that I had been hit, that I was dying, but I felt no fear. If dying was like this, without pain, there was nothing to worry about.

I was in a dream world. A stupor clouded my brain. Visions swam before me. . .With astonishing clarity I saw my mother's face. She cried, "Shame! Shame! Wake up, Saburo, wake up! You are acting like a sissy. You are no coward! Wake up! "

Gradually I became aware of what was happening. The Zero plunged earthward like a stone. I forced my eyes open and looked around to see bright, red, flaming scarlet. I thought the plane was burning. But I could smell no smoke. I was still groggy. . .I blinked several times. What was wrong? Everything was so red! I groped blindly with my hand. The stick. I had it. Still unable to see, I pulled the stick back. Gently. The plane began to recover from its wild plummeting. I felt the pressure push me into the seat as the Zero eased out of the dive and returned to what must have been level flight. The wind pressure abated; no longer did it beat with such force against my face. A wild, panicky thought gripped me. I might be blind!' I'd never have a chance to return to Rabaul.

I acted instinctively. I tried to reach forward with my left hand to grip the throttle, to gain more power. I strained, but my hand refused to move. Nothing! In desperation I tried to clench my fingers.

There was no sensation. Just numbness. Then I shifted my feet to the rudder bar. Only my right foot moved, and the Zero skidded as the bar went down. My left foot was numb. I gritted my teeth and strained. There was no feeling, no sensation of any kind.

My whole left side seemed to be paralyzed. I tried for several minutes to move my left arm or leg. It was impossible. Still I did not feel any pain. I could not understand it. I had been hit. Badly. But I could feel nothing. I would have welcomed pain in my left arm and leg; anything, to let me know my limbs were still intact.

My cheeks were wet. I was crying; the tears poured out. It helped, oh, how it helped! The stiffness began to go away. The tears were washing some of the blood out of my eyes.

Still I could not hear anything. But I could see again! Just a little, but the red began to fade. The sunlight streaming into the cockpit enabled me to see the outline of the metal posts.

The range finder was a blur in front of me. It kept improving, and soon I made out the circles of the instruments. They remained fuzzy; although I could see them, it was impossible to read the dials. I turned my head and looked out the side of the cockpit. Great black shapes slid past the wings with tremendous speed.

They had to be the enemy ships. That meant I was only about 300 feet over the water. Then sound came to me. First I heard the drone of the engine, then sharp, staccato cracks. The ships were firing at me! The Zero rocked with the blast waves of the bursting flak! Strangely, I did nothing. I sat in the cockpit without even trying to take any evasive action. The sounds of the bursting shells fell away. I could no longer see the black shapes on the water. I had flown out of range. Several minutes passed. Still I did nothing but sit in the cockpit, with difficulty trying to think.

My thoughts came in fitful snatches. I wanted to go to sleep again. Through my stupor I realized I could never fly all the way back to Rabaul. Not the way I felt. I would never even make Buka, less than 300 miles away. For a few minutes the thought of diving at full speed into the sea attracted me as the solution to my disability.

I was being stupid. I tried to force myself awake. I cursed at myself: this was no way to die! If I must die, I thought, I should go out like a man. Was I some untried fledgling who didn't know how to fight? My thoughts came and went, but I knew that as long as I could control the plane, as long as I could fly, I would do everything in my power to take one or more of the enemy with me.

I was silly, but I felt I would be cheating some enemy pilot if I crashed into the sea merely because I accepted the inevitable so readily. I knew the great value of aerial victories to a fighter pilot. If it had to be, why not in combat? Why go out alone and unseen, a silent splash and an explosion heard by no one?

I could no longer even rationalize. Where were the fighters?

I cursed and yelled for the Wildcats to appear. "Come on!" I screamed. "Here I am! Come on and fight!"

For several minutes I must have raged like a madman in the cockpit. Slowly I came to my senses; little by little I realized the ridiculous futility of my actions. I began to appreciate the incredible luck which had kept me alive so far. I had survived many crises before, but none so serious as this. Bullets had ripped by inches away from my head, and more than once had actually grazed my arms, breaking the skin but causing me no further injury. What was the matter with me?

I had a chance to live! Why throw it away? And suddenly I wanted to live, I wanted to reach Rabaul.

The first thing to do, I realized, was to check my wound.

I still did not know where I had been hit, or how seriously.

I was regaining confidence in myself, finally thinking and acting sanely. But I still could not move my left hand. I snapped my right hand in the air, flinging away the glove.

I brought my hand to my head, gingerly, afraid of what I might find. My fingers, moving over the helmet, felt slippery and sticky. I knew it was blood. Then they felt a slit in the helmet on top of my head. The depression was deep, and greasy with blood. I moved my fingers down, probing gently. How deep could it be? Something hard met my fingers. I was afraid to accept the truth. My fingers were deep, well past the helmet. That something "hard" could only be my skull, laid open by bullets. Maybe it was cracked. The thought was sickening. Bullets could have reached the brain, but not penetrated deeply. Something I had once read about combat wounds came back to me. The brain cannot feel pain. But maybe the bullets were the cause of the paralysis on my left side.

These thoughts came slowly. How can you sit in the cockpit of a damaged airplane, half blind, half paralyzed, sticking your fingers through a hole in your head, and be objective about the matter? I realized what had happened, I felt the blood and the hole in my head, but I am certain its significance never really penetrated my thoughts. I knew it; that was all.

I moved my fingers down over my face. It was puffy and swollen. I felt tears in the skin; pieces of metal, perhaps. I was not certain. But there was blood there, too, and I felt several loose patches of skin.

The Zero droned on, its engine beat steady. My head continued to clear. More and more I acted rationally. I sniffed. No odor of gasoline, so neither the engine nor the fuel tanks had been hit. That was my

most cheering realization since the battle. With the undamaged tanks
and a reliable engine, the fighter could have plenty of miles left in it.
The wind seemed to increase as my mind cleared. It buffeted at my
head. I stared ahead, squinting. The front windshield glass was
missing. No wonder it felt so strong; it was beating into the cockpit at
more than 200 miles an hour. I felt the blood drying on my face. But
the top of my head was still wet, and the wind tugged at the deep
crease in my skull, which felt as though it were still bleeding. I must
plug something into the wound, I knew, or I would soon black out
again, this time from loss of blood.

Sudden pain engulfed me. My right eye! It began to throb as the
pain steadily increased. I felt it with my fingers, and jerked them away.
The pain was becoming unbearable. I placed my hand over my right
eye again; my vision remained the same. I was blind in the eye!

Every Japanese fighter pilot carried with him four pieces of
triangular bandage in the pockets of his flight suit. I pulled one out
and tried to moisten it with saliva by biting the end.

I had absolutely no saliva in my mouth! I was terribly thirsty. My
mouth felt dry, like cotton.

I kept biting and chewing; the end of the bandage slowly became
damp. Leaning forward to get away from the steady wind pressure, I
wiped my left eye with the moistened bandage. It worked! Little by
little my vision cleared, and in less than a minute I could make out
clearly the ends of my wings. I sighed with relief.

Only for seconds. As I sat back I felt a stabbing pain in my head,
then another. The pain came and went in waves. For moments I would
feel nothing, then a shock as if a blunt-edged hammer had struck me
against the skull. I wasted no time in applying the bandage to the head
wound, but as soon as I took my hand away the wind snatched the
bandage and whipped it away through the shattered glass.

Despair swept over me. How was I to get a bandage around my
head? I *had* to stop the bleeding! My left hand was useless, and I could
use only my right in applying the bandage. But my right hand was
necessary to hold the stick and to work the throttle. The shrieking
wind in the cockpit further complicated the situation.

I pulled free a second piece of bandage. No sooner had I laid it in
my lap than it was blown away. The third and fourth went as quickly.
What could I do? I was almost frantic. The pain in my head had
increased; it was now a deep throbbing, each succeeding wave of agony
more intense than before.

I still had the silk muffler around my neck. I untied the knot and pressed one end beneath my right thigh, so that my weight would hold it down in the wind. Then I took out a jackknife, holding it in my teeth while I opened the blade. The muffler fluttered wildly in the wind. I held the knife in my right hand and transferred the end of the muffler to my teeth then cut out a piece. The wind blew it away. Again I cut the muffler, and again the shrieking wind tore it out of the cockpit.

I didn't know what to do. Despair returned. I searched frantically for a solution. There was only one piece of the muffler left.

Of course! I should have realized before. I bent forward to escape the wind, and began to squeeze the muffler below the edge of my helmet, working it up into the wound. But I had to sit up to continue. The longer I remained leaning forward, the worse the pain became.

Finally I thrust the stick into the crook of my leg and steadied the airplane in this fashion. Then I leaned forward and moved the throttle all the way forward in its slot, holding it in position. When I pulled back with my leg the Zero rose steadily in a long climb. I didn't care how erratically I was flying, so long as I could control the airplane.

At 1,500 feet I eased off on the throttle and returned to level flying. Then I pulled the cushion loose from the seat so that I would be as low as possible in the cockpit to escape the wind blast. Wedging my leg tightly against the stick to hold the plane steady, I slipped out of the seat to my knees, wedging the cushion with my shoulder to act as a wind buffer. Slowly I managed to move the muffler further under my cap, pressing it against the wound. I have no idea how long it took me to do this, but it seemed forever. It was impossible to see out of the cockpit, and once the Zero jerked wildly and dropped off on one wing as I hit a violent updraft. If the airplane went out of control I was lost. I couldn't touch the rudder bar at all.

Finally I was through. The muffler was taut beneath my helmet, and pressed tightly against the wound. I crawled back to my seat and brought the fighter back to an even level. My head felt better at once. The bleeding stopped.

My feeling of relief after the strain of working the muffler into position was overpowering. Soon an overwhelming desire to sleep assailed me. I fought it desperately, but could not shake it off. More than once I fell asleep, my chin resting against my chest. I shook my head, hoping the pain would keep me awake. But every thirty or forty seconds my shoulders jerked as I slipped against the straps.

More than once I snapped awake to find the Zero in an inverted position. Once I came to, flying upside down, and was so loggy I failed to move the controls. In a few seconds the engine coughed alarmingly. It was enough to bring me awake and I jerked the controls over to right the plane.

The drowsiness. Shaking my head. Slower and slower. The wonderful, warm, comforting embrace of sleep. Everything I was so peaceful. *Wake up! Wake up!* I screamed to myself. *Wake up!*

I came to with the Zero skidding wildly to the right, the wings straight up and down. *I had to stay awake!*

How? How to overcome the frantic urge to go to sleep, not to succumb to it all, to forget everything in the wonderful peace of slumber? It felt so good, so warm, so comfortable.

The fighter jerked suddenly. I was upside down again! *Stay awake!* I shouted to myself. I became angry at my failure to resist the desire to sleep. I lifted my hand from the stick and struck myself on the cheek as hard as I could. Once, twice, three times, hoping the pain would jar me to full consciousness.

I could not continue this indefinitely. Soon I tasted salt in my mouth. Blood spilled out on my Ups and trickled down my chin. My cheek puffed up still more and became seriously bloated. It felt as though a giant rubber ball were expanding within my mouth. There was no alternative; I must continue to strike myself to stay awake. Perhaps food would help overcome the drowsiness. I took my lunchbox and gulped down several mouthfuls of fishcakes. I was as sleepy as ever.

I ate some more, chewed it carefully, then swallowed.

In a moment I was violently ill. The plane heeled over out of control, as spasms of nausea wracked my body. Everything came up, spewing over my legs and the instrument panel. I was nearly insane with the stabbing pains from my head. Even this sudden new agony failed to keep me awake. Again and again I struck my cheek with my fist until I no longer had any sensation there. In desperation I banged my hand down on top of my head, but to no avail. I wanted to sleep. Oh, to go to sleep, to forget everything, to know that the slumber would never end! Delightful, warm sleep!

The Zero reeled and lurched. No matter what I did, I could not keep the wings level. I seemed to hold the stick in one position and never realized when my hand dropped to the left or right, sending the plane over in a wild skidding turn.

I was ready to give up. I knew I could not continue on like this. But I swore I would not go out like a coward, merely diving the plane into the ocean for one bright flash of pain, and then nothing. If I must die, at least I could go out as a Samurai. My death would take several of the enemy with me.

A ship. I needed an enemy ship. Out of an overwhelming despondency, I turned the Zero and headed back toward Guadalcanal. Several minutes later my head cleared. No drowsiness. No overwhelming pain. I could not understand it. Why dive to my death now, if I could reach Buka, or even Rabaul? I turned the fighter again and headed north. In a few minutes the desire to sleep engulfed me once more. I became groggy. Everything seemed to swirl around. What was I doing, flying north? An enemy ship! I remembered now; I must find an enemy ship and dive. Crash into it at full speed. Kill as many of the enemy's men as I could.

The world was misty. Everything dissolved into a haze. I must have turned back to Guadalcanal five times, and as many times reversed my course for Rabaul. I began to shout to myself, over and over again. I was determined to stay awake. I yelled and shrieked. *Stay awake!* Gradually the urge to sleep diminished. I was on the way back to Rabaul. But merely flying north was no guarantee I would ever reach my home base. I had no idea of my position. All I knew was that I was flying in the general direction of Rabaul. I was a considerable distance north of Guadalcanal, but did not know exactly how far away. I searched the sea, but found none of the islands in the chain which stretches up to Rabaul. With only my right foot working the rudder bar, it was probable that I had edged toward the eastern part of the Solomons.

I drew the ocean chart from beneath my seat. It was smeared with blood, and it took me several minutes of spitting on the map and rubbing it against my suit to clear some of the blood away. But for the moment it was no help. I tried to orient myself by the sun's position in the sky. Thirty minutes passed, and still no islands appeared. What was wrong? Where was I? The sky was absolutely clear, and the ocean stretched without a break to the horizon.

Something was lifting me up from my seat. Was I in a downdraft? Everything felt so strange! I was upside down again, and did not realize the plane had rolled around until my body tugged at the seat belt. Slowly I regained normal position. Something flashed beneath the wings. What could that be? I looked down. It was just a blur, something dark, stretching endlessly just below the fighter.

The water! I was almost in the water! In panic I leaned forward and shoved at the throttle, the next moment hauling back on the stick. The Zero responded with a rapid climb to 1,500 feet. I throttled back and went on at minimum cruising speed.

An island! Dead ahead, an island! It was on the horizon, looming out of the water. Elated, I laughed loudly to myself, I would be all right now, I could get my position and be sure I was heading for Rabaul. I went on and on, anxious for a close look at the coastline.

The island failed to appear. Where was it? Was I having hallucinations? What was the matter with me? The "island" passed to my right, a low-hanging cloud.

Again I tried to read the compass. It was still blurred. I spit on my hand and rubbed my left eye. Still I could not read the dial. I leaned as far forward as possible, my nose almost against the glass. At last, I could see. The reading shocked me. I was holding a 330-degree heading! No wonder I had not seen any islands for nearly two hours. The Zero was moving out to the center of the Pacific Ocean.

I took out the chart again, and estimated my position as sixty miles northeast of the Solomons. It was only a guess, but the best I could do. I made a ninety-degree turn to the left and headed for what I hoped would be New Ireland, which is just northeast of New Britain and Rabaul.

Again and again the waves of drowsiness assailed me. I lost count of how many times the plane dropped off on a wing, or how many times I frantically brought the Zero out of inverted flight. I staggered through the sky, leaning down often to check the compass reading, and yanking the stick over until I was back on what I hoped was my heading for New Ireland.

The head pains increased and helped to keep me awake. Then I was suddenly shocked to full consciousness. Without any warning the engine went dead. There was a strange hissing sound and then only the shriek of the wind ripping into the cockpit. Instinctively I shoved the stick forward to gain speed. This way I'd keep from stalling out and the propeller would continue revolving. I made every move with a deftness which, when I thought about it later, was startling. The mind adapts itself to such emergencies perfectly. I knew, even without thinking about it, that the main fuel tank had been drained.

I had one tank left, but only a short time in which to transfer the fuel feed. I must be quick and sure when I changed the fuel-supply cock. Normally I had no difficulty in manipulating the cock with my left hand. But now it was paralyzed. I had to do it with my right hand. I reached across my body. Not far enough. I strained. Still my hand would not reach the other side of the cockpit.

The Zero dropped slowly toward the ocean, gliding without a tremor. I jerked my arm forward with all my strength and opened the fuselage tank.

The fuel would not suck through. The automatic pump leading to the feed lines had been sucking air for too long, and the lines were dried out. I reached for the emergency hand pump and worked it savagely. There was so little time left! The pump worked at once. With a satisfying roar the engine burst into life and the Zero surged forward. I wasted no time in going back to 1,500 feet.

All my months of training for overwater flights now came to my help. I had once established a record in the Navy for flying with a lower fuel consumption than any pilot. If I kept going now at the minimum possible consumption I could get from the airplane, I had perhaps one hour and forty-five minutes left in the air. I adjusted the propeller pitch and throttled back to only 1,700 revolutions per minute. I adjusted the fuel air mixture to the absolute minimum to keep the engine from stalling.

The Zero flew on slowly. I had less than two hours in which to reach a Japanese-occupied island. Less than two hours to live, if I failed.

Another hour passed. Nothing met my eyes in the vast ocean and the blue sky. Suddenly I sighted something on the water. An atoll! No mistake this time, no cloud in front of me. It was definitely an island. Its shape became apparent as I drew closer. Green Island, the horseshoe-shaped coral reef which I had noticed on the way to Guadalcanal. I checked the island against the map. Hope leaped within me . . . I was only sixty miles from Rabaul!

Sixty miles. Normally, only a brief hop. But now conditions were anything but normal. My situation could not have been worse. I had enough fuel left for only forty minutes of additional flight. The Zero had been shot up badly, and the drag of the smashed cockpit, as well as the metal skin which had been chewed up by bullets, seriously affected the airplane's speed. I had been badly wounded, and was still partially paralyzed. My right eye was totally blind, and the left eye none too good. I was exhausted, and it took all my effort to keep the plane on an even keel.

Another island, dead ahead. This time it was no cloud looming on the horizon. I recognized the mountains. This was New Ireland; no mistake about it. I knew that if I could cross the peaks, which reached to a height of 2,400 feet, I could make Rabaul. It seemed as if I faced an endless series of obstacles before I could reach my home base. Thick clouds gathered around the peaks, and a violent rain squall lashed the mountains and the island. It seemed impossible to get through. Exhausted physically and mentally, half blind, and in a badly damaged fighter, how could I get through a squall which was extremely dangerous even under normal conditions?

I had no choice but to detour. It was a bitter decision, for the fuel gauge dropped lower and lower. I had only minutes left in the air. I bit my lips and turned to the south. The plane moved slowly down the George Channel between Rabaul and New Ireland. Two foaming wakes in the water slipped beneath the wings. Soon I saw two warships, heavy cruisers by their looks, steaming south under full speed. They were making more than thirty knots, headed for Guadalcanal.

I almost wept at the sight of the Japanese warships. I felt like ditching the plane right then and there—one of the cruisers could swing around and pick me up. My hope was fast running out on me; Rabaul seemed a million miles away. I circled once over the two warships, ready to descend for a water landing.

I could not bring myself to do it. The two cruisers were on their way to the fighting off Guadalcanal. If they stopped to pick me up—which was questionable—their firepower would be delayed where it was urgently needed. There could be no ditching.

(I learned weeks later that the two cruisers were the *Aoba* and the *Kinugasa,* each of 9,000 tons. They had been making full steam, headed for Guadalcanal at more than thirty-three knots. Along with seven other warships, they stormed the Allied convoy at Lunga, sinking four enemy cruisers and damaging another cruiser and two destroyers.)

I turned again toward Rabaul. The fuel gauge showed barely twenty minutes of flight time remaining. If I failed to reach Rabaul, however, I would be able to crash land on the beach. Then the familiar volcano showed over the horizon. I had done it! Rabaul was in sight!

I still had to land. It seemed an impossible undertaking with my left side so completely paralyzed. I circled over the airfield, undecided, not knowing what to do. I didn't know that I had been given up for lost, that all the other planes except for one shot down over Guadalcanal had landed almost two hours ago. Lieutenant Sasai told me later he could not believe his eyes when he identified my Zero through his binoculars. He screamed my name, and the pilots came running from all over the field. I couldn't see them from the air through my still-damaged left eye. All I saw was the narrow runway.

I decided to ditch in the water just off the beach. The Zero went down slowly. Eight hundred—seven—four—one—then I was only fifty feet above the water. I changed my mind again. The vision of the airplane crashing into the sea, and my wounded head slamming forward, was too much. I felt I would never live through the impact.

I pulled up again and turned for the runway. If I concentrated, I felt, I could make it.

The fuel gauge was nearly at the bottom. I adjusted the propeller to its highest pitch, gunned the engine, and climbed back to 1,500 feet. It was now or never. The Zero dropped down when I pushed the stick forward. I lowered the wheels, then the flaps. The airplane's speed dropped sharply. I watched the long lines of fighters parked on each side of the runway rushing up to me. I had to miss hitting the planes! Bring her back! I was too far to the left, and yanked back on the stick to go around again.

After the fourth circle of the field, I went in for another landing attempt. Once I was in a glide, I lifted my right foot and switched the ignition off with the top of my boot. With even a drop of fuel in the tanks the Zero would explode if I crashed.

The coconut trees on the edge of the field loomed before my eyes. I slipped over them, trying to judge my height by the treetops. Now ... I was over the runway. There was a sharp jolt as the Zero struck the ground. I pulled back on the stick and held it against the seat with all my strength to keep the plane from swerving. The Zero rolled to a halt near the Command Post. I tried to grin, and a wave of blackness swept over me.

I felt I was falling, tumbling end over end into a bottomless pit. Everything seemed to be spinning wildly. From a great distance I heard voices calling my name. They shouted *"Sakai! Sakai!"* I cursed to myself. Why didn't they keep quiet? I wanted to sleep.

The blackness lifted. I opened my eyes and saw faces all around me. Was I dreaming, or was I really back at Rabaul? I didn't know. Everything was so unreal. It was all a dream, I was sure. It couldn't be true. Everything dissolved into waves of blackness and shouting voices.

I tried to stand up. I gripped the edge of the cockpit and rose to my feet. It was Rabaul. It was no dream, after all! Then I collapsed, helpless.

Strong arms reached in and lifted me from the airplane. I gave in. I didn't care any longer.

CHAPTER TWENTY-THREE

I REGAINED consciousness staring up at the sky. Something jerked and shook my body. I turned and recognized Sasai and Nakajima. The two officers had climbed onto the Zero's wing and carried me down from the plane.

Nishizawa's voice burst through the murmuring of the crowd which had gathered. "Call a car—quick!" he shouted. He raged at the orderlies. "Quick! To the operating room. Go phone the chief surgeon! Quickly, you slow son of a bitch!" I couldn't go to the hospital. Not yet. I must report to Captain Saito before anything else. We always reported to the Command Post. The need to turn in my report for the day clamored urgently in my mind.

I raised my right arm, protesting to Sasai and Nakajima to put me down. "I have to report," I choked. "Let me go to the Command Post."

"Damn your duty!" Nakajima thundered back at me. "That can wait. We're taking you to the hospital."

I insisted and yelled that I had to turn in my report. The next moment Nishizawa stepped forward and grabbed me under the arm. Ota slipped along my left side, and the two pilots carried me into the Command Post. Nishizawa kept muttering, "Stupid bastard. Doesn't even know what he looks like. Crazy, that's what he is!"

I hardly recall standing—trying to stand—before Captain Saito, who stared at me incredulously. I think I spoke to him, but everything began to black out again. All of a sudden I wanted to go to sleep. That was it. Sleep. What was I doing here, anyway? Then there was only blackness.

Nishizawa and Ota carried me to the car (they told me later) waiting outside the Command Post. Nishizawa hurled the driver from the seat and slid behind the wheel, driving fast—but carefully to avoid any bad bumps—for the hospital. Sasai and Ota stayed with me in the back seat, supporting me.

The chief surgeon was waiting for me in the operating room. He cut off my torn uniform and at once began to work on my wounds. Through my sleep I felt blinding stabs of pain from time to time as the doctor cut into my scalp. (He saved two jagged pieces of 50-caliber bullets to show me later.) I felt a knife blade scraping against my skull.

I awoke almost as he finished. I stared up at him as he bent over me. My eyes—I remembered my eyes. Suddenly panic gripped me. "My eyes! " I shouted, "Doctor, what about my eyes?"

"You are seriously wounded," he replied. "I can do nothing further for you here." He peered at my face closely. "You'll have to be sent back to Japan where a specialist can work on you."

A feeling of disaster engulfed me. I feared for my right eye. I could see nothing on that side. The thought of being blinded horrified me. I would be useless as a fighter pilot. But I had to fly; I *had* to fly fighters again!

Four days passed slowly in the hospital. Bandages covered my body. The doctor withdrew four pieces of metal stuck in my flesh, as well as steel splinters from my cheeks. On the fourth day I felt slight movement in my left hand and leg. The muscles barely twitched, but at least they moved! On the other hand, the head wound began to rot in the high tropical humidity, and my right eye remained blind.

Meanwhile, the fighter sweeps and bombing raids against Guadalcanal continued without letup. Every day I heard the thunder of the planes as they raced down the runways and took off for the distant battlefield.

Rabaul had its own daily visitors, the high-flying Fortresses, which attacked the two airfields. Every time the enemy bombers approached I was carried to a shelter with the other patients.

Each evening Sasai and Nakajima visited me. They suggested that I return to Japan. Only the temperate climate of the home islands and a leading specialist could cure my eye injuries, they said. I refused to go home. I was irrational and irritable. I insisted I could be cured right here at Rabaul, that there was no reason why I couldn't be flying again in a few weeks.

If I had only known! It is difficult to explain my feelings, my reluctance to leave the hellhole that was Rabaul. I realize now that I bordered on the hysterical from the nightmare prospect of having to end my career as a pilot. There was the matter of honor, as well. I felt I was honor-bound to remain at Rabaul as long as I could. Even if I could not fly, I could help the green pilots. I might be able to warn them of the mistakes which could cause their death. All the reasons melted into one; my return to Japan meant a final judgment by an eye specialist, and I feared and rebelled against what I might be told.

Sasai and Nakajima abandoned their arguments. The matter was ended on the morning of August 11, when Captain Saito, the commander of the Lae Wing, came to my bedside. He was as kind to me as he could possibly be, and equally adamant.

"I know how you feel, Sakai," he said, "but I have taken all factors into consideration. My orders are that you will be sent home to Japan on rotation, and assigned to the Yokosuka Naval Hospital. You will leave tomorrow by transport plane. The surgeon has told me that your only hope lies with the doctors at Yokosuka."

He smiled at me. "Your going home will do as much for us as it will for you, Sakai. We will all know that the best medical care in Japan will be yours." He rose to his feet.

For several moments he looked at me, then leaned down and placed his hand on my shoulder. "You have done a marvelous job for all of us, Saburo," he said softly. "Every man who has ever flown with you is proud to have known and to have fought with you. When your wounds are healed, come back to us." Then he walked away.

That evening Sasai came to visit me. He was visibly tired from the day's mission over Guadalcanal. I told him of the orders sending me home the next day. In a little while all my old friends had assembled in the room for a modest farewell party. No one sang, or talked loudly, or cracked any jokes. We merely talked quietly, mostly about Japan.

But the Americans had other ideas about our small gathering. What had turned out to be a quiet few hours ended up in a mad dash for the shelters, the other pilots carrying me out of the hospital. I gritted my teeth with shame and bitterness. I felt so helpless! Here were the same men whom I had led into combat, and now they were carrying me around like a half-blind, crippled child! I wanted to scream and shout and tear the bandages off my body. But all I could do was to lie there with my eyes tightly closed.

Early the next morning I limped slowly to the pier; a barge waited to take me to the flying boat anchored on the water, you, Saburo. Much more than you will ever know."

Sasai held my hands tightly in his own. "I'm going to miss you, Saburo. Much more than you will ever know."

Tears started down my cheeks; I could not hold them back. I choked up and could only hold his hands.

Sasai withdrew his hands, unbuckled his belt, and handed it to me. I stared at the famed engraved Roaring Tiger. "Saburo, this belt was given to me by my father. One for myself, and one each for my two brothers-in-law. One of us has already died. I know little of the magic qualities of the silver tiger, but I wish you to keep this buckle and wear it for me. I hope it will help to bring you back here to us."

I protested, but to no avail. Sasai would not have it otherwise. He placed the buckle and belt in my pocket, then clasped my hands again. 'Til see you again, Saburo. Don't say farewell! We shall meet again, and soon, I hope."

He helped me into the barge. In a moment it was chugging toward the waiting plane. Nishizawa, Ota, Yonekawa, Hatori, Nakajima, and all my friends waved from the pier. They were shouting for me to hurry back, to fly with them again.

In a few moments they were blurred. I could still see only a few feet with my left eye. I stood as straight as I could on the barge, my right hand raised, as they blurred into dim and unrecognizable forms. Then I cried like a child.

There were few passengers in the flying boat, myself, an orderly assigned to take care of me on the return trip home, and several war correspondents. We stopped at Truk and Saipan to refuel.

It was a long time since I had walked on my home soil. I had no idea of what conditions would be like back in Japan, but I was totally unprepared for the shock of Yokohama. We landed in the Yokohama harbor early Saturday evening. There was little purpose in reporting that night to the hospital, and I went into the city, where I could take a taxicab to my uncle's house in western Tokyo.

These people—they had absolutely no idea of what the war really was like! I gaped in astonishment at the bustling crowds, at the bright signs and lights. I could not believe the sounds which met my ears, of thousands of voices, of laughter, and unconcern. Didn't they know what was really going on down in the southwest Pacific?

At every newscast, blaring loudly into the streets, the radios boomed forth with the "Warship March," broadcasting details of tremendous victories against the Americans in the sea battles which raged off the Solomons. I heard nothing but incredible lists of American shipping destroyed, of hundreds of airplanes shot down.

The crowds of people in their light and colorful summer clothes stopped outside the stores and the corners where the radios trumpeted. Every time the announcer mentioned another major defeat over the enemy loud cheers and cries resounded through the streets.

The nation was drunk on false victories. It was hard to believe that a destructive war was going on. In the stores I saw that only certain commodities were being rationed, but that the daily necessities of life were available in abundance.

I wanted to get out of the city, and quickly. Everything at Lae and Rabaul seemed so unreal! Could these two separate worlds exist simultaneously? The blood and dying only short hours away by airplane, and the cheering for nonexistent victories here at home?

I waved down a cab and gave him my uncle's address. We passed through Yokohama and entered Tokyo. Several minutes later a policeman halted the vehicle and stared through the window at me. My uniform was blood-stained and I was still swathed in bandages.

"What happened to you?" he demanded.

"I've just returned to Japan from the front," I answered sourly.

"So!" he cried. "So you were hurt at the battlefront! Where? Tell me; and how?"

"I'm a pilot," I spat. "At Guadalcanal. I was shot up in a fight."

"Guadalcanal!" The young policeman's eyes gleamed. "We hear a lot about that nowadays. I understand that only yesterday we had a smashing victory over the Americans. The radio said that our Navy sank five cruisers, ten transports, and ten destroyers. It certainly must have been an exciting spectacle to watch!"

That was *too* much. "I'm sorry, sergeant," I snapped at him, "but I'm late." I shouted at the driver. "Go ahead. At once! "

Many years had gone by since the first time I had walked into my uncle's home. The house stood unchanged, a link to an era which now seemed a million years in the past. For several minutes I stood on the sidewalk, taking in the familiar structure, the lights, the sounds. A strange feeling of peace descended upon me. My irritation fled, and I opened the door, exactly as I had done in my childhood, and, using the same words I had always cried upon entering the house, shouted, "Here I am! I'm home!"

A startled "Who's that?" came from the kitchen. I grinned; it was my aunt.

"It's me!" I called back.

There was silence for a moment. "It's me! Saburo! " I shouted in joy.

My uncle's voice burst through the house, a startled *"What?"* Then they came running out to the portico.

For almost a full minute they stared at me. My uncle, my aunt, and my two cousins Hatsuyo and Michio, unable to speak, stood with their mouths open in astonishment. I returned their gaze patiently as their eyes took in my bloodstained uniform and the bandages.

My uncle's voice was a querulous whisper. "It really is you, Saburo?" I could barely hear his words. "It is Saburo; it is not a ghost I am seeing?" He strained forward, afraid that I might vanish into thin air.

"No. It is no ghost," I answered. "It is really I. I'm home once again."

This was like returning to life. The battles, the dying, the wounds, squeezing the trigger, flicking in rolls to escape pursuing fighters, cowering in the mud of the bomb shelters . . . all of it fled, all of it became unreal, remote, a shadowy world which never existed but which hung over my shoulder like the ghost my uncle had believed me to be.

To sit in a home like this again! To talk with my uncle and aunt, to see Hatsuyo and Michio again, to relax! To know there would be no bombs tonight, no Fortresses cruising high above 20,000 feet, no Mitchells and Marauders screaming in, no blasting explosions or shrieking fragments of steel or fiery tracers into the billets ... it took a long time to relax as the evening wore on. Every now and then I shook my head in amazed happiness over it all. We had so many things to talk about! It was almost three years since I had spent a night with this family.

Hatsuyo was no longer the high-school girl I remembered. I stared at her, trying to realize that this beautiful young woman really was my same cousin. Even Michio, a wild boy in the lower grades when I had gone to high school, was a husky young man. I kept staring at Hatsuyo, trying to catch up with all the years which had passed so strangely and—now that I was seeing them again—so quickly!

I stayed the night at their home. It was the first night in many years that I had enjoyed a deep and sound sleep. Not even my wounds, which had kept me awake for the last week, disturbed me.

The next morning I left by train for Yokosuka. The everyday life of the people in the city seemed even more startling than the night before. The passengers, especially the young girls and women, looked at me only once. They grimaced at my appearance and looked the other way. Their deliberate concentration to avoid looking at the bloody bandages unnerved and enraged me. No longer was I the leading ace of Lae and Rabaul, the man whom Captain Saito asked to come back, the pilot who cried with his other fliers. I was a bloody, dirty', and, yes, it was true, a distasteful sight to my own people. I was disgusted.

No sooner had I reported to the Yokosuka hospital than an orderly took me to the chief surgeon's room. I was puzzled; today was Sunday. Except for dire emergencies, the chief surgeon would not be on duty. He surprised me by greeting me personally.

He smiled at my astonishment. "I left word that I was to be notified the moment you showed up," he explained. "I've just come from my billet. You see, I received a special letter from Captain Saito of your Lae Wing, requesting me to do everything possible for you." He looked at me for a moment. "Captain Saito went to great pains to tell me of what you have done in the Pacific. I understand that you are the leading fighter ace of all our pilots?"

I nodded.

"I can well understand your captain's apprehension, then. Come," he took my arm, "we will begin work on you at once."

A few minutes later I was in the operating room. The surgeon scraped off the rotten flesh from my head wound. He worked quickly and surely, and paid no attention to my gasps as the knife cut and scraped along the skull. When he had cleaned out the wound and applied fourteen new stitches, he personally brought me down to the eye department.

"We have called in the best man in all Japan to work on you," he explained. "Doctor Sakano was drafted from his civilian practice into the Navy, and is now a lieutenant commander. There is no better eye surgeon in our country. When we heard from Captain Saito, we notified Doctor Sakano to be on call for your arrival."

So I was coming to the fateful moment. I would know soon just what the decision was to be, whether I would see again, whether I could take to the air. I tried to think of everything but my eyes; I didn't want to think about it. It was no use.

The doctor examined me. Several minutes later he stood up. His face was serious and he spoke slowly.

"There is not a minute to waste. I must operate on your eyes—*now*. Listen to me carefully; your sight will depend upon what I do to you in the next hour."

He paused. "Sakai, I cannot apply any anesthetics. If you wish to see, if you wish me to save at least one of your eyes, you must be prepared to endure all the pain while you are fully awake."

I was in a daze. I nodded dumbly, afraid to trust my voice. They placed me on a high bed. Then several orderlies tied me down with straps and ropes. I was unable to move my arms or legs even a fraction of an inch. A strap went across my forehead to keep my head steady, and a nurse clamped her hands against my temples for added safety. The doctor told me to set my eyes on a red lamp hanging from the ceiling.

"Look at it, Sakai," he warned. "Look at it. Never take your eyes away from that light. You are not to blink, you are not to even turn your eyes to the sides. Listen to me carefully! You can blind yourself for life if you do not do exactly as I say!"

It was horrible. More than that, it was the most frightful pain I had ever known. I had always regarded myself as capable of withstanding great pain. The *Bushido* code had taught me patience, perseverance under the most trying conditions.

But *this!* I had to stare at the light. Stare at it until I saw only the red bulb, filling everything. Until the doctor's hand swam into view, looming and unreal, the sharp, pointed steel in his hand, bringing it closer and closer and closer.

I screamed. More than once I shrieked like a madman with the terrible agony. I felt I could not stand it for another moment. Finally nothing mattered any longer except that the pain be stopped. My desire to fly again, my desire even to see, none of it mattered any more. *The pain!* Once I screamed at Sakano: *"Stop! Stop it! Gouge it out, do anything, only stop it!"* I tried to squirm away from that knife, I tried to slide under the straps. They were much too tight. The doctor shouted back at me every time I yelled. *"Shut up!"* he roared. "You *must* endure this! Otherwise you will go blind. Stop your screaming!"

The torture lasted more than thirty minutes. It seemed a million years to me; it seemed that it would never stop. When it was over, I was too weak even to move a finger. I lay on the bed, sucking in air, helpless, while the chief surgeon leaned over me, trying to comfort me as my chest heaved and I sobbed.

For a month I was confined to my hospital bed. I was steeped in misery. Life meant little to me. I dreamed during the day and night of that long flight back to Rabaul, of all the occasions when I could have shoved the stick forward and plunged into the ocean. It would have been only a brief moment of pain.

Dr. Sakano visited me often to study my eyes. "I did everything I could," he told me, "but your right eye will never recover. Not fully. You will be able to see things perhaps one or two feet in front of you, but that is all. Your left eye will be perfectly all right."

His words were a thundering sentence of death—of living death—to me. A fighter pilot, with only one eye. I laughed bitterly and the doctor went away.

My head wound healed rapidly, and the doctor permitted me to walk around the hospital. Every week I put in an application to be discharged and sent back to Rabaul. And every week the application was rejected.

Finally the chief surgeon personally returned the latest application. He was obviously angry. "I tell you, Sakai," he complained, "it will be many months before you can even think of returning to Rabaul. My orders are explicit. You are to have at least six months' convalescence before you can be assigned to any duty—here at home or overseas."

I felt like a fugitive, a deserter from the battlefront. I thought of all the pilots, of Nishizawa and Ota and Sasai, going out every day in their Zeros to engage in battle. I was afraid even to listen to the war news over the radio. It reminded me too much of Rabaul.

One day I had visitors. A nurse came into my room. "There are visitors downstairs," she said. "Would you like to have them come to your room?"

I had no idea who they could be. It was Thursday, and my cousin Hatsuyo came to see me, bringing flowers for my room, each week end, when she could get away from her job in the munitions factory. I had written my mother not to attempt the long trip from Kyushu, for within the next several weeks I would be transferred to the Sasebo Hospital. Yokosuka was more than 700 miles by rail from Fukuoka in northern Kyushu, where my mother had moved to live with her daughter and son-in-law.

But I had not expected these visitors. Two people entered the room. I strained to see them. My eye still was unable to make out faces at a distance of more than six or seven feet.

"Fujiko-san!" I gasped her name. Fujiko, even more beautiful than I had remembered her, stood in the doorway with her father, Professor Niori. I had not seen her since our one meeting more than eighteen months before in Osaka.

They bowed to me, and I returned the greeting. Still we had not spoken except for my crying out her name. The nurse offered them chairs and withdrew.

Her father spoke: "Hatsuyo-san wrote us that you were at this hospital. How we have worried about you, Saburo-san! It is a great relief to see you again; we feared for your health. It is wonderful that you seem so much better than we believed." I stammered in reply; I had failed to write Fujiko for many months. My apologies were halting and embarrassed, for Fujiko had written me often when I was at Lae, and the mail from home brought many gifts from her.

Her father waved away my stammered apologies. "It is of no matter," he said. "We know of the marvelous things you have done at the front and we are so proud of you! But now, tell us, how are your wounds? Will you be able to leave here soon?"

"I was hit in four places," I answered. "The doctors have done a wonderful job. Except," I added bitterly, pointing to my right eye, "for this. I am blind in this eye and the doctors say I will remain this way for the rest of my life."

My reply startled Fujiko. She jerked her hand to her mouth, her eyes opening wide at what I had said.

"It's true. All of it," I emphasized. "There are no two ways about it. I am disabled. The loss of this eye means the end to my life as a fighter pilot."

Professor Niori interrupted. "But. . . then won't you be discharged from the Navy?"

"No. No, I do not think so," I replied. The sarcasm welled up in me. "You can not understand this here at home, sir, but the magnitude of this war is beyond your comprehension. I do not think I will be discharged at all. The Navy will find use for me as an instructor, or I will be assigned to some command post duty on the ground."

There was a brief silence. It gave me time to reflect that these two people had come more than 500 miles from their home in Tokushima simply to welcome me home, to try and cheer me up. I was behaving disgracefully, and I thanked them deeply for their trouble and their great kindness.

Fujiko shook her head at me. She was obviously annoyed at the formality of my voice. She tried to speak, but the words did not come. Finally she turned quickly to the elderly man at her side and cried, "Father!" Her eyes were wide and appealing.

Professor Niori nodded gravely and cleared his throat. "When do you think you will be reassigned?" he asked. He looked straight at me. "I think we will go ahead with the arrangements for the wedding . . . that is, of course, if it is all right with you, Saburo-san!"

"W—what?" I croaked. I could not believe his words. The wedding arrangements! My head reeled. "I—I beg your pardon, sir?" I blurted out.

"Forgive me, Saburo-san," he answered. "I know this is a very clumsy way of bringing this matter before you. Let me say it otherwise."

The old professor rose to his feet and spoke solemnly. "Saburo-san, will you accept my daughter, Fujiko, as your bride? We have taken the utmost pains to raise her as a decent woman, and we have taught her to be exemplary in all the necessary and chosen fields. I would be exceedingly happy if you were to accept my offer and I could be your father-in-law." I could do no more than gasp. His words were like bells ringing in heaven.

Fujiko stared at my wide eyes and blushed; she lowered her head and looked into her lap.

I tore my eyes away from her and stared at the wall. The irony was bitter; how many days had I stared in my despair at that same wall?

Finally I regained my voice. But I could hardly talk. My own words choked me. I had to force them out. I hated myself for what I was saying. But there was no way out.

"Professor Niori. I. . . Sir, I am so greatly honored to hear your words. They are happiness itself. But..." I choked and forced back the tears, "I—I cannot. I cannot accept your offer." There. It was done. The words were out. I had said it.

"What?" His voice was incredulous. "Are—are you already engaged to someone else?"

"No! Oh, no! Do not even think such a thing, I beg of you! I must decline, but for an entirely different reason. Professor Niori, I can't say yes! It is impossible! Look at me, sir, look at me! I do not deserve Fujiko-san. Look at my eyes!" I cried. "I am half blind!"

Relief swept over his face. "Oh, come! Saburo-san, you belittle yourself without need. Don't heap abuse upon yourself because you have been wounded! Your wounds are honorable, they bring no disgrace to you. Do you not understand your own position? All Japan acclaims you, they sing your praises. Do you not realize that as the greatest ace of our country you are a national hero?"

"Professor Niori, you do not understand! I am only telling you the truth, sir, the truth you yourself cannot see," I insisted. "There is no condescension in my words. A hero is a fleeting thing. He is a creature of the moment. And I am not a hero! I am a flier who cannot fly. I am a pilot who is half blind! What good am I; of what use am I any longer! Hero, indeed; you know our country has no individual heroes."

He was silent for a while. "Perhaps I expressed myself improperly, Saburo-san," he continued. "But you must realize that this is not a matter which has been decided upon suddenly. My wife and I took to you immediately upon our first meeting. I understand your feelings, but you must understand one thing above all. My wife and I, as well as Fujiko, believe you are the only man who can make her happy. It is our hope, our trust, that our daughter will do the same for you."

I felt as though my heart would break. Could this fine and wonderful man not understand what I was driving at? "How can you judge a man at only one meeting?" I cried. "How can you make this decision with so little to go on? Fujiko-san's entire life, her happiness, all hinges on the one time you have met me. I cannot understand your actions—although no honor ever offered me has been greater than that you brought to me tonight."

I spread my arms in exasperation. "There must be many other young men for Fujiko-san who are so much better suited than myself! Thousands of them, with all the advantages of complete educations, with more promising futures. What can I offer your daughter, Professor Niori? What can I give her? I beg you again, look at me in another light! Look at me! What future do I have as I am now?"

Fujiko remained quiet no longer. She raised her head and stared at me. I wanted to run from the room. "You are wrong, Saburo-san," she said quietly. "Oh, you are so wrong! You make too much fuss over your eye. Whether you are half blind or not matters not at all to me. We are to be wedded as one. The same things in life which lie ahead for any man are yours, too.

"If it be necessary, Saburo-san, if it be necessary, I can be of help. I do not want to marry you merely for the sake of your eyes!"

"You are wrong, Fujiko-san," I replied. "I know you are brave, that what you say about yourself is true. But now you are talking from sentiment. You cannot decide your entire life upon passing emotions."

"No, no, no," she repeated, shaking her head. "How can you so misunderstand me? This is no fleeting sentiment. Do you not realize that I have dwelt upon this meeting tonight for many months? I know what I am saying! "

There was no use in continuing the conversation in this fashion. I was afraid that at any moment I would break down. "Professor Niori and Fujiko-san," I said with as much authority as I could inject into my voice, "I am not trying to belittle you. This is not a matter for bargaining. I repeat, sir, you have bestowed upon me tonight the greatest honor I have ever known. But I cannot accept your magnificent offer. I refuse to allow my emotions to govern my thoughts or actions. I have always been a proud man. I cannot marry Fujiko-san. I cannot accept the honor of marrying this girl, whom I do not deserve. That is the reason why I must say no. I will not do this to her."

I refused to listen to the professor's words. He pleaded with me, but I would only repeat the same words, over and over again. Soon Fujiko broke down; she flung herself into her father's arms and wept aloud. I could have killed myself for what I was doing, for the sorrow to which I was subjecting her. But I knew that I was acting properly, that what I was doing was for her good. A marriage with me might bring temporary happiness, but in later years it would be Fujiko who would suffer.

Nearly an hour later they left the room.

T do not know how long I stared at the doorway after them. Then I turned and collapsed, weak and almost helpless, on the bed. That was the worst hour I had ever known. But what else could I have done? A thousand times I asked that question of myself. A thousand times the same answer came back to me. There wasn't any other way out of it, but this realization did me little good. I had cast aside the most beautiful thing which had ever entered my life.

Two days later, Hatsuyo came for her weekly visit. She did not greet me with her usual smile, and did not trouble to conceal her displeasure.

"How could you have done it, Saburo?" she asked as soon as she was at my bedside. "How could you have hurt Fujiko so much!"

Hatsuyo told me that Fujiko had sobbed uncontrollably when she visited Hatsuyo in Tokyo on her return from the hospital. Professor Niori begged my uncle and Hatsuyo to do everything in their power to make me change my mind.

Hatsuyo looked eagerly at me. "They say, Saburo, that perhaps you acted so because they displeased you with their words. My father and I know their family so well. They are such wonderful people. Why did you do it?" she cried.

"Hatsuyo, please try to understand," I begged of her. "You lived with me as a child for several years and you, of all people, should know me well. As much as I am hurt by what I had to say, I do not regret my decision. I honestly believe that I acted for Fujiko's good, for her own happiness."

She rejected my words. "They told us that you refused because you had been wounded."

"You should know better than to say that. It is only part of the reason. I have loved Fujiko with the deepest devotion ever since I first met her. My feelings for her are no less today, my love is no weaker. All through the long months at Lae and at Rabaul, Fujiko was to me woman eternal. Do you, too, fail to understand? I refused because I *do* love her! "

"You are not making sense, Saburo."

"Listen to me, then. During all the time I was overseas, during all the weary months in the Pacific, Fujiko never left my mind. I wanted her to be so proud of me, and I did well.

"Perhaps this is not the nicest thing to discuss with you, Hatsuyo, but I must be frank. Rabaul was a major military base, and there were more than 10,000 Japanese stationed there at all times. In addition, we often had with us for a while a full division of Army troops.

"What do you think men do when they are away from home, away from their own women? We had brothels at Rabaul, just as we have here in Yokosuka! When we went to Rabaul for a rest, more than a few of the pilots never even left those brothels. Not all of us, but a great many.

"But I never did so. My pride would not allow it. I wished to remain as pure in body as was possible for Fujiko, when the day came that I could ask her hand in marriage.

"Before my injury I could have come to her as Sakai, the great ace, the fearless flier, a man worthy of her hand. But now? *No!*" I shouted at Hatsuyo. "I will not be pitied! Do you think I could stand to have Fujiko *pity* me? Never! Now do you understand me?"

Hatsuyo held my hand tightly and nodded. "I know, I know," she whispered.

She looked into my eyes. "I do know you, Saburo, much better than you realize. I know how badly you want to fly again. But I cannot help feeling sorry for Fujiko."

"She will be happier for it. She..."

But Hatsuyo interrupted me by throwing her arms around my neck and hugging me closely. "Poor Saburo! Have hope . . . you must have faith. You will fly again. I know you will!"

CHAPTER TWENTY-FOUR

IN OCTOBER the Navy transferred me to the Sasebo Navy Hospital. The change of surroundings was more than welcome; I would be closer to home, and could see my family again.

By now the torrid summer was gone, and the train ride proved comfortable. I opened the windows wide and soaked in sunshine and the soothing autumn wind. Japan was as beautiful as ever and now, with autumn color on the mountains and hills, the passing countryside took on the appearance of a strange and wonderful fairyland. Trees and shrubs lay in crimson splashes on both sides of the tracks. They had turned yellow and scarlet and green and brown in a riot of blending hues.

Three hours after we left Yokosuka, Fujiyama swam into view. I will never tire of looking at this most beautiful of all mountains. The graceful lines curved gently to the summit, still uncapped with snow, but half hidden in swirling mist made brilliant by the sun. Fuji-san. It reminded me of Fujiko, who was, indeed, named after the mountain, but who was now equally as remote for me.

The country lay quietly, at peace. There was no war here, not within the hundreds of farms and paddies which lay neat, clean, and prosperous on both sides of the tracks. What war? I saw only what I had always seen, now even more beautiful than when I had viewed it as a younger man. My perspective was different. Now I could compare the serenity and dignity of all this with the volcanic misery which was Rabaul, the sandy runway gouged out of the jungle at Lae. No wonder an aura of comfort and well-being radiated from my home soil!

And yet, I mused, not one of these people, the children, the farmers, young and old, the village elders, the postmen and the police, the merchants, nor one of them had crossed Guadalcanal from twenty thousand feet and looked down to see the vast ocean alive, teeming with a strange and terrible life, row upon row of American warships and transports. And there were so many more lying over the horizon I had not seen!

In this respect, too, my perspective had changed. Our pilots from the Lae Wing were unique, I had discovered at Rabaul. The incredible one-sided margin of victories was by no means shared by other wings. And the Army, what of the Army, with its pilots who sadly lacked the fine temper of training which we had been afforded, whose planes blundered into enemy entrapments?

No longer was I myself inviolate. It had been the enemy's turn then, and no less than a miracle had brought me here on this train as it swayed along the tracks leading to Sasebo. A man sees the war differently after the doctors have scraped away rotten flesh from his skull, have dug jagged steel splinters from his body, and comforted him with the staggering living-death sentence, "It is not so bad, Sakai, you will be only half blind." *Only* half blind!

My mother waited to greet the train at the Fukuoka station. We stopped only briefly, and no through passengers were permitted off the train. I leaned as far out of my window as I could, waving frantically to catch her attention. The joy in her face when she saw me was the most wonderful thing I had known in so many long months! She was older—oh, so much older!—now that all her sons had left for war.

I shouted to her. "I am all right now!" I cried, "I am all right, Mother! Don't worry about me. Everything is all right now!"

The train was moving again. She stood on the platform, her eyes brimming with tears, slowly waving the rising sun flag, crying, *"Banzai! Banzai!"* after me as the train pulled away.

The doctors at Sasebo ordered another month's convalescence in the hospital. No longer did I argue with them, implore them to return me to Rabaul. I felt drained out; I cared little what their orders might be.

The month passed slowly, but my first week end was gladdened by a visit from my mother. She was still the same wonderful woman! Convinced that what I needed best were the favorite foods of my childhood, she had cooked an entire meal to bring along with her. I feared the moment when I would have to tell her of losing the sight of my right eye. To my astonishment she did not appear upset at the news. "It does not make you any less a man, my son," she said calmly. And that closed the subject for her. She offered to come every week end. It would have been wonderful to see her so often, but I begged her not to. She was old and no longer could stand the arduous rail journey. Train travel was becoming more and more difficult. With war materiel taking up so much space, passenger accommodations were restricted and at best were acutely uncomfortable.

In November there occurred an event which, under any other circumstances, would have been one of the greatest moments in my life. Now it meant little. Orders were received by the hospital promoting me to the rank of Warrant Officer. The long climb upward from a recruit seaman, with its brutal discipline and endless punishment, was ended. Step by step I had forged my way through the ranks, and now the reward had come. It was a hollow victory, but it had its compensations. My new status meant I could complete my convalescence at home. I snatched at the surgeon's offer and left at once for the Fukuoka suburbs, where I joined my family.

The next month was wonderful. It was the first time in ten years I had spent thirty consecutive days with my mother, and her happiness was a joy to behold. Everything was quiet and peaceful. Almost every day my mother asked, "When do you think the war will be over, Saburo?" I knew she had in mind my two brothers who were now overseas. And every time she asked I could only tell her the truth; I did not know.

Then she would look around, to be sure no other person was within earshot. "Saburo, tell me," she implored in a half whisper, "are we really winning? Is everything they tell us true?" Again I could only repeat, we must win. But she was happy. There was no denying that. I knew that she wished there was some way my convalescence period could be made to continue indefinitely.

Several weeks after I arrived at my sister's home I had a visitor from Tokyo, a news correspondent sent by the *Yomiuri Shimbun,* one of the largest newspapers in Japan. He told me his paper had sent him down from Tokyo to get an exclusive interview with Japan's leading ace (I wondered how many enemy planes Nishizawa and Ota had shot down by now; I was sure they had surpassed my own victories); the entire country wanted to read my own words on the war.

I questioned my liberty to talk to this man. Disciplinary action could be swift and harsh if I spoke out of turn. I called the

Administration Officer at Sasebo and told him my problem. He was evasive and insisted there were no specific regulations in the matter.

"I have no authority to discourage you from talking with a reporter," he concluded. "But I must remind you that your conversation will be entirely at your own discretion, and that you may be held responsible for anything you say. Also, bear in mind that this desk neither approves nor disapproves of any officer giving an interview. Just be careful."

That was certainly a negative reply. I returned to my room and told the correspondent that my superiors did not favor the interview he requested. But he would not be shaken so easily.

"It is not that I meant to bother you," he pleaded, "but that I have traveled seven hundred miles from Tokyo just to talk to you! Let me ask you only a few questions. Please! Just five minutes will do."

Fool that I was, I should have known better. His ability to twist and weave through a conversation was uncanny. His "five minutes" became three days! Every morning he commuted to my home from his hotel and took many notes.

Never have I encountered such tact! He made me talk almost about everything. His questions kept away from the war, until I discovered that the stories of my personal accounts 'were of the war. He soon found out that I had lost all optimism, and that our Navy fliers at Rabaul, despite their many successes, were now waging an uphill battle at Guadalcanal, and virtually without any cooperation from the fighters and bombers of the Japanese Army.

"We need more fighters and more experienced pilots," I told him in a fit of anger. "Every Zero fighter should be pulled off the line and run through a complete overhaul after one hundred and fifty hours in the air. This has nothing to do with battle damage. Even if the airplane never fires a shot and is never fired at in return, it requires that overhaul. Now, we can't do that any more. We consider a Zero in excellent condition if it is only slightly shot up and has a complete overhaul after two hundred hours.

"Do you know what it means for a pilot to go into combat with an airplane that won't answer every demand at the controls? Only the best of our fliers can take that kind of a ship into battle and come out alive. If the new pilots we're sending overseas as replacements don't measure up to the standards of the men with whom I flew, then heaven help them. The American Navy pilots we encountered over

Guadalcanal were the best I have ever fought, and their tactics were superb. And their planes are certain to improve."

The reporter was more than satisfied. He could not conceal his elation as he thanked me profusely and bid me goodbye.

I was to find out later, however, that I had committed a major error even in talking to him at all.

A week later I returned to the Sasebo Hospital and filed a request for a final medical checkup which would qualify me for reassignment. It was accepted! They assigned me to a cot in the hospital, and told me I would remain for several days until they could complete the examination.

Early the next morning I was summoned to the Administration Office at Sasebo Headquarters. The roof had caved in; the personnel captain's face was red from his anger.

"Warrant Officer Sakai," he shouted, "you are an idiot! I just received a wire from Navy Military Headquarters in Tokyo, telling me that they have suppressed in its entirety the interview you gave that reporter from the *Yomiuri Shimbun*. Have you taken leave of your senses, saying the things you did?

"Now you listen to me, Sakai. Tokyo has reprimanded me sharply for my lack of surveillance over the men under my command. I will not stand for this kind of stupidity! I tell you now that you will release not one single word about your combat duty without first clearing with the Public Information Officer. Do you understand? Any repetition of the nonsense which you just issued will result not only in your court-martial, but mine as well! And no one, no one, you understand, is going to do that to me! "

I understood perfectly. I was to be gagged, but I could sympathize with my superior's position. It was all very simple, Sakai, just keep your mouth shut.

I returned to the hospital, brooding at the tongue-lashing I had just received.

Someone called my name. An orderly stood stiffly at attention in the doorway, saluting. "What is it?" I snapped.

"You have a visitor, sir. A tall naval flier is waiting for you in the visitor's room. I think he said his name is Nishizawa."

"What?" I shouted. "Nishizawa! Can it really be he?"

I forgot everything that had happened and dashed madly from the room, nearly knocking the startled orderly off his feet. I opened the door to the visitor's room and stared in.

A tall, lean man paced slowly in the room, a cigarette in his mouth. It *was!* He hadn't changed a bit.

He looked up at me, smiling broadly, and shouted, "Sakai!" I yelled his name. "Nishizawa!" The next second we were pounding each other on the back, happy beyond all words.

I held my good friend at arm's length. "Let me look at you!" I cried. "You look wonderful. No wounds?" I asked hastily.

"None, Saburo," came the welcome answer. "I left Rabaul in November. Not a scratch on me. It seems that all those bullets just never caught up."

I was elated. "Hah! We named you properly, all right," I said. "Truly you are our own Devil, my friend, to have come through Lae and Rabaul without a mark on you. Nishizawa, it is simply wonderful to see you again.

"Tell me, how did things go after I left? By now you must be the Navy's leading pilot. Oh, I can just imagine you over Guadalcanal."

He waved his hands in protest. "You make too much of me, Saburo," he complained. "I am not even sure of the exact figure. Maybe, around fifty or so. But I am still far behind you." He smiled. "Perhaps you do not realize it, but you are still the best of all our pilots."

"Ah, you talk like a fool, old friend," I said. "I have seen you fly too many times. I am afraid, Nishizawa, that you shall be our leading ace before too long. But, tell me, what are you doing at Sasebo?"

"They sent me home to the Yokosuka Wing," he answered, his face turning glum. "An instructor. That's what they made me, an instructor! Saburo, can you picture me running around in a rickety old biplane, teaching some fool youngster how to bank and turn, and how to keep his pants dry? Me! "

I laughed. He was right; Nishizawa just wasn't the instructor type.

"Well," he continued, "after a little time at that, I felt disgusted. So I volunteered to go overseas again, just as soon as they would let me. I received my orders this morning; I'm reassigned to the Philippines. That's why I had to see you today. We take off tomorrow morning."

"So soon?"

"It is the way I wish it to be, Saburo," he replied. "Flying around Yokosuka is not for me. I want a fighter under my hands again. I simply have to get back into action. Staying home in Japan is killing me."

I knew how he felt. Indeed, I knew too well. But . . . there were other things to discuss, our other friends.

"I envy you, Nishizawa. But come, tell me about Rabaul, let me hear about everyone else. Where is Lieutenant Sasai now? And Ota, is he with you? What about my wingmen, Yonekawa and Hatori? Tell me all about them!"

"*What?*"

He stared at me, his face blank. Despair crowded his eyes. "So they did not tell you . . .

"What are you talking about?"

He waved his hand feebly.

"What is the matter with you, Nishizawa? Weren't they sent home with you?"

He turned away, his back to me. His voice choked. "Saburo, they are . . ." He put a hand to his forehead. Then he spun around. "Dead."

I couldn't believe it! . . . It was impossible!

"*What are you saying?*" I yelled at him.

"They are all dead. You and I, Saburo, you and I. . . we are the only ones still alive."

It couldn't be true! My knees buckled. I leaned against a table, while my mind tried to comprehend this tragedy.

Nishizawa began to talk. "Lieutenant Sasai was the first. We made a sweep to Guadalcanal on August twenty six. It was not as you remember, Saburo. I don't know how many Wildcats there were, but they seemed to come out of the sun in an endless stream. We never had a chance. Our formation went to pieces. We had to scatter so quickly that no one saw Sasai's plane go down. We thought that perhaps he had been hurt and had gone ahead of us. But when we returned to Rabaul, he was missing He never came back."

Nishizawa sighed wearily. "Then it was Ota. Just one week later. Every time we went out, we lost more and more planes. Guadalcanal was completely under the enemy's control. Ota went the same way as Sasai. No one saw his plane go down. He just didn't come home.

"Then, about three or four days after that, Yonekawa and Hatori were shot down. Both of them died the same day.

"Of all the men who returned with me, only Captain Saito, Commander Nakajima, and less than six of the other pilots who were in our original group of eighty men survived."

I was stunned. Nishizawa remained silent, waiting for me to speak again. It seemed so unreal! How could they all be dead?

Four of my best friends. They were all killed while I lay helplessly in the Yokosuka Hospital. Now I understood why I had failed to learn of their loss before. Nishizawa and Nakajima had made sure that the news did not reach me, not when the operation on my eyes had just been performed.

Their faces swam before me. I remembered Ota, laughing from his cockpit as we looped over Moresby. Yonekawa and Hatori, who clung grimly to my tail through all the air battles, always alert to protect me, to keep me from being killed. Sasai, he ... And now they were ... dead. I sobbed aloud, without shame, like a child. I could not stop. My body shook helplessly.

Nishizawa grasped my hand, begging me to stop. "Saburo, *please!*" he implored. "Please stop it!" I looked up at him.

"I am an accursed man!" he choked at me. "I never saw Sasai and Ota going down! I never even knew they had been lost. Our best friends, Saburo, our best friends, and I didn't do anything to help them! I must be Satan's bastard," he raged, "going after other planes while they died around me!"

He sat down again. "No, no, it is not true. There was nothing I could do. There were just too many enemy planes, just too many." His voice trailed off.

We sat silently for a long time, looking at each other.

What more was there to say?

CHAPTER TWENTY-FIVE

I WAS discharged from Sasebo Hospital during the last week of January, 1943. The long months of medical attention were over. I reported to my original outfit, the Tainan Fighter Wing of the 11th Air Fleet, now stationed at Toyohashi in central Japan.

I had first joined the wing during its formation in September of 1941 at Tainan on Formosa. Of the 150 pilots who had left Tainan during the great Japanese sweep across the Pacific, less than twenty were now alive. These veterans formed the core of the new wing, the majority of the members of which were green pilots rushed through training schools at Tsuchiura and other air bases.

Commander Tadashi Nakajima personally greeted me when I arrived at Toyohashi. Neither he nor I ever thought that we would meet here, instead of back at Rabaul. Thank heaven that Nakajima was my superior officer again. He engaged in no nonsense about my not being able to fly, and the very next day I went aloft. Only—in a Flying Fortress! This was the same B-17 which the Army had captured at Bandung, Java, in March of 1942. Every man of my original outfit went up in the great bomber. We got a tremendous kick out of flying the bomber, which impressed us with its excellent controllability and, above all, the precision workmanship of its equipment. No large Japanese airplane I had ever seen was in its class.

The next day I returned to my first love—the Zero. I can never describe the wonder of the feelings which came back to me as I took the lithe fighter into the air. She handled like a dream. Just a flick of the wrist—she was gone! I went through all sorts of acrobatics, standing the Zero on her tail, diving, sliding off on the wings. I was drunk with the air again.

As an officer I acquired an entirely new perspective of the war. Enlisted men were denied access to the secret combat reports which the Navy distributed to its officer personnel. Several days after my arrival at Toyohashi, Nakajima wordlessly showed me the report of our withdrawal from Guadalcanal on February 7, 1943, exactly six months after the Americans had landed. The radios blared of strategic withdrawals, of tightening our defense lines, but the secret reports revealed a staggering defeat and appalling losses.

Two full divisions of Army troops were gone, annihilated by the savagely fighting enemy. The Navy had lost the equivalent of an entire peacetime fleet. Rusting in the mud off Guadalcanal were the blasted hulks of no less than two battleships, one aircraft carrier, five cruisers, twelve destroyers, eight submarines, hundreds upon hundreds of fighters and bombers, not to mention the crack fighter pilots and all the bomber crews.

What had happened to us? We had stormed through the Pacific with impunity. Time and again we had whipped the enemy fighter planes. But the secret reports from the front told of new enemy fighters far superior to the P-39s and P-40s.

And for the first time I learned what really had happened at Midway last June. *Four carriers!* And nearly 300 airplanes, with most of their pilots, lost! It was unbelievable.

My heart sank when I saw the new pilot arrivals assigned to the Tainan Wing. They were eager and serious young men, unquestionably brave. But determination and courage were no substitute for pilot skill, and these men lacked the fine temper which they would need against the Americans who stormed the Pacific in every increasing numbers. These recruits with their shining faces— were they to fill the yawning gulf left by such men as Sasai and Ota? How? How in the name of heaven could they be expected to do *that?*

Their training at Toyohashi was severe. From sunup to sundown the instructors ran them through their paces. Classroom studies, and more and more flying. Teach them to hold their formations. That's a control stick you're holding there, not a broom handle! Don't just fly your airplane, become a part of it! This is how you save fuel... squeeze your trigger for short bursts, don't burn out your guns. All the lessons of the past battles relived again, trying to implant the invaluable lessons, the little tricks, the advantages in these new men.

But we didn't have enough time. We couldn't watch for individual errors and take the long hours necessary to weed the faults out of a trainee. Hardly a day passed when fire engines and ambulances did not race down the runways, sirens shrieking, to dig one or more pilots out of the plane they had wrecked on a clumsy take-off or landing.

Not all the new pilots were so ill equipped to master the training planes and fighters. Many appeared as gifted in the air as the great aces in 1939 and 1940 had been. But their numbers were distressingly few, and there would be no painless interval for them to gain many hours in the air or any combat experience before they were thrown against the Americans.

Less than a month after Guadalcanal fell, we were called in for a special officers conference, to hear news of a further disaster. The report remained classified throughout the rest of the war and was never revealed to the Japanese public. Behind locked doors, I read that a Japanese convoy of more than twenty ships—twelve transports, eight destroyers, and several smaller auxiliaries—had attempted to land Army troops at Lae, my old fighter air base. At least 100 enemy fighters and bombers attacked the convoy on the open seas with determined runs, sinking *all* the transports and at least five of the destroyers. The news carried implications of a disaster greater than

Guadalcanal, for it meant that the enemy now dominated the skies as far north as Lae, and that we were helpless to stop his incredibly effective attacks against our shipping.

Several days later the Tainan Air Wing was ordered to transfer without delay to Rabaul. Commander Nakajima asked me if I would accompany him back to the southwest Pacific. How could he believe I wished to do otherwise? Nakajima told me that, despite the loss of my right eye, he was convinced I was better than the new pilots. That night Headquarters posted a list of the men who were transferring to Rabaul. My name was included.

But we failed to reckon with the Chief Surgeon at Toyohashi. He was outraged when he read my name on the list. He stormed into Nakajima's office and vented his wrath on the unhappy commander. "You are out of your mind!" he bellowed. "Do you want to kill this man? What is wrong with you, even to consider allowing a one-eyed pilot to go into combat? He wouldn't stand a chance! The whole thing is preposterous! I will not allow Sakai to transfer to Rabaul!" We could hear them shouting at the other side of the field.

Nakajima protested that I was better than most of the new fliers, that, two eyes or one, nothing could replace my skill behind the controls of a Zero nor, for that matter, my long combat experience. The surgeon refused to budge an inch. Now Nakajima became angry. They argued back and forth for several hours, but in the end it was the surgeon who emerged triumphant. He persuaded Nakajima to change his mind.

As he left the commander's office I ran up to him and begged him to change his mind. He stared unbelievingly at me. He tried to speak, but his face turned redder and redder, until he yelled, *"Shut up!"* at me and stalked off, muttering that all fliers were crazy.

I was reassigned as a flight instructor to the Omura Air Base, near Sasebo.

The new wing arrived at Rabaul on April 3. Before a week passed, I read in the battlefront reports, they had carried out major attacks against Guadalcanal, Milne Bay, Port Darwin, and other critical targets. In four missions enemy fighters and antiaircraft guns shot no less than forty-nine of the wing's planes out of the air.

Disaster followed disaster. On April 19, a horrible rumor, shortly thereafter confirmed, spread among the officers. On the eighteenth, Admiral Isoroku Yamamoto, the esteemed Commander in Chief of the Imperial Japanese Navy, was killed. I read and reread the action report. Admiral Yamamoto was a passenger in one of two bombers escorted by Zero fighters when several of the American's new P-38 fighters ripped through the Zero cover and blasted both bombers from the sky.

And I sat at Omura, training new pilots. I found it hard to believe, when I saw the new trainees staggering along the runway, bumping their way into the air. The Navy was frantic for pilots, and the school was expanded almost every month, with correspondingly lower entrance requirements. Men who could never have dreamed even of getting near a fighter plane before the war were now thrown into battle.

Everything was urgent! We were told to rush the men through, to forget the fine points, just to teach them how to fly and shoot. One after the other, singly, in twos and threes, the training planes smashed into the ground, skidded wildly through the air. For long and tedious months, I tried to build fighter pilots from the men they thrust at us at Omura. It was a hopeless task. Our facilities were too meager, the demand too great, the students too many.

I felt I was rusting away. There was no longer any doubt that our country was in trouble. The civilian populace was not aware of this fact, nor were the students, nor any of the enlisted men. But those officers who saw the reports, who had been in combat, realized the gravity of the situation. The majority adhered to their unshakable belief that Japan would emerge the victor, but the victory parties and glad cries were fewer and further between than before.

Not even my remoteness from the field of battle reduced the immediacy or the pain of the war. In September of 1943, I was shocked to learn that an old and close friend, one of Japan's greatest pilots, NAP 1/C Kenji Okabe, had been shot down and killed over Bougainville. He had been a classmate at Tsuchiura, and was the ace who set our Navy's all-time record by shooting down seven enemy planes in a single day's action.

Was there no end to their deaths?

As I read on I felt like weeping. After Okabe's sensational day in the air over Rabaul, Admiral Ninichi Kusaka, the commander of the nth Air Fleet, had requested Naval Headquarters in Tokyo to award his pilot a medal for his outstanding valor. Nothing had changed. Tokyo had refused the request on the basis of "no precedent," exactly as it had refused Captain Saito a year before. Admiral Kusaka, however, was not to be turned aside so easily. Irritated at the decision from Headquarters, the Admiral had bestowed upon Okabe, in a special honor presentation, his own ceremonial sword.

Three days later Okabe burned to death when his Zero fell in flames.

CHAPTER TWENTY-SIX

IN APRIL of 1944, after long and wearying months of training student pilots at Omura, I was transferred to the Yokosuka Air Wing. Prior to the war, Yokosuka was a coveted assignment, since it was an Imperial Guard air unit which protected the air gateway to Tokyo. Now, it was just another wing. The days of coveted assignments were past.

With the secret reports available to me as an officer, I had been able to maintain a true appraisal of the war. The secret documents were a far cry from the drivel shouted over the radios to the unsuspecting populace. Everywhere in the Pacific our units were being forced back. Incredibly powerful American task forces, fleet units the size of which staggered the imagination, roamed the Pacific almost at will.

I read report after report, telling of the murderous havoc raised by these swift-striking fleets. The enemy's Army air force had grown tremendously in power. By the hundreds, their P-38S soared above the reach of our fighters, choosing combat at will. New types of fighters and bombers appeared almost daily, and our pilots' stories of their vastly improved performance boded ill for the future. We were still hanging on at Rabaul, but no longer did that once-mighty bastion threaten Moresby and the enemy's other bases. Rabaul suffered in more ways than one. The Americans were using it for bombing practice, to break in their new replacements.

Soon after I reached Yokosuka, I requested leave and took the train from the naval base to Tokyo, only ninety minutes away. My uncle's family welcomed me as if their own son had returned for a visit. I knew that any time I could leave the base for several hours or longer, this was my "home."

That night, after dinner, Hatsuyo began to chide me about the fact that I had not yet married. Her teasing seemed fully as serious as it was fun, and I shot back, "Why arc you still single, my dear cousin? What is wrong with you, that you have not yet selected for yourself a nice husband?"

My uncle and aunt interrupted the fireworks, laughing at us. "The both of you," my uncle mocked us, "so choosy!"

I grinned. "I don't see why Hatsuyo-san hasn't picked out a husband. Just look at her. She is as pretty as any movie star in the country. And how many girls today can boast of being an accomplished pianist?" I grinned. "I do believe," I said to them, looking at Hatsuyo, "that you could select for her an excellent husband."

My uncle and aunt smiled at my remarks. But not Hatsuyo. She glared at me and looked the other way, her eyes averted. "What is wrong, Hatsuyo-san?"

She ignored me. I was startled; she was angry. I changed the subject at once.

"Hatsuyo-san, will you favor me, please? The piano? It is a long time since you have honored me with a recital."

She looked at me questioningly.

"Remember when I first enrolled at school? You played, let me see ... Yes, I remember now. Mozart. Will you play it again?"

For reply Hatsuyo walked to the piano and sat down. As her fingers caressed the ivory keys, who would have thought a war was raging across thousands of miles in the Pacific! I closed my eyes and in my mind saw the flickering blue exhausts of fighters and bombers taxiing down runways, hurling dust and stones behind them, lifting with a thundering crescendo of power off the ground, to disappear into the night, many of them not to return.

And here I sat, in the Tokyo suburbs, relaxed, my body whole and well, my stomach full, basking in the warmth and affection of these people who loved me no less than a son. And others were dying. It was a strange world.

The music stopped. Hatsuyo sat at the piano for several moments, then turned and looked at me strangely. Her eyes were wide and questioning, and she spoke softly. "Saburo-san, I have another I wish to play, especially for you. Listen carefully. It will tell you something I cannot myself express in words."

She looked so strange! Then a flush spread over her face and she quickly averted her gaze.

She played for a long time. The music rolled from the piano, lifted quietly and drifted through the room, then crashed and soared. I looked at this girl. I knew her, and yet I knew her not at all. Never had I seen Hatsuyo like this. What did she mean when she said, "It will tell you something I cannot myself express?"

Suddenly I realized I was looking at Hatsuyo, not as a young girl, not as my cousin, but as a woman! For the first time I really saw her, intent at the keyboard, her fingers flashing up and down, her face tense as she poured her soul into the music.

Hatsuyo? And I? The thought was staggering. But, she was no longer a child. Wake up, Sakai, you fool! She is a woman. She is telling you, now, this moment, that she is in love with you! I knew now what she meant. In a rush of emotion, I wished to respond. It could not be, I told myself. But it was; it is! It is Hatsuyo. You are in love with her, you fool, and you did not even know how she felt. I remembered the hospital, when she threw her arms around me and sobbed that she was sure I would fly again.

So she had loved me, and for much longer than I would have dared imagine. It was so strange. At that moment I knew that I, too, was in love. With her. But what could I do? I had suffered those dark months long ago, when Fujiko cried at my refusal. Were the reasons now any the less compelling? Could I throw away the love of Fujiko then, because I was half blind, and do less than to refuse Hatsuyo's unspoken plea to me?

How could I now humble my pride, ignore these same beliefs, pretend that miraculously I could see again clearly and well enough to take to the air as the ace I once was? Could I do all that and retain my integrity? No!

So far as Hatsuyo was concerned, her message was wasted on me. I gave no indication that I knew what she was telling me, that I wished fervently to respond. When Hatsuyo finished playing, I waited as long as courtesy required, then retired for the evening, pleading weariness. But I did not fall asleep for many hours.

During my assignment to Yokosuka, I visited Tokyo often. In the eighteen months of my absence, the capital city had changed. The color and gaiety were gone. People no longer laughed as quickly or as heartily. The streets were dreary and lifeless. The people moved along, heads bent, intent on their own problems. The "Warship March" no longer generated enthusiasm. Too many sons of these same people, too many husbands and brothers and uncles and nephews, were never to come home again.

But Tokyo still did not truly reflect the war, although the shouting was over. The stores had run short of commodities, and strict rationing was now in force. People braved the wind and the cold in long queues, waiting for bowls of steaming broth. The homeland remained untouched, however, except for that one single raid back in 1942, the daring flight of Doolittle's bombers, which raced over the city and fled for China. Tokyo and all our cities had remained unviolated by the thunder and the screaming pieces of steel from American bombs.

War came to Japan in June of 1944. The effect on our population was unmistakable. On June 15 the people of Japan were shocked to hear that twenty bombers, tremendous giants of the air which dwarfed the powerful B-17, had flown an incredible distance from China to attack a city in Northern Kyushu. The raid did little damage, and twenty planes were hardly enough to cause national excitement. But in the homes and the stores, in the factories and on the streets, everywhere in Japan, the people talked about the raid, discussed the fact that our fighters had failed to stop the bombers. They all asked the same questions. Who was next? When? And how many bombers would come?

The newscasters gave them something else to worry about. The Americans had invaded Saipan. In more ways than one, the war had come home. Saipan was not very distant. The maps were unrolled, and our people looked for the tiny dot which lay not so far off our coastline. And they looked at each other. They began to question—never aloud, but in furtive conversations—the ceaseless reports of victories. How could we have smashed the enemy's ships, destroyed his planes, decimated his armies, if Saipan had been invaded? It was a question which everyone asked, but which very few dared to answer.

No sooner did we receive the news of the Saipan attack than powerful units of our fleet sailed for the Marianas to engage in what everyone at Yokosuka knew would be one of the decisive battles of the war. We were no longer invading foreign islands, we were guarding the very portals of our homeland.

The next morning the Yokosuka Wing received orders to transfer to the island of Iwo Jima. Our high command feared that, with Saipan secured, the Americans would strike next at that strategic point. With Iwo Jima in their hands, all of Japan was imperiled. Those great battles in the Marianas are history. Saipan fell before the terrible enemy onslaught. Our Navy sustained a crushing defeat and the American task forces roamed the Pacific, all-powerful, indomitable, and fearless.

The fact that Iwo Jima was not invaded in the summer of 1944 surprised us all. The island was barely able to defend itself! A fraction of the force which took Saipan could have stormed Iwo's beaches and crushed the token resistance which our skeleton forces then on the island could have mustered. For some unknown reason the invasion was delayed for many long months, during which time the Army and Navy poured men and weapons onto the strategic little isle.

When the Yokosuka Air Wing received orders to establish an air defense of the island, we were able to spare only thirty Zero fighters for the task. Thirty fighter planes, essentially the very same Zero with which I had fought in China nearly five years before. That was all! Yet no invasion came. We considered this turn of events nothing less than a miracle.

Commander Nakajima was back at Yokosuka. One month after he had left Toyohashi for Rabaul, Tokyo had ordered him to return to Japan for reassignment to Yokosuka, where he was to help turn out new fighter pilots at a record rate. Now, after a year on the homeland, he was leaving again, but for a campaign of more epic proportions than any he had ever undertaken.

I received orders to report to his office. "Sakai, why don't you come with me this time?" he asked. "You know how anxious I am to have you flying with me again. I don't care what any doctors say, you were, you are now, an excellent pilot. You prove it every time I see you fly."

He paused. "Let us be entirely honest, Saburo. You know better than any of us the questionable ability of these new pilots. I fear for their lives once they face the new American planes. We need something to bolster their morale, to give them a greater will to fight.

"You see, Saburo, I need you with me. Desperately. You are almost a god to these men. With you flying with us, their morale will soar. They will follow you anywhere."

"You need to ask me, sir?" I burst out. "You ask me if I will go with you? How many times have I tried! How many times have I been told no! 'You cannot fly, Sakai.' 'You are half blind, Sakai.' 'You are no good any more, Sakai.' Of course I want to go! I *want* to go with you, sir, I want to fight again! " Times had changed. No surgeon rose in heated protest to prevent my leaving. The niceties of keeping a one-eyed pilot out of the war no longer existed. We could not afford to worry about such minor details any longer. Japan herself was endangered, and a one-eyed pilot with my combat experience was no longer a liability.

I had come into my own again. My country needed me.

We received orders to leave at once for Iwo Jima. We did not even have time in which to contact our families. There were no farewells.

On the morning of June 16 we took off from Yokosuka and moved into formation as we headed for the distant island. We never made Iwo. After 100 miles of wild flying through a low, thick overcast and torrential rains, we were forced to turn back for Yokosuka. Japan's rainy season had begun. Nakajima and I could have made it to Iwo, as could several other fliers. But the majority of the thirty pilots in our group were inexperienced men. The storms would have detached them from our formation in no time and that would have been their end.

Iwo Jima is a tiny island 650 miles south of Yokosuka. It is barely two miles across at its widest point. On a global map, Iwo seems to be the last of a long series of stepping-stones in the Bonin group which extends from Yokosuka to Guam. Maps are notoriously misleading, however, and in the vast reaches of the Pacific the distance between each small outcropping of land can assume terrifying proportions. Without radar, indeed, without even radios in our Zero fighters, we dared not risk the loss of most of our planes.

Our experience in such matters had been tragic. Early in 1943, several squadrons of Army fighter planes, manned by pilots who had absolutely no experience in long-distance flying over the ocean, left Japan for a base to the south. En route, they encountered severe weather conditions, but refused to turn back. Almost every plane disappeared in the endless reaches of the Pacific.

We tried again the following morning, June 17. This time we flew less than 100 miles from Yokosuka before the storms forced our return, although ironically the weather over Iwo Jima and the Marianas was reported perfect! We languished in our billets, listening to radio reports from our island garrisons, telling of the enemy air attacks all through the day and on into the night.

Four times we took off for Iwo, and four times the raging storms foiled our flight. On June 20, when we made our fifth attempt, the weather conditions were still far below minimum safety standards.

Nakajima, however, was determined to get through. The inexperienced pilots glued their eyes to the wings and tails of the lead Zeros, and we fought our way through the violent updrafts and blinding sheets of rain.

None of us knew it at the time, of course, but this was the day our major fleet units suffered a disastrous beating by the planes and guns of the enemy task force rampaging through the Marianas.

Finally we came out of the storm front. Several minutes later, after we had flown 650 miles, Iwo's volcanic hump loomed out of the water. Nakajima began a wide circle over the second air strip, over Mount Motoyama, in the center of Iwo. I had thought the dusty runway of Lae bad, but this was impossible! Landing on the deck of a pitching and rolling aircraft carrier would have been simpler than descending to the monstrosity below us. Two sides of the landing strip were steep rock walls. Even the slightest skid on landing and ... a ball of fire. At the end of the runway there waited for any unwary pilot who missed his brakes a towering cliff.

Nakajima refused to take his men onto the forbidding runway. He led the formation back to the first airfield on the southern slopes of the volcanic island. Here was a wide, long runway. One after the other, the fighters dropped from the air.

More than ninety planes lined the long runway. Not an inch of parking space for our fighters was left.

Nakajima waved his arm above his cockpit to signal the other fighters to follow him. A long, winding road led from the main airfield to the second strip. The distance was more than a mile, and the smaller runway was at a level higher than the one we were leaving. I felt ridiculous as I jockeyed the Zero along on the road. This was my first— and my last—experience climbing the side of a mountain in a taxiing fighter plane. And in a convoy of thirty fighters.

A battalion of Army troops watched our queer convoy, with its clouds of dust and blatting motors, their mouths gaping open in disbelief. Many of them pointed their arms at us, laughing loudly and jeering. It was hardly funny to us. Taxiing the Zero up that tortuous slope with a fighter in front of me and a whirling propeller immediately behind, while we all tried to negotiate the hairpin curves, was as hazardous as maintaining tight formation in a thick fog.

Fortunately, we had arrived at Iwo during a temporary lull in the fighting. Only the day before the island had rocked and heaved beneath the impact of thousands of shells from the American task force which steamed off shore. Now they were back at Saipan, steadily reducing the fortifications on that island to wreckage.

For three days the war spared Iwo. Not that it was a place where any sane man would voluntarily want to remain. It was as dreary, hostile, and uncomfortable as Rabaul, if not more so. But we were left to our own devices, and took advantage of the lull in the fighting to soak in the hot springs which bubbled through the rocks from one end of the island to the other.

The war never seemed stranger to us. We knew by now that our fleet had been shattered in the Marianas sea fight and that practically all of the carrier pilots in the battle had died. There was no doubt that the overwhelming might of the American invasion forces, supported by many hundreds of planes and the thousands of heavy guns on the ships, would annihilate our troops on Saipan to the last man. And we soaked in hot baths on Iwo Jima.

Our officers were desperate. They knew all too well the need for help at Saipan. But what could we do? A mass assault by our fighters would have only a temporary and meaningless effect, for Saipan lay nearly 600 miles south of Iwo. On the other hand, we could not sit comfortably on our islands while our friends were blasted to bits. There was still another factor. If we left Iwo Jima unattended by dozens of fighters ready for instant flight, then the Americans could—in those unguarded hours—storm the island's defense and move in against weak opposition.

Finally it was decided that the fighters would remain, but that the bombers would attack the American warships cruising off Saipan. Each attack would be made at night, the unescorted bombers leaving in groups of eight or nine.

When I watched these planes roaring down the Iwo runways, their blue exhausts illuminating the wings and fuselage, the old days at Lae flashed back into my mind. I finally began to understand what had motivated the crews of the Mitchells and Marauders which pounded Lae, day and night, without fighter escort, hurling their defiance in the teeth of dozens of Zero fighter planes.

Now I saw the other side of the picture, but it was worse. In the early months of 1942 the American twin-engine bombers had a fighting chance. With the Bettys it was different. Let a fighter plane catch a Betty in its sights for a second or two, let an antiaircraft shell spill its hot fragments into the fuselage, and the odds were that there would be no more bomber, but a roaring mass of flames disintegrating into the water.

The hours between each take-off and the return of the surviving bombers seemed interminable. Our pilots carried out their bombing runs with the utmost gallantry and scored some hits. But what did it mean? These were only fleabites!

And every night perhaps one or two planes limped back to Iwo Jima with fuselage and wings holed, the crews desperately tired, their eyes haggard from watching their friends going down, one after the other, even before they were within attack range. The few pilots who returned to the island told us of fighters coming in after them in almost total darkness, and finding their planes unerringly in the gloom, of tracers bursting bright as day when all the guns on the American ships opened up at them. Brilliant explosions, cobwebs of spitting tracers which seemed to be impenetrable walls of fire blocking their path as they swung into their bombing runs.

In a few days there were hardly any of the twin-engined Mitsubishi bombers left on the island. Then Iwo threw in its torpedo bombers, single-engined planes (Jills) which attempted zero-level torpedo attacks. They fared little better than the larger planes.

On June 24 the quiet lull which had settled over Iwo Jima disappeared. It was about 5:20 a.m. when the air-raid alarms set up a terrific din across the island. Early warning radar had caught several large groups of enemy aircraft less than sixty miles to the south—and coming in fast.

Every fighter plane on the island—more than eighty Zeros— thundered down the two runways and sped into the air. Mechanics dragged the remaining Bettys and Jills to shelter.

This was it! The long wait was about to be rewarded. I had a Zero under my hands again, and in another few moments I would know— by the acid test of actual combat—if I had lost my skill.

An overcast at 13,000 feet hung in the sky. The fighters divided into two groups, forty Zeros climbing above the cloud layer, and the other forty—my group—remaining below.

No sooner had I eased out of my climb than an enemy fighter spun wildly through the clouds, trailing a long plume of flame and black smoke. I had only a brief look at the fighter—it was a new type, unmistakable with its broad wings and blunt nose, the new Grumman

I had heard so much about—the Hellcat. I swung into a wide turn and looked up . . . another Grumman came out of the clouds, diving vertically, smoke pluming behind.

Hard on the heels of the smoking fighter came scores of Hellcats, diving steeply. All forty Zeros turned and climbed to meet the enemy planes head on. There was no hesitation on the part of the American pilots; the Grummans screamed in to attack. Then the planes were all over the sky, swirling from sea level to the cloud layer in wild dogfights. The formations were shredded.

I snapped into a tight loop and rolled out on the tail of a Hellcat, squeezing out a burst as soon as the plane came into the range finder. He rolled away and my bullets met only empty air. I went into a left vertical spiral, and kept closing the distance, trying for a clear shot at the plane's belly. The Grumman tried to match the turn with me; for just that moment I needed, his underside filled the range finder and I squeezed out a second burst. The cannon shells exploded along the fuselage. The next second thick clouds of black smoke poured back from the airplane and it went into a wild, uncontrolled dive for the sea.

Everywhere I looked there were fighters, long trails of smoke, bursts of flame, and exploding planes. I looked too long. Flashing tracers poured directly beneath my wing and instinctively I jerked the stick over to the left, rolling back to get on his tail and snapping out a burst. Missed. He dove out of range, faster than I could follow.

I cursed at myself for having been caught without warning, and with equal vehemence I cursed my blind eye, which left almost half of my area of vision blank. As quickly as I could I slipped out of the parachute straps and freed my body, so I could turn around in my seat, making up for the loss of side vision.

And I looked without a second to spare. At least a half-dozen Grummans were on my tail, jockeying into firing position. Their wings burst into sparkling flame as they opened fire. Another left roll—fast!—and the tracers slipped harmlessly by. The six fighters ripped past my wings and zoomed in climbing turns to the right.

Not this time! Oh, no! I slammed the throttle on over-boost and rolled back to the right, turning after the six fighters with all the speed the Zero would give me. I glanced behind me—no other fighters in the back. One of these was going to be mine, I swore! The Zero closed the distance to the nearest plane rapidly. Fifty yards away I opened up with the cannon, watching the shells move up the fuselage and disappear into the cockpit. Bright flashes and smoke appeared beneath the glass; the next moment the Hellcat swerved crazily and fell off on one wing, its smoke trail growing with each second.

But there were more fighters on my tail! Suddenly I didn't want to close with them. Weariness spread over me like a smothering cloak. In the old days, at Lae, I would have wasted no time in hauling the Zero around and going for them. But now I felt as though my stamina had been wrung dry. I didn't want to fight.

I dove and ran for it. In this condition it would have been sheer suicide to oppose the Hellcats. There would have been a slip, a second's delay in moving the stick or the rudder bar ... and that would be all. I wanted time in which to regain my breath, to shake off the sudden dizziness. Perhaps it was the result of trying to see as much with only one eye as I had before; I knew only that I couldn't fight.

I fled to the north, using over-boost to pull away. The Hellcats turned back and went after fresher game. And then I saw what was to me the most hideous of all the hundreds of air battles in which I had fought. I glanced down to my right and gaped.

A Hellcat rolled frantically, trying to escape a Zero which clung grimly to its tail, snapping out bursts from its cannon, no more than fifty yards behind. Just beyond the Zero, another Hellcat pursued the Japanese fighter. Even as I watched, a Zero plunged from above and hauled around in a tight diving turn after the Grumman. One after the other they came in, in a long snaking file! The second Zero, intent upon the pursuing Hellcat fighter, seemed entirely unaware of a third Hellcat following in its dive. And a third Zero, watching the whole proceedings, snapped around in a tight turn and caught the trailing Hellcat without warning.

It was an astonishing—and to me, a horrifying—death column which snaked along, each plane following the other before it with determination, firing at the target before its guns. Hellcat, Zero, Hellcat, Zero, Hellcat, Zero. Were they all so stupid that not one pilot, either Japanese or American, guarded his weak spot from the rear?

The lead fighter, the Grumman, skidded wildly as it hurled back smoke, then plunged toward the sea. Almost at the same moment the pursuing Zero exploded in a fireball. The Hellcat which had delivered the death blow remained in one piece less than two seconds; cannon shells from the second Zero tore its wing off, and it fell, spinning wildly. The wing had just ripped clear of the fighter when a blinding flash of light marked the explosion of the Zero. And as the third Hellcat pulled up from the explosion, the cannon shells of the third Zero tore its cockpit into a shambles.

The five planes plunged toward the sea. I watched the five splashes. The last Zero rolled, turned, and flew away, the only survivor of the melee.

I circled slowly, north of Iwo, sucking in air and trying to relax. The dizziness left me, and I turned back to the battle area. The fight was over. There were still Zeros and Hellcats in the sky, but they were well separated, and the fighters of both sides were forming into their own groups.

Ahead and to the right I saw fifteen Zeros swinging into formation, and I closed in to join the group. I came up below the formation and . . .

Hellcats! Now I understood why the surgeon, long ago, had protested my return to combat so vigorously. With only one eye my perspective was badly off, the small details were lost to me in identifying planes at a distance. Not until the white stars against the blue wings became clear did I realize my error. I wasted no time in throwing off the fear which gripped me. I rolled to the left and came around in a tight turn, diving for speed, hoping the Grummans hadn't seen me.

No such luck. The Hellcat formation broke up and the planes turned in pursuit. What could I do? My chances seemed hopeless.

No—there was still one way out, and a slim chance at that. I was almost over Iwo Jima. If I could outmaneuver the other planes—an almost impossible task, I realized—until their fuel ran low and forced them to break for home. . . .

Now I appreciated the speed of these new fighters. In seconds they were closing in. They were so fast! There was no use in running any further. . . .

I snapped back in a tight turn. The maneuver startled the enemy pilots as I climbed at them from below, swinging into a spiral. I was surprised; they didn't scatter. The lead fighter responded with an equal spiral, matching my maneuver perfectly. Again I spiraled, drawing it closer this time. The opposing fighters refused to yield a foot.

This was something new. An Airacobra or a P-40 would have been lost trying to match me in this fashion, and not even the Wildcat could hold a spiral too long against the Zero. But these new Hellcats—they were the most maneuverable enemy planes I had ever encountered. I came out of the spiral into a trap. The fifteen fighters filed out of their spirals into a long column. And the next moment I found myself circling in the center of a giant ring of fifteen Grummans.

On every side of me I saw the broad wings with their white stars. If ever a pilot was surrounded in the air, I was.

I had little time in which to ponder my misfortune. Four Grummans broke out of their circle and dove at me. They were too eager. I rolled easily out of the way and the Hellcats skidded by, out of control. But what I thought was only a slight roll set me up for several other fighters. A second quartet flashed out of the ring, right on my tail.

I ran. I gunned the engine to give every last ounce of power and pulled away sufficiently to get out of their gun range for the moment. The four pursuing planes didn't worry me; it was the first quartet. How right I was! They had climbed back from their skidding plunge and were above me, diving for another firing pass.

I slammed my right foot against the rudder bar, skidding the Zero to the left. Then the stick, hard over to the left, rolling sharply. Sparkling lights flashed beneath my right wing, followed by a plummeting Hellcat.

I came out of the roll in a tight turn. The second Grumman was about 700 yards behind me, its wings already enveloped in yellow flame from its guns. If I hadn't known it before, I knew it now. The enemy pilots were as green as my own inexperienced fliers ... and that could be a factor which would save my life.

The second fighter kept closing in, spraying tracers all over the sky, tracers which fell short of my own plane. Keep it up! I veiled, keep it up! Go ahead, waste all your ammunition; you'll be one less to worry about. I turned again and fled, the Hellcat closing in rapidly. When he was about 300 yards behind, I rolled away to the left. The Grumman passed below me, still firing at empty air.

I lost my temper. Why run from such a clumsy pilot? With out thinking, I rolled back and got on his tail. From fifty yards away I snapped out a cannon burst.

Wasted. I failed to correct for the skid caused by my abrupt turn. And suddenly I didn't care what happened to the fighter in front of me ... another Grumman was on my tail, firing steadily. Again—the left roll, a maneuver which never failed me. The Hellcat roared past, followed by the third and fourth fighters in the quartet.

Another four planes were almost directly above me, ready to dive. Sometimes, you have to attack in order to defend yourself. I went into a vertical climb, directly beneath the four fighters. The pilots banked their wings back and forth, trying to find me. I had no time to scatter them. Three Hellcats came at me from the right. I narrowly missed their tracers as I evaded with the same left roll.

The fighters were back in their wide ring. Any move I made to escape would bring several Grummans cutting at me from different directions. I circled in the middle, looking for a way out.

They had no intention of allowing that to happen. One after the other, the fighters peeled off from the circle and came at me, firing as they closed in.

I cannot remember how many times the fighters attacked nor how many times I rolled away. The perspiration rolled down my body, soaking my underclothes. My forehead was all beads of sweat, and it began to drip down onto my face. I cursed when the salty liquid trickled into my left eye. . . . I couldn't take the time to rub it with my hand! All I could do was to blink, try to keep the salt away, try to see.

I was tiring much too quickly. I didn't know how I could get away from the ring. But it was very clear that these pilots weren't as good as their planes. An inner voice seemed to whisper to me. It repeated over and over the same words . . .*speed . . . keep up your speed . . . forget the engine, burn it out, keep up your speed! . . . keep rolling . . . never stop rolling.* . . .

My arm was beginning to go numb from the constant rolling to the left to evade the Hellcats' tracers. If I once slackened my speed in flicking away to the left, it would be my end. But how long could I keep that necessary speed in rolling away?

I must keep rolling! As long as the Grummans wanted to keep their ring intact, only one fighter at a time could jump me. And I had no fear of evading any single plane as it made its firing pass. The tracers were close, but they must hit me exactly if they were going to shoot me down. It mattered not whether the bullets passed a hundred yards or a hundred inches away, just so I could evade them.

I needed time to keep away from the fighters which raced in, one after the other, peeling off from the wide ring they maintained about me.

I rolled. Full throttle.

Stick over to the left.

Here comes another!

Hard over. The sea and horizon spinning crazily.
Skid!
Another!
That was close!
Tracers. Bright. Shining. Flashing.
Always underneath the wing.
Stick over.
Keep your speed up!
Roll to the left.
Roll.
My arm! I can hardly feel it any more!

Had any of the Hellcat pilots chosen a different approach for his firing pass or concentrated carefully on his aim, I would surely have been shot out of the air. Not once did the enemy pilots aim at the point toward which my plane was moving. If only one fighter had spilled its tracers into the empty space leading me, toward the area where I rolled every time, I would have flown into his bullets.

But there is a peculiarity about fliers. Their psychology is strange, except for the rare few who stand out and go on to become leading aces. Ninety-nine per cent of all pilots adhere to the formula they were taught in school. Train them to follow a certain pattern and, come what may, they will never consider breaking away from that pattern when they are in a battle where life and death mingle with one another.

So this contest boiled down to endurance between the time my arm gave out and I faltered in my evading roll and the fuel capacity of the Hellcats. They still had to fly back to their carriers.

I glanced at the speedometer. Nearly 350 miles an hour. The best that the Zero could do.

I needed endurance for more than my arm. The fighter also had its limits. I feared for the wings. They were bending under the repeated violence of the evading roll maneuvers. There was a chance that the metal might collapse under continued pressure and that the wing would tear off from the Zero, but that was out of my hands. I could only continue to fly. I must force the plane through the evasive rolls or die.

Roll.
Snap the stick over!
Skid.

Here comes another one.

To hell with the wings! Roll!

I could hear nothing. The sound of the Zero's engine, the roaring thunder of the Hellcats, the heavy staccato of their .50-caliber guns, all had disappeared.

My left eye stung.

The sweat streamed down.

I couldn't wipe it.

Watch out!

Stick over. Kick the bar.

There go the tracers. Missed again.

The altimeter was down to the bottom; the ocean was directly beneath my plane. Keep the wings up, Sakai, you'll slap a wave with your wing tip. Where had the dogfight started? Thirteen thousand feet. More than two and a half miles of skidding and rolling away from the tracers, lower and lower. Now I had no altitude left.

But the Hellcats couldn't make their firing runs as they had before. They couldn't dive; there was no room to pull out. Now they would try something else. I had a few moments. I held the stick with my left hand, shook the right vigorously. It hurt. Everything hurt. Dull pain, creeping numbness.

Here they come, skidding out of their ring. They're careful now, afraid of what I might do suddenly. He's rolling. A rolling pass.

It's not so hard to get out of the way. Skid to the left. Look.

The tracers.

Fountains geysering up from the water. Spray. Foam.

Here comes another one.

How many times have they come at me this way now? I've lost count. When will they give up? They must be running low on fuel!

But I could no longer roll so effectively. My arms were going numb. I was losing my touch. Instead of coming about with a rapid, sharp rolling motion, the Zero arced around in a sloppy oval, stretching out each maneuver. The Hellcats saw it. They pressed home their attacks, more daring now. Their passes came so fast that I had barely time for a breather.

I could no longer keep this up. I must make a break! I came out of another left roll, kicked the rudder bar and swung the stick over to the right. The Zero clawed around in response and I gunned the fighter for a break in the ring. I was out, nosing down again and running for it, right over the water. The Hellcats milled around for a moment in confusion. Then they were after me again.

Half the planes formed a barricade overhead, while the others, in a cluster of spitting guns, hurtled after me. The Hellcats were too fast. In a few seconds they were in firing range. Steadily I kept working to the right, kicking the Zero over so that she jerked hard with each maneuver. To the left fountains of white foam spouted into the air from the tracers which continued narrowly to miss my plane.

They refused to give up. Now the fighters overhead were coming down after me. The Grummans immediately behind snapped out their bursts, and the Hellcats which dove tried to anticipate my moves. I could hardly move my arms or legs. There was no way out. If I continued flying low, it would only be a matter of a minute or two before I moved the stick too slowly. Why wait to die, running like a coward?

I hauled the stick back, my hands almost in my stomach. The Zero screamed back and up, and there, only a hundred yards in front of me, was a Hellcat, its startled pilot trying to find my plane.

The fighters behind him were already turning at me. I didn't care how many there were. I wanted this fighter. The Hellcat jerked wildly to escape. Now! I squeezed, the tracers snapped out. My arms were too far gone. The Zero staggered; I couldn't keep my arms steady. The Hellcat rolled steeply, went into a climb and fled.

The loop had helped. The other fighters milled around in confusion. I climbed and ran for it again. The Grummans were right behind me. The fools in those planes were firing from a distance of 500 yards. Waste your ammunition, waste it, waste it, I cried. But they were so fast! The tracers flashed by my wing and I rolled desperately.

Down below, Iwo suddenly appeared. I rocked my wings, hoping the gunners on the ground would see the red markings. It was a mistake. The maneuver slowed me down, and the Hellcats were all over me again.

Where was the flak? What's wrong with them down on the island? Open up, you fools, open up!

Iwo erupted in flame. Brilliant flashes swept across the island. They were firing all the guns, it seemed, spitting tracers into the air. Explosions rocked the Zero. Angry bursts of smoke appeared in the air among the Hellcats. They turned steeply and dove out of range.

I kept going at full speed. I was terrified. I kept looking behind me, fearing that they had come back, afraid that at any second the tracers wouldn't miss, that they'd stream into the cockpit, tearing away the metal, ripping into me.

I passed Iwo, banging my fist on the throttle, urging the plane to fly faster. Faster, faster! South Iwo appeared on the horizon . . . there, a cloud! A giant cumulus, rearing high above the water. I didn't care about the air currents. I wanted only to escape those fighters. At full speed I plunged into the billowy mass.

A tremendous fist seemed to seize the Zero and fling it wildly through the air. I saw nothing but livid bursts of lightning, then blackness. I had no control. The Zero plunged and reared. It was upside down, then standing on its wings then hurtling upward tail first.

Then I was through. The storm within the cloud spit the fighter out with a violent lurch. I was upside down. I regained control at less than 1,600 feet. Far to the south I caught a glimpse of the fifteen Hellcats, going home to their carrier. It was hard to believe that it was all over and that I was still alive. I wanted desperately to get out of the air. I wanted solid ground beneath my feet.

I set down at Iwo's main strip. For a few minutes I relaxed in the cockpit, exhausted, then climbed wearily down from the Zero. All the other fighters had long since landed. A throng of pilots and mechanics ran toward the plane when it stopped, shouting and cheering. Nakajima was among them, and he threw his arms around my neck, roaring with joy. "You did it, Sakai! You did it! Fifteen against one . . . you were marvelous!" I could only lean against the plane and mumble, cursing my blind eye. It had nearly cost me my life.

An officer pounded me on the back. "We were going crazy down here," he shouted. "Every man on the island was watching you! The gunners, they couldn't wait for you to come over the island, to bring those planes into their range. Everybody had his hands on the triggers, just waiting, hoping you'd come our way. How did you do it?" he asked in amazement.

A mechanic ran up to me, saluting, "Sir! Your plane. It—it doesn't... I can't believe it. . . there's not a single bullet hole in your fighter! "

I couldn't believe it, either. I checked the Zero over from one end to the other. He was right. Not a single bullet had hit the fighter.

Later, back at the billet, I learned that the first group of Zeros which had flown above the clouds had fought a far easier battle than our own formation. The large Hellcat formation had climbed from the overcast directly beneath their own planes, and they had the advantage of diving, surprising the American pilots before they even knew what happened. NAP I/C Kinsuke Muto, the Yokosuka Wing's star pilot, had a field day, shooting down four of the Grummans. The other pilots confirmed his victories. Muto flamed two Hellcats before they could even make an evasive move.

But the day's toll was staggering. Nearly forty—almost half of all our fighters—had been shot down.

CHAPTER TWENTY-SEVEN

THE DAY following the savage air battle which cut our numbers in half, I came down with a severe case of diarrhea, which might have been expected, inasmuch as Iwo's entire water supply came from rainwater collected in tanks, cans, and other containers.

My mental condition was no better than my lessened physical ability. The loss of forty planes and pilots in a single action staggered me. Equally disturbing was the sight of our inexperienced pilots falling in flames, one after the other, as the Hellcats blasted their outmoded Zeros from the sky. How much like Lae the battle had been! Except that now the obsolescent planes were Zeros, and the inexperienced pilots were Japanese. The war had run full circle.

The diarrhea sapped my strength and kept me bedridden for a week. My recovery was slow.

The evening of July 2 excitement spread through the billet. Orderlies dashed back and forth outside, rushing from the radio shack to the Command Post. I went out and stopped one man, who told me that our radio monitors were receiving a sudden increase in enemy message transmissions. Although the majority of such messages were in code, which we could not decipher, the transmissions came from enemy units not too far from the island.

An attack was under way. That much was clear, as well as the fact that it would come very soon. All pilots reported to the Command Post for orders. I was refused permission to fly; the commander felt I was still too weak properly to handle my fighter.

The next morning all pilots reported to the airfield at four o'clock. Several scout planes took off immediately to search the ocean. Nothing happened during the next hour. I returned to the billet to catch some more sleep. At six o'clock bugles shattered the island's quiet, announcing that an attack was under way. Men ran across the fields to handle their guns, and the forty fighters sped down the runways to take up their interception positions. I walked out to the yard in front of the barracks to watch the action.

Far to the south at least fifty planes appeared, headed directly for us. Hellcats. The forty Zeros circling overhead turned to meet the enemy fighters in a head-on attack.

I had only one or two minutes to watch the fierce air fight. A new sound came to my ears ... planes diving! I turned and saw a squadron of Avengers in four separate flights hurtling down against the main strip. Their attack was timed perfectly; our forty fighters had been drawn into battle by the Hellcats, leaving the island wide open for the bombers' run.

I was still running for the billet when thundering explosions shook the ground beneath my feet. That was enough for me! I dove for the ground, burying my face in the volcanic ash. I tried to grovel my way into the dirt, to get away from the steel splinters which hurtled through the air. The explosions continued unabated for several minutes. Every time a bomb went off the ground beneath me heaved. Dust was everywhere. Then the noise ended.

I rolled over on my back. The Avengers were moving off to the south.

I stood up and looked at the columns of smoke and dust towering over the airfield. Another attack! A second Avenger squadron sliced through the billowing smoke clouds, plunging directly toward our runway. The bombers appeared to be headed directly at me. I turned and ran as fast as I could, throwing myself on the ground behind a large rainwater tank behind the billet.

Almost at the same moment I saw the bombs fall from the Avengers. I stared at them in hypnotized fascination ... they grew in size, swelling rapidly, as they plunged through the air. I ate some more dirt.

A blast of hot air punched the ground and flung me over. Shattering explosions hammered at my ears. I opened my eyes; there was only dust and smoke boiling up from the ground. I was more shaken up and frightened than hurt. I had suffered no injury, except the bruises from diving for the protection of the soil. Gradually my ears recovered. I heard the billet collapsing, and dashed out of the way as the water tank fell apart with a roar.

The air battle was still going on. I watched the planes, listened to the racing engines and the coughing sounds of cannon from the Zeros, the staccato bark of the Hellcat guns. What was I doing on the ground? To hell with the diarrhea! I ran out of the shelter toward the Command Post.

The sight of a third wave of bombers screaming down on the field stopped me in my tracks, and I turned and fled again for shelter. This time their aim was poor; the bombs hurtled beyond the airstrip and dug craters just beyond its end. This time I made it to the Command Post, a flimsy tent, still undamaged by the bombs.

I told a grim-faced Nakajima that I wanted to fly. "All the operational planes are off the ground, Sakai," he answered unhappily. "Besides, I thought the doctor said you weren't fit to fly?"

"There's nothing wrong with me, sir," I snapped back. "And there is a fighter available." I pointed out a Zero standing at the end of the runway.

"That ship had a bad engine when it was checked before," the commander replied. "But it may be all right now. The mechanics have been working on it for several hours." He looked up. "All right, go ahead."

I threw a salute and ran out of the tent. "Sakai!" I turned; it was Nakajima. "Take care of yourself, Sakai," he called. "This is no longer Lae ... take care."

Several men were dragging the Zero off the runway, trying to get the airplane to a revetment before the next bombing. I shouted for them to swing the fighter around again. While I was in the cockpit a mechanic clambered up onto the wing. "The engine's been irregular, sir!" he shouted over the din as I started her up. "It should be all right now! "

The engine caught perfectly. I wasted no time in warming the fighter up, but gunned her for take-off. The wheels had just lifted when I saw the fourth Avenger squadron plummeting down for its attack. I was in no position to oppose the bombers when I was barely off the ground. I dropped the nose and skimmed over the water to gain speed, pulling up twenty miles away.

The bombers had completed their runs, and now a fifth wave of planes hurtled through the smoke and dust to lay their eggs. Not a single fighter opposed them. Every Zero in the air except for my own was battling for its life against the Hellcats.

I returned to Iwo at 13,000 feet, heading for the scrambling dogfight. The battle was over. Now that the Avengers' bombs were expended, the Hellcats broke off with the Zeros and turned away to escort the bombers back to the carriers. There was nothing I could do; I returned with the remaining Zeros to the Iwo strip.

Again the Hellcats had slashed our ranks badly. Again half of all the fighters which took off to intercept the American planes were lost: twenty out of forty Zeros! In two battles the American fighters shot down sixty out of eighty Zero fighters. It was incredible.

NAP 1/C Muto and Ensign Matsuo Hagire were the lights in an otherwise dark morning. Each destroyed three Hellcats, and a number of other pilots put in claims for one fighter shot down. But these victories were incidental. Our planes had done nothing against the Avengers.

The two airstrips were in a shambles. It seemed impossible to land, but somehow all the pilots snaked their way around the craters which pitted both runways.

The enemy would continue to come. And what could we do? Even if every pilot in the air shot down several of the enemy's fighters, we were powerless to stop the bombers from working over our airfields and other defenses. All through the afternoon and well into the night our staff officers tried to find a way out of our dilemma. There was no rest that evening. Ground crews worked until dawn to clear the runways and fill the craters.

The pilots heard nothing of what had occurred in the staff conference. We went to bed early—in the few shacks and tents which remained standing—anticipating another morning attack.

The Americans did not disappoint us. Again every Zero fighter on the island raced into the air. The results were even worse than we had anticipated. Nine Zeros, most of them badly shot up, came back to land at Iwo. In three battles, we had now lost seventy-one out of eighty fighters!

Again we did nothing to foil the bombers. Moreover, their aim had improved. Iwo was in incredible chaos, most of its installations wrecked, the field again pitted with bomb craters. Exactly eight bombers were left on the ground—eight torpedo planes which had been protected by their shelters. Almost every other bomber and fighter under repair or hidden in its shelters was destroyed.

After landing we trudged back to the Command Post. Not a man had the energy or the spirit to talk. We sprawled on the ground, weary and despondent, watching the men running frantically over the runways, trying to fill in the holes, fighting the flames which roared fiercely in the wrecked buildings.

Several minutes later Commander Nakajima walked slowly from the Command Post tent and approached our group. We rose to attention. Nakajima waved his hand, telling us to be seated. The commander was visibly agitated, and he talked in a low, faltering tone. He told us that the staff officers had argued all through the night, that they disagreed as to what action against the Americans we should take in the future. One group insisted that we had no choice, that continuing to throw interceptors at the enemy raiders was useless. In a few days we would find ourselves without any planes at all. Therefore, the only thing to do was to strike back with all the strength we could muster at the American task force, which one of our scouts had located 450 miles south-southeast of the island.

The second group agreed, in theory, to the attack plan. "But" they argued, "what can only nine Japanese fighters and eight single-engine bombers do against the enemy task force? The Americans can launch from all their carriers at one rime *several hundred* interceptors!" The American fleet was the same force which, on June 20, had virtually wiped out all our carrier-borne planes in the Marianas.

The argument, Nakajima, said, was ended conclusively when the Iwo Wing commander, Captain Kanzo Miura, finally accepted the plan to hit back at the American fleet. Miura set our departure for noon on July 4—the enemy's Independence Day.

We never made the attack as planned. Anticipating that we might employ the occasion for a raid against their fleet, the rampaging American pilots returned to Iwo on the morning of the fourth and tore the island's facilities into a flaming, smoking ruin.

We could not even take off. Again the runways were rendered useless. We sat around the Command Post, just as we had done before, while the staff officers argued among themselves. Captain Aliura (we found out later) refused to budge from his position. "We are being bled white," he told his staff. "The end is clearly in sight if we continue fighting only defensive battles. What should we do? Stay here and see every last plane shot out of the air while the enemy fleet is unmolested? No! We will attack, and this same day! As soon as the runways are repaired, I want every plane off the ground."

Nakajima related the details of the meeting to us. "I realize," he concluded, "what we are sending you out to do. There is no use in my saying otherwise; you will be flying to almost certain death. But," here he hesitated, "the decision has already been made. You will go."

He looked into the eyes of each man. "And may good fortune accompany you."

The commander withdrew a sheet of paper from his pocket and read off the names of the pilots selected to man the planes for the flight—a one-way mission, it seemed.

There was no excitement among the pilots. Each man rose when his name was called and saluted. Mine was the ninth name to be announced; I would lead the second V formation of the nine Zeros. Muto, easily the best pilot among us, would lead the third V. Nakajima selected a lieutenant to lead the fighter squadron.

Nakajima came up to me, obviously unhappy. He placed his hand on my shoulder. "I hate myself for sending you out today, my old friend," he mumbled. "But," he sighed wearily, "there seems nothing else for us to do. Sakai. I... good luck! " I had no words for a reply. I offered my hand. We clasped in silence, then Nakajima turned and walked away.

We broke up our group almost wordlessly. The pilots selected for the mission left to pack their belongings. I stared at the few personal things I had brought with me to Iwo. I thought of the men who would deliver them to the families of the dead. How would my mother act when they handed her the bundle, tell her how it happened?

The hours slipped by very quickly. It's ironic, I thought. Only a few days ago I thought each minute had become a lifetime, when those fifteen Hellcats were gunning for my blood.

Muto approached me in my tent, and asked for any ideas I might have on the mission. I looked at him for several moments. "Muto, I . . . I don't know. Ideas? There aren't any *good* ones. When we reach those ships this afternoon, the enemy fighters will swarm all over us. All I can say is . . . we have our orders. We'll go. That's all."

I felt sorry for the young pilot. I personally was no longer a great asset to my country. The difficulties I had experienced in evading even the inexperienced American pilots told me beyond any doubts the extent to which my half blindness had hobbled my dogfighting abilities. But Muto ... he was Nishizawa, Ota, and Sasai all in one. A brilliant pilot. He did not belong in the air with us today. To throw away his life on such a hopeless mission was sheer stupidity. With one of our newer fighters at his disposal, Muto was our best chance to destroy a dozen, perhaps two dozen, enemy planes. He was the kind of pilot who belonged over Japan, ready to defend the country against the B-29s which were certain to attack in ever greater strength. And now . . . what a waste!

Muto, of course, realized none of these thoughts? He smiled at my remarks. "All right, Sakai. I know. If the gods smile .. he shrugged. "Otherwise, let us at least die together like the friends we are."

An hour later all the pilots chosen for the attack mission lined up at attention before the Command Post. Behind the tent, fastened to a high pole, a broad, white banner flapped wildly in the wind. Imprinted against the white were the ancient words, *"Namu Hachiman Daibosatsu."* A literal translation would read: "We believe in the Merciful God of War." The banner was a replica of the emblem used by a Japanese warlord in the sixteenth century, when an endless series of local civil wars rocked the length and breadth of Japan.

When we were at Lae our fliers had never resorted to such psychological crutches as morale boosters. To me the theatrical display was a sign of weakness, and nothing else. It betokened mental retrogression on the part of our officers, who attempted to impress themselves with the fire and fury of the ancient times when wars were decided for the most part by individual courage and skill. But those days were centuries past! I was no staff officer, I participated in no campaign planning, and heaven knows I was far from being even an amateur strategist. But certain things were obvious! Our own officers were resorting to what amounted almost to modern witchcraft. They were beating the drums of patriotism, trying to convince, not only their subordinates, but themselves, as well, that we could recoup the tremendous losses we had suffered by emotional displays and threats shouted at the "cursed Americans."

How could these men so resolutely refuse to recognize truth? Did it take a world upheaval to make them realize that our Zero fighter—which long ago had been the world's best—could be outflown, outdived, outclimbed, and outgunned by the Hellcat, as well as by many other new planes I had not yet seen?

I looked at the banner. It had been there for many days, but today for the first time I really saw it. Were we to put our faith in this symbol of supernatural strength? How was this to help us gain victory? Would it stop the flaming tracers of the Hellcats' guns?

As a fighter pilot, I appreciated better than most the wisdom of relying upon my own strength and my own skill to escape the death which in a dogfight was never more than a split second away. I could count only upon myself and my wingmen. and the assistance I knew I would always receive from my fellow pilots. Had I gone into battle only shouting historic phrases, I would never have survived this long. All of this was now drastically altered. My skill in preserving my life against every assault no longer counted. Not one of the seventeen pilots standing at ramrod attention before the Command Post entertained even the faintest hope that he would ever see his friends alive. Or that he himself could possibly survive.

I loved my country dearly, and never would I hesitate a moment to defend Japan with my life. But there is a vast gulf between defending one's land even to the last and wantonly wasting one's life. To me, the ancient warrior's incantation meant something else.

"Namu Ami Dabutsu!" The ancient Buddhist chant, *"I believe in Buddha."* The prayer murmured by those among my people who were breathing their last on their deathbeds, or who offered solace and comfort to those among them who were dying. I believed in Japan, but not in the so-called merciful god of war. I was willing to die for my country, but, only in my faith, in the tradition of the Samurai, as I had been taught all my life, as a man, as a warrior!

The thought soothed my anger. By the time Captain Miura came out of the tent to address us, I was relaxed. The captain climbed onto the podium of empty beer cases. He looked slowly from man to man, unhappy, regarding us as if it were the last time he would see our faces.

"You will strike back at the enemy," he began. "From now on our defensive battles are over. You men are the fliers chosen from the Yokosuka Air Wing, the most famous in all Japan.

I trust that your actions today will be worthy of the name and the glorious tradition of your wing."

He hesitated for several moments. "In order for you to perpetuate the honor which is ours, you must accept the task which your officers have put before you. You cannot, I repeat, you cannot hope for survival. Your minds must be on the word *attack!* You are but seventeen men, and today you will face a task force which is defended perhaps by hundreds of American fighter planes.

"Therefore, individual attacks must be forgotten. You can not strike at your targets as one man alone. You must maintain a tight group of planes. You must fight your way through the interceptors, and . . ." Captain Miura drew himself up straight, *"you must dive against the enemy carriers together!* Dive—along with your torpedoes and your lives and your souls."

A great roaring sounded in my ears. What was he saying? Had I heard him right? ". . . a normal attack will be useless. Even if you succeed in penetrating the American fighters, you will only be shot down on the way back to this island. Your death will be ineffective for our country. Your lives will be wasted. We cannot permit this to be."

His voice boomed at us. "Until you reach your targets, the fighter pilots will refuse to accept battle with the enemy planes. No bomber pilot will release his torpedo in an air drop. No matter what happens, you will keep your planes together. Wing to wing! No obstacle is to stop you from carrying out your mission. You must make your dives in a group in order to be effective. I know that what I tell you to do is difficult. It may even seem impossible. But I trust that you can do it, that you will do it. That every man among you will plunge directly into an enemy carrier and sink the vessel."

For another minute he looked at us. "You have your orders," he snapped.

I was stunned! We had been sent out before this on missions where our chances of survival seemed hopelessly remote. But at least we had the chance to fight for our lives! This was the first time a Japanese pilot had actually been *ordered* to make a suicide attack.

In our Navy it was an unwritten convention that, once a plane was crippled on the high seas far from its base, the pilot would dive against an enemy warship or transport, since he had no chance to return home. We were not the only pilots to do so; it had happened with the Americans, with the Germans, with the British ... it would always happen so long as men fly and fight. But no Japanese air commander had ever told his men, "Go out and die!"

(The celebrated *Kamikaze Special Attack Corps* was organized four months later in the Philippines, by Vice-Admiral Takijiro Onishi. Before he proceeded with his "suicide" planes, as they are described elsewhere, he queried the pilots under his command and received an overwhelming assurance that they would, if necessary, sacrifice their lives to defend their country. The *Kamikaze* operation, however, was an elaborately planned campaign, eventually utilizing airplanes specifically designed for such operations. In the beginning, however, the planes which were to dive against ships were loaded with bombs and escorted by Zero fighters whose pilots were under specific instructions to return to their base. In this fashion they operated as fighter escorts and provided eyewitness testimony to the results of the attack. At Iwo, it was entirely different. Even the Zeros, which carried no bombs on the mission, were expendable. Captain Adiura, who gave us our orders, died in action, while Admiral Onishi committed *harakiri* after Japan's surrender.)

Miura's talk had a tremendous shock effect upon the assembled pilots. Whatever the reaction of the men toward deliberately sacrificing their lives, the captain's words, his manner of speaking, and his background of outstanding valor in combat buoyed the spirits of most of them. No longer did they approach the mission with the purely negative attitude of departing without any chance. Now it was different. Now that they *knew* they would never return, the men took on an air of determination. Their lives were no longer to be wasted. The sacrifice of their small number would be more than compensated for by the loss of one or more huge enemy ships, possibly causing the death of thousands of Americans.

I was in a turmoil. I had a cold, sinking feeling of revulsion in my brain. I was neither furious nor desperate. My heart and my emotions might perhaps be called frozen. The ancient words returned to me. "*A Samurai lives in such a way that he will always be prepared to die.*"

The Samurai code, however, never demanded that a man be constantly prepared to *kill himself.* There is a great gulf between deliberately taking one's life and entering battle with a willingness to accept all its risks and hazards. In the latter case death is acceptable and there can be no regrets. Man lives with his head held high; he can die in the same fashion. He forfeits neither his personal honor nor that of his country, and he has the satisfaction of having given his nation his best. It has never been difficult to become so exalted in the heat of combat as to defy the worst odds, to fight when necessary, to attack when outnumbered. All these things comprise the life of a marl dedicated as a warrior.

But how does one quietly and objectively decide in a few hours to go out and kill oneself?

It was to be remembered, however, that we were still in the Navy, where orders are orders.

A chilled silence followed the end of Captain Miura's address. Presently we saluted, the captain left the area, and the pilots broke up into small groups.

I told the two men assigned as my wingmen, "You understand fully the captain's orders?" They nodded. "I trust you are prepared, then, for what we must do. My only instructions to you are these: stay with my plane until we arrive at our target. Never break away from my V formation. No matter what happens, stick with my plane."

They both were so serious. Young-old men! All of twenty years old.

Muto and his two wingmen joined us. Muto grinned broadly and joked. "Well, since all of us are going to die in a few hours, we might as well look at each other. I want to be sure to remember all your homely faces later on." He broke the tension; we laughed and sat down on the ground. Muto kept up the laughter and jokes. After a few minutes, however, the laughter became forced and the jokes stale.

Several pilots dropped from the mission came up to us. They brought gifts, all they could find among their meager personal supplies: some cigarettes, candy, and bottles of soda. The gifts themselves were, of course, an expression of their attempt to cheer us up, to tell us of their regret that we, not they, had been selected for the fatal dives. The significance of this was not lost on us. Supplies at Iwo were almost totally exhausted, and we were sure that these sparse offerings meant that everything left among the other pilots was gone.

Their eyes were wide and sad, telling us more than could be said with inadequate words. Muto no longer joked. He sat silently, lost in his own thoughts. The very air seemed to crackle with the tension which had again arisen among us.

It was time to take off on the last mission.

The other three pilots came out of the tent, and we all walked down to the fighters. Standing alongside my plane, I looked at my parachute. Then, as one man, all nine pilots flung their chute packs onto the volcanic ash of the runway.

The Zero wouldn't start. I turned the engine switch back and forth, right and left. Finally she caught, vibrating badly. The engine was no good.

For two days this plane had fought in combat, and the stringent power demands of the dogfights had nearly burned the engine out. When I switched from one generator to the other, the propeller dragged almost to a stop, instead of slowing down slightly. Unless I used both generators the propeller stayed dead.

Normally I would never have attempted a take-off with a plane in this condition. But now? I was embarrassed. I looked at the other fighters. Mechanics were working on at least four of the other eight planes; my difficulties were not unique.

But who required a plane in perfect working order? Remember, Sakai, this is a one-way flight. You need cover only 450 miles in the air, not 900. You're not coming back from this mission. The engine's condition no longer seemed important. I waited for the fighter to warm up.

The eight bombers sped down the runway, one after the other. The first Zero moved into take-off position. I followed, taxiing slowly, my wingmen behind me.

On both sides of the runway the mechanics and other pilots stood at attention, their caps off, waving handkerchiefs as we thundered down the strip and into the air. We formed into our V's and turned toward the distant enemy fleet.

I felt drained of all emotion, cold and lifeless. I turned; Iwo Jima was a speck on the horizon, growing smaller as we bored through the air, dwindling to a dot on the vast ocean.

I felt so small. One man, in an insignificant fighter plane, and the ocean stretching endlessly below me.

I looked back again, barely able to make out Iwo. The horizon blurred and wavered before my eye. I felt dizzy and upset.

My mother's face, tenuous and filmy, filling the sky. A vision, but so real!

She smiled at me. She didn't know that soon I must die, that I was about to kill myself. I stared at her face. The vision faded slowly and disappeared.

A terrible loneliness gripped me. I was lost in an endless sea. Everywhere below me there was only water, with the sky above. The horizon was misty and unreal, blurred with distance.

I looked at the fighters in front of me, the bombers ahead and below. They did not seem to be moving, but were poised in midair, rocking gently, rising and dipping easily on the invisible swells of air. Was it all real?

I shook my head to clear away the fog. Music! Listen! A piano . . . the *Moonlight Sonata* . . . Hatsuyo had played that for me... .

Hatsuyo! Her face appeared .. . was it a vision? The music began to fade, then swelled louder and louder, crashing and thundering in my ears.

I had never told her. "Hatsuyo, I love you!" I cried. No one knew. No one but me. I thought of her . . . I turned back and looked for Iwo Jima. I saw only the endless ocean.

The music vanished. The sky was clear again. The drone of my engine beat strongly in my ears. The Zeros kept in perfect formation, precise, exact, moving together toward their flaming, blood-letting destiny.

The loneliness fled. You are too maudlin, Sakai, I cursed. You are a pilot. A Samurai. You wallow in your emotions. The mission . . . do what you must do!

I tried to plan the last moments in the air, the best method of diving into a carrier. What was the weakest spot? The stack; dive into the stack? Take all three fighters and plunge together at the thin hull at the waterline? Hope there would be planes lined up on the deck, their tanks filled with fuel, their bombs loaded? Dive into the planes, explode their bombs and fuel tanks, and in a split second transform nearly 30,000 tons of ship and thousands of men into a shrieking, fiery, bloody Hell?

The ocean flowed beneath me. The minutes passed quickly until we saw, far off to the right, a column of smoke, flayed by the wind, drifting slowly over the water. This was the first landmark, Pagan Island, jutting 300 feet from the water, a barren, hideous mass of volcanic rock, steaming and glowing with the heat of its fires far below the surface. It resembled the pictures of Hell I had seen in my Buddhist books when I was a child. It was ironic. The last piece of land I was to see in my life was bubbling, boiling, flaming, and hideous.

Forty minutes later black clouds appeared on the horizon before us. They towered many thousands of feet above the surface, lashed the sea below with high winds and torrential rains. I looked at the map. The enemy task force, as pin-pointed by our scouts, should be lying somewhere beneath those fierce squalls.

Now that we were so close, I thought of nothing but the warships cruising along beneath the storm. Everything except the ships and the dive I was to make was blotted from my mind. The old excitement was there, too. It was the same all over again! I thought only of combat, the ships, my plane, the dive, and the interceptors which might appear.

We were within the routine scouting radius of the enemy fighters. They might spot our formations at any moment. And the warships' radar were certain to have caught us in their scopes.

The eight bombers nosed down, our fighters close behind. At 16,000 feet we dropped into a thin cloud deck, were engulfed for several seconds in blinding white, then broke through and continued to descend.

At 13,000 feet something bright flashed in the sky. There . . . far ahead and several thousand feet above us. The brilliant flash was repeated. It could only be sunlight glancing off a plane's wing.

I saw the first fighter. A Hellcat, its broad body and wings unmistakable, dropping through the clouds. Another. More. How many were there? Look at them! Dropping through the clouds, one after the other, a seemingly endless column of the dangerous fighters. I fired a burst from my guns to warn the other pilots. The squadron leader and Muto banked their wings in response. The American radar had pin-pointed our position perfectly. The column of fighters descended from the clouds less than a mile ahead of us, and only half a mile above.

I counted the enemy planes as they ripped through the fluffy overcast. I lost count at seventeen. They saw us! The seventeenth fighter—the last one I had time to count—rolled abruptly to the left and dove. Immediately the other fighters swung around and screamed down at us.

Miura's words boomed at me. "*. . . refuse to accept battle . . . keep your planes together. . . .*"

Fine words. But how? Look at those fighters come! Hellcats were everywhere, many of them pulling out of their dives to attack from beneath our planes, even still more of them continuing to burst through the clouds to take us from above. A second column of more than twenty fighters pounced wildly on Muto's trio of fighters. Still another column, more than thirty planes, it seemed, came out of their dives, climbing rapidly, gunning for the bombers from beneath.

I held my breath as the Hellcats clawed into the bombers. In two blinding explosions the first and second bombers disappeared, blown into tiny pieces of wreckage as their torpedoes went off with shattering roars which shook my plane.

Now the Hellcats were within firing range of Muto's trio. The three Zeros sliced up into a wicked loop, evading the Hellcats. They did not attempt to return the fire, as they could have done. I pounded my fist helplessly against the glass. Muto had a dead shot! He could have rolled to the right and gunned two fighters from the air without even trying.

Another Hellcat column raced in against my formation. I hauled back on the stick, going up and around in a tight loop, my two wingmen sticking to me. The column was too long. We came out of the loop to find several fighters plunging in, their wings ablaze with their firing machine guns.

I rolled. Fast. More fighters. Another loop.

Twice.

Roll to the left!

Snap out of it. Here they come; how many are there?

Take her up and around.

"...*refuse to accept combat...*"

You can follow orders just so far. I could not follow mine. Not now. Not with the sky filled with Hellcats I could evade just so long and that would be all.

I snapped around in a tight turn at a diving Hellcat. He flew right into my shells. The fighter flipped wildly through the air and then dropped for the ocean, trailing a fast-growing plume of smoke.

I had no time to watch him go down. I kicked the rudder bar and yanked the stick over hard. Just in time. A Hellcat skidded crazily past the Zero. And still they came in, one after the other.

I didn't even have time to jettison the belly tank. Then the last of the column was past, dropping toward the ocean, beginning their long pull-outs to come back again. I jerked the toggle and the tank dropped free. I turned back. My wingmen were still with me. Good! They had followed my instructions to the letter, concentrating entirely on my plane, matching me turn for turn.

I was soaking wet. I tried to wipe the sweat away from my face. No time. All sixteen fighters of the column which had jumped my planes were out of their dives, skidding around in long climbing turns, coming back at us.

Again an eternity of diving, looping, skidding, rolling. Stick over, back, forward, right left. Kick the rudder bar. Skid her around. Bright, flashing tracers. They missed, and continued to miss. The American pilots had poor aim.

I glanced at the bombers. It was a slaughter: Slow, sluggish with their torpedoes, they wallowed helplessly in the air, unprotected by the Zeros which fought frantically to fend off the Hellcats.

A ball of fire disappeared in a searing burst of light. Another torpedo had exploded.

In less than a minute seven bombers were gone. Not even the fuselage or a whole wing of one plane remained. Seven bombers had disappeared in as many explosions.

The Zeros fared hardly any better. I saw two of our fighters engulfed in flame, swooping and rolling crazily. The pilots didn't even try to get out. They stayed with their fighters, burning to death.

I failed to see a single Hellcat in trouble. Except for the one fighter I had shot up, there were just as many of the Grummans in the air. We had little or no chance of evading combat by attempting to outmaneuver a horde of fighters which, it seemed, could match us turn for turn. The Hellcats were fully as agile as our own planes, much faster, and able to outclimb and out-dive us. Only the inexperience of their pilots saved us. Had they been better, every Zero would have been shot down in less than a minute. As it was, mine was the only Japanese formation to be seen anywhere in the sky. The Hellcats which had wiped out the other planes now joined the original sixteen fighters which had worked us over.

Flashing blue wings and white stars. Wings blazing with firing guns. Above us. Below us. To the right and to the left. Hellcats everywhere.

They reminded me of Lae, when twelve of us tried to shoot up a single bomber. We shredded our own formations in our eagerness to get at the enemy. Now the Hellcats were doing the same. Their organization was gone. They skidded wildly, frantically evading their own fire, trying to get out of the way of other pilots hungry for blood. I watched a fighter come at us, guns blazing, then forced to roll away as another Grumman sliced in from the side, paying no attention to the air space around him.

Their eagerness saved our lives. We flew in the middle of a tremendous Hellcat formation. The enemy fighters spent more time trying to avoid collisions than firing at us. But I saw no way of breaking off the fight. We were 400 miles from Iwo Jima, and still fifty miles or so from the American carriers which we had not yet seen and might not be able to find. Even if we did, how were we to break through more than sixty Hellcats, each of which was so much faster than the Zero?

Fate gave us a slim chance. The running air fight drifted toward a cumulus cloud hovering over the water.

A Hellcat flashed by, leaving an opening in the ranks of the circling fighters. I rolled over and shoved the stick forward, diving with full power into the protecting invisibility of the cloud. I glanced back. My two wingmen were still with me. For several minutes the world went mad. I saw nothing as the raging winds within the cloud flipped the Zero crazily. Then it was over. I was out, the fighter again in control. I turned to see two Zeros, far below my own plane, spinning wildly as they hurtled free. In a few seconds they were out of their spins and climbing to rejoin me.

The sky was clear of Hellcats. We had flung them off.

The irony of our survival! We had escaped almost insuperable odds, only to save ourselves to die. We reformed into a V and turned to the south again. We were relieved at our escape, but the immediate future justified no elation.

The clouds thickened as we drew nearer to the enemy fleet. They became thicker and thicker, and the airspace between the cloud bottoms and the ocean surface dwindled to a mere 700 feet.

Blinding sheets of rain fell with such force that at times the Zero heeled over dangerously on one wing, buffeted by the weight of the water pouring down like an avalanche. We had to keep going. The clouds dropped lower and lower toward the ocean. We were in a long, gradual descent, maintaining altitude directly beneath the storm base. Then we were only sixty feet above the surface, whipped into foaming whitecaps.

If anything, the storm increased its fury. The wind shrieked louder than the roar of the engine. The Zero buffeted and shook from the terrible force of the rain slamming against the wings and fuselage. For long moments the torrents blinded me, covering the windscreen with an impenetrable flood.

We could go no lower. We were blind now. I saw only sheets of rain all around me, forcing us toward the ocean surface; the water became indistinguishable from the rain. Another foot lower, and for all I knew, we would smash into the sea. Thirty minutes went by. The storm raged unabated. Still we saw nothing but rain and, at brief moments, the storm-blasted ocean surface. According to my map, I was supposed to be directly over the enemy task force. We had failed even to catch a glimpse of the vast fleet.

The sky grew darker. It was past 7:00 p.m. I was worried. Even if we succeeded in fighting through the rain, the fast-approaching darkness would hide the fleet from our sight. There was no moon at this time of the month.

I had to make a decision quickly. If we kept forging ahead, groping indefinitely in the darkness, the ocean surface blinded to us, our fuel would give out and we would crash without any hope of survival. A death without meaning, without purpose. . . .

I glanced back at the two fighters hugging my tail. What about those two men? They were following me without question, ready to accept whatever I chose. If I winged over and dove full speed into the water, they would be no more than a fraction of a second behind my plane when it crashed. Their fate lay in my hands, and the thought upset me.

What use to go on? To plunge into the ocean, to let the men back at Iwo *think* that either we had reached the enemy ships, or had been blown out of the air trying? Was that the course of honor?

No! I checked the compass and swung around in a wide turn, the two other Zeros close behind. I was not even sure of my location at the moment; we had fought wildly, fled into the cloud, and then wandered blindly through the storm. I might be anywhere over the water . . . even a 180-degree turn could send me due south, instead of back toward Iwo Jima. But I must turn, I must try!

Captain Miura's grim words came back to me. ". . . *you must dive against the enemy carriers together!*"

I almost turned back again to search for the ships. I was still an officer in the Imperial Navy, where orders were absolute. For any man to question those orders, just or unreasonable, was unheard of. Even if we made home, how could I again face the same wing commander who had sent me out on this mission?

It was a tremendous struggle. I was beside myself with indecision and anguish. I know now, years later, that I acted in the only sensible way. But even today I cannot describe in words the emotional struggle required to overcome the years of strict and brutal discipline, the lifelong adherence to orders. In those terrible moments in the Zero's cockpit, I fought successfully to break the chain of discipline and tradition.

Even if the three of us found the enemy ships, even if we penetrated the fighters, even if our dives were perfect, what could we accomplish with our three small, light fighter planes, without bombs, carrying only some cannon shells and machine-gun ammunition which would explode briefly and then be gone? These two young pilots behind me, trusting their lives to me, had shown outstanding skill in following me doggedly through the violent evasive maneuvers to escape the Hellcats. They had flown unflinchingly into the heart of a thunderhead, no mean feat in itself. They deserved a better fate than to sink in the wreckage of their planes beneath the ocean; they belonged in Japan, they deserved the opportunity to fly and fight again.

So my decision was made. But a long and dangerous flight lay ahead of us, filled with more dangers than I cared to face. There was the matter of orientation. Our engines were anything but in good operating shape. NAP 2/C Hajime Shiga's plane, especially, was in dangerous condition. The violent thermals within the thunderhead had torn the engine cowling clear off his plane. I waved for him to draw abreast of my own fighter, and he signaled by hand that his engine was faulty and might quit at any moment.

What could I tell him? I waved back for him to stay close to me. NAP 2/C Yji Shirai's plane was in better shape, and after Shiga's plane had taken its new position, he drew up on the other side.

A few minutes later I checked my course with the setting sun, now showing brilliantly through the broken clouds. We were past the squall; each passing minute took us into clearer and calmer air.

The minutes dragged on slowly. Again I was in the position dreaded by all fliers: over the ocean with darkness setting in, with no way to check with any accuracy my location, with fuel running low, and a destination which would be shrouded in darkness as a protection from marauding enemy bombers.

I marveled at the fighter's engine, which continued to beat with amazing regularity. One generator had burned out; the motor's continued operation was astounding.

I took no precaution to conserve fuel, as I had two years before when I limped home from Guadalcanal to Rabaul. I did not see how the overtaxed engine could function under such stringent conditions. By now I cared little if it failed. I was trying: that was enough. If the plane actually lost its power I would be spared the moment I dreaded more and more with every passing second. I would lose honor when I returned to Iwo Jima. That I appreciated only too well. The prospect of standing before Captain Miura terrified me.

Two hours after I had turned back for Iwo, the ocean was lost in total darkness. I saw absolutely nothing below me, only the stars which gleamed brightly in the sky. Nearly another hour went by. This was it. The fateful moment. If I had set the fighter on its correct course, Iwo should be below me now. If not . . . at least I would never feel the freezing embrace of the ocean when the Zero struck.

Several more minutes passed. I stared at the horizon, hoping to see something, a blur, a black shape lifting its outline against the stars. Something was there. Something big, black, irregular, rising steeply at one end. *Iwo!* We were back!

I nosed down, followed by Shiga and Shirai. Iwo lay shrouded in gloom, blacked out, as we circled overhead. Out of the darkness there appeared four weak lights. They were like blinding, wonderful beacons to me. Lantern lights, along the runway of the main strip. They flickered briefly in the signal to land. The men on the island had recognized the sound of our engines. A feeling of relief washed over me and I almost went limp with the sudden cessation of the strain which had been building up for almost three hours during the return flight.

Four lights barely showed the runway. Normally we used twenty, but the others had been destroyed by bombs. Four lights or forty, what did I care! After what we had been through, I felt I could have landed in darkness. Then I was down, taxiing off the runway as the two fighters landed behind me. The lights went out.

A crowd of pilots and mechanics ran toward our planes. For a moment I stared at them as they approached. I hardly felt able to face them. I dropped to the ground and walked to the Command Post. No one tried to stop me as I walked through the crowd, looking neither to the left nor to the right. Every man understood my feelings, and they stepped aside as I walked across the field, my two wingmen following.

In the darkness I stumbled against a body. I stepped back suddenly. There was no movement, no sound. "Who's that?"

I shouted. No reply. I approached the man who cowered on the ground. I could barely make out the pilot's uniform. I bent down to look at his face.

"*Muto!*"

The flier sat in dejection, his head resting on his arms. "Muto, were you wounded?"

The unhappy man lifted his head and looked at me. "No," he said slowly, "I wasn't wounded."

He rose to his feet and stared in wonder at Shiga and Shirai, who waited behind me. "You . . . you brought back your wingmen, too!" he gasped.

He stared at the ground, moaning. "Sakai . . . Sakai . . . spit on me, my friend. Spit on me."

Tears streamed down his face. "I was forced back," he cried in anguish. *"Alone!"*

On the ground before Muto were the gifts of the other pilots who had welcomed him when his lone fighter appeared over the ocean and landed on the island. Again the modest gifts—all the other men had in the world—testified to their attempts to cheer up the dejected pilot.

I grasped his shoulder. "I know how you feel, Muto. But nothing can be done now. It is too late. All that is over with. It is in the past."

I shook him slightly. "Muto." I pointed to the Command Post. "We—we will go in together."

He nodded. We could not look at each other. And then something snapped inside me. Suddenly cold anger at everything which had passed this terrible day gripped me. I thought of Muto, brilliant in the air, already an ace, willing to fight at any time, anywhere ... I thought of him weeping abjectly, sorrowful, fearing that he had shown himself a coward when he had been sent out on a fool's mission.

I swore that, no matter what happened, if any superior officer attempted to vent his wrath on the young pilot by beating him, I would throw all caution to the winds and throw myself on that man and reduce him to a pulp. I have no idea what brought on the sudden burst of anger. One moment I was fearing our audience with our superior, the next I seethed with rage.

Captain Miura sat impassively at his desk. He listened, intent on every word, as I told him what had occurred, of the swarms of Hellcats, of the burning fighters which never had a chance, of the bombers which exploded, one after the other, seven within a minute.

Miura lifted his eyes and looked deeply into mine. "Thank you, Sakai," he said quietly. That was all.

Then Muto spoke. Much of what he said, of course, was confirmation of my own words. Again the captain spoke but three words. "Thank you, Muto."

We saluted and stepped back. Captain Miura sat without moving a muscle of his body, his face dark, agony in his eyes. I felt grief for this man who had ordered his men on a mission doomed to failure before it began, but who had done so because he felt he had no other choice, because it was best for Japan. Right now, however, Captain Miura appeared only as a man grieving for the men—his men—who would never return.

Shiga and Shirai left the tent with us. A man ran after us; it was Commander Nakajima. He grasped my shoulders, relief on his face. "Sakai! " he exclaimed. "I despaired ever of seeing you again!"

"But—" I protested.

"You have no need for apologies," he interrupted before I could speak further. "Do you not think I know you so well, my friend? Every man on this island knows what happened today, that the only thing for you to do was to return. Don't scowl so! We will still have our chance, we will still strike back. It is good to have you here again, Saburo. Very good." Nakajima's words melted the ice in my heart. He understood, then. I was not alone with my feelings. But not even his kind words could drive away completely the anger which revolted me.

The other fliers ran up to us, offering cigarettes, candy, what food they had. Other men had gone ahead to the billet and rushed some warm food for us to eat. One after the other, the pilots came in with canned goods they had foraged somehow from other installations on the island.

We could only say our thanks, and refuse. I could never have forced a morsel down my throat.

An hour later an orderly rushed into the room, his chest heaving from the exertion of the long run from the radio shack. "A message just came through," he shouted, "from South Iwo. One of the bombers just landed there. The crew is safe! "

So another man in the air today had shared my feelings! The pilot had released his torpedo and run for it, fully aware that not in a thousand years could he have broken through the wall of fire thrown up by the Hellcats.

The news washed much of the tension away. It was good to know that Muto and I were not the only ones who had broken with the "unbreakable chain" of tradition and orders.

CHAPTER TWENTY-EIGHT

THE AMERICAN task force gave us little time to brood over our misfortunes. The day after our return from the ill-fated mission, the enemy greeted us with a thundering salvo from sixteen warships cruising off the island.

Breaking away from their fleet's main body, eight cruisers and eight destroyers steamed leisurely toward the island. After a few probing salvos of shells which burst with tremendous concussion on the island, the warships moved in at point-blank range.

For two days we cowered like rats, trying to dig ourselves deeper into the acrid volcanic dust and ash of Iwo Jima. For forty-eight hours the warships cruised slowly back and forth, their sides livid with flashing fire, belching forth masses of screaming steel which shook the island from one end to the other.

Never have I felt so helpless, so puny, as I did during those two days. There was nothing we could do, there was no way in which we could strike back. The men screamed and cursed and shouted, they shook their fists and swore revenge, and too many of them fell to the ground, their threats choking on the blood which bubbled through great gashes in their throats.

Virtually every last structure on Iwo Jima was tom to splintered wreckage. Not a building stood. Not a tent escaped. Not even the most dismal shack remained standing. Everything was blown to bits. The four fighter planes which had returned from our last sortie were smashed by shells into flaming pieces of junk.

Several hundred Army troops and naval personnel were killed, and many more injured. We were virtually without supplies. We were short on ammunition.

Iwo lay dazed and helpless. The men's ears rang shrilly from the ceaseless detonations of the thousands of shells which had shrieked onto the small island. There remained on hand to defend the vital island of Iwo Jima less than a battalion of Army troops.

These men walked about in shock, stupefied by the terrible bombardment they had suffered. Their brains were addled; they spoke incoherently.

Iwo Jima lay naked.

Equally dazed were the small group of naval fliers who had survived the terrifying shelling. We were few in number, but we were determined to defend our island against the invasion which every man believed was but perhaps hours away, perhaps days at the most. We formed a tiny "Iwo Marine Company" of pilots without planes. Our pathetic little group vowed to fight to the last man alongside the surviving Army troops. We received weapons and ammunition, and accepted the fact that our cause was lost.

How could we doubt our impending destruction? If the Americans had taken Saipan, which seemed likely by now, if they had absolute supremacy of the air, if their warships sneered at our fleet and cruised insolently up and down off Iwo Jima, were they not able to storm our few defenses?

Iwo Radio kept calling frantically for reinforcements from Yokosuka. We begged for more fighters. We begged for anything which could fly! Yokosuka could do nothing. The thirty Zero fighters which we had flown to Iwo Jima were all the fighter planes available. There were no more. Chaos reigned within the high command in Tokyo.

Glad cries and shouts of happiness awoke us one morning shortly after the usual devastating bombardment. The Navy could spare us no planes, but we were not forgotten. Several transport ships appeared over the horizon, making for the island. We ran down to the shore, shouting and laughing at the unexpected good fortune, only to see the ships erupt in geysers of flame and water, sunk before our very eyes by American submarines which had waited in anticipation of just such a move.

That last catastrophe was decisive. It was obvious to us all that we could offer only token resistance, that within an hour or two after a landing the Americans would control Iwo. Who then, of all the men on the forsaken hump of volcanic ash, with its bubbling sulphur springs, could have foreseen the actual turn of events? Who among us would have dared to prophesy that the Americans would throw away their priceless opportunity to take the island with minimum casualties on their side? We felt we had but a few days in which to remain alive.

The Americans did not come. Every hour of the day lookouts posted from one end of the island to the other, searching the sea from Mt. Suribachi, looked for the invasion fleet. From time to time a nervous lookout would imagine he saw something on the ocean surface and would sound the alarm. Bells, bugles, sticks beat against drums, anything and everything which could make noise broke the quiet of the island with a terrific clamor. We would rush from our cots, grim-faced, ready to fight, clutching our weapons, but nothing ever hap-

We did not know, of course, that the Americans already had turned for the Philippines. They did not return to Iwo Jima for another eight months. Eight months during which Lieutenant General Tadamachi Kuribayashi moved onto the island, bringing with him 17,500 soldiers, as well as nearly 6,000 naval personnel. He built Iwo Jima into a mighty fortress, buttressed with pillboxes, powerful cave defenses, elaborate tunnels. He poured men onto the island until Iwo Jima could contain no more.

(Many of Japan's military leaders stated later that the war would have ended sooner if the Americans had attacked Iwo Jima in July of 1944, instead of waiting so long to do so. To these men the Philippines invasion was a vast and costly operation, highly successful for the Americans, but an insignificant campaign which did little to hasten the defeat which was already in sight.

(The long-expected invasion came finally on February 19, 1945, in the form of a stupendous gathering of military strength. According to the United States Navy, that invasion force required a total of 495 ships, including seventeen aircraft carriers. The official American government information stated further that the incredible number of 1,170 fighters and bombers was employed against Iwo Jima.

(A total of 75,144 American fighting men engaged in the most bitter struggle of the entire war in their attempt to take the island. Of these, the Americans counted 5,324 men killed, as well as 16,000 wounded. The island was not declared secure until March 16, when the last Japanese defenders were killed.)

After several false invasion alarms, a message from Yokosuka astounded us. The Yokosuka command informed us that all staff officers and pilots were to return to Japan by courier planes which were already on their way to us.

The unexpected reprieve elated the fliers. We had been prepared to die fighting on the ground ... and now life was offered us again! We dropped our guns and ran to the main strip to join with the mechanics and other ground personnel in filling the hundreds of craters which pitted the runway.

We had never expected a miracle of this nature, and so had made no attempt to repair the field after the July 4 debacle. I was among the fliers turned coolie, and went at my labors with feverish determination. Not all the men were pleased, of course. There were those who would remain behind. The maintenance crews, for example, as well as the Army garrison. Not one man among them spoke a word against the decision to leave them behind, but their faces indicated clearly their envy and, as was to be expected, often their resentment.

Late that afternoon the first of the courier planes landed. They were obsolete bombers, which sneaked in low over the water, one by one, to escape detection by the radar of any American ships which might be prowling the area. Yokosuka was taking no chances. It was fortunate indeed for us that no American fighters appeared during the landing and departure of the courier planes. Seven twin-engined bombers arrived to take back the men selected to return to Japan.

Even here the military caste system was rigidly adhered to. Not even our desperate plight could negate centuries of tradition. Each evacuee filed into a bomber in the order of his rank. No other factor was considered.

My own group of eleven noncommissioned officers and enlisted men were left behind. There were so many officers of higher rank before us that no room was left. We stared hollowly as the last plane lurched into the air and headed for Japan.

The next day a single plane returned to the island to pick us up. I gaped in disbelief at the flying wreck which staggered onto the runway. Not only was the plane obsolete, but it was so badly in need of repair that it seemed impossible for it to fly. The plane had barely managed to reach Iwo. With the eleven of us aboard, it reeled and swerved dangerously down the runway. It could not reach flying speed, and the pilot taxied back, one engine spitting and belching forth clouds of smoke.

For two hours the mechanics worked silently to repair the bad engine. The two hours were like weeks to us. We kept looking at the sky, afraid that Hellcats would burst out of the blue to pour tracers into the weary old plane. A single fighter could doom us to remain on the island.

Finally the mechanics were through, and the engine turned over as smoothly as its battered parts would allow. The ground crew looked so forlorn as we climbed aboard that I turned and called to them, "We'll be back! And soon, with new fighters!"

They waved to us, afraid to entertain any hope. None of them dreamed that for nearly eight months Iwo would be ignored by the enemy.

We were airborne only ten minutes when the airplane shook violently. A steady vibration rattled our teeth. I looked out the window at the right engine, which vibrated and shook wildly in its mountings. How was this incredible old junk pile going to carry all of us 650 miles to Japan?

The copilot, a youngster about twenty years of age, walked back through the cabin. "Warrant Officer Sakai? Sir, could you come forward and help us out?" He was pale and shaking almost as badly as the airplane.

I knew the answer before he had finished speaking. "Turn around," I snapped. "With that engine we'll never make Japan. You'll have to go back for some more repair work."

The crew obeyed me at once. Back at Iwo, we had a long, worried inspection of the troublesome engine. It looked like fouled plugs. We inserted new spark plugs and took off again.

The bomber cruised steadily toward Japan. But our worries were far from over. An hour and a half later we were in the middle of a violent rainstorm. Sheets of water battered heavily at the flying wreck. The plane leaked like a sieve. The copilot returned again and asked me if I would come forward.

The pilot was hardly any older—twenty-two at the most. "Sir? Should we try to go over the cloud deck or fly beneath it?"

"Take it below," I ordered.

The storm continued without letup, at times hemming us in to zero visibility. It was fully as bad as the storm I had encountered only days before, trying to find the American task force off Saipan. The bomber skidded wildly, plunged up and down in the murderous air currents.

We went lower and lower until the pilot was skimming directly over the foaming water.

Beads of sweat dripped down his face. He was becoming panicky. In desperation he turned his pale face to me and bleated plaintively, "Sir, where are we now? "

That was the silliest question I had ever heard from a pilot. For a few seconds I was speechless with astonishment. "Get out of that seat! I'm taking over!" I shouted. He wasted no time in clambering out of his seat to relinquish the controls.

It was dead reckoning all the way. For another ninety minutes I flew blind, fighting the sluggish plane through the winds and rain. Then the familiar peninsulas south of Tokyo Bay hove into view.

Cries of jubilation shook the bomber as the crew and passengers cheered.

We landed at the Kisarazu Bomber Base across the bay from Yokosuka. I looked around at the broad airfield. Japan! I was home again! On my own soil! There had been so many times when I was convinced that never again would I see my country. What a difference from Iwo Jima, only a few hours' flight from here!

To me and to the ten other men who had come out of the volcanic Hades behind us, the pure and sweet water of Japan seemed the most desirable thing on earth, water which did not have the horrible, gritty taste of the collected rain on Iwo. Every one of us ran across the field to an open pipeline by the control tower. We turned the faucet on and let the cool liquid gush forth. I drank and drank, enjoying immensely the feel and taste of the water as it washed down my throat and into my body.

But Iwo Jima was too close behind me. Muto and I must have thought of the same thing together, for suddenly we could drink no more. We both thought of our friends who had died only a few days before from wounds inflicted by the shells pouring onto the island, spitting out volcanic dust and crying to us in their agony, "Water! Water!" begging for the water of which there had been none.

CHAPTER TWENTY-NINE

A month after my return to Yokosuka I was promoted to the rank of ensign. After eleven years I had reached the status of a regular officer. It was an all-time record in the Navy.

Several men who died in the midget submarine attack against Pearl Harbor received double promotions and were moved up to officer rank, ten years after their enlistment. Their award, however, was more in keeping with tradition, since the promotions were posthumous. I was the first Japanese enlisted man to achieve my memorable regular officer's status—alive—within the space of eleven years.

Muto and I were reassigned to the Yokosuka Air Wing. We were not to be sent back to Iwo Jima; so acute was the shortage of pilots and planes that the high command was forced to leave the island without air protection for many months to come.

That the Philippines were now destined for invasion was clearly apparent, and a flow of planes and pilots bolstered our forces in the islands. We saw Commander Nakajima off when he left for his new post at Cebu.

My new assignment included a welcome change from the disastrous beatings we had suffered at Iwo Jima. In addition to my training duties with new fliers, I was made a test pilot.

The high command had ordered mass production of new fighter planes to replace the Zero. Even the most obstinate staff officer could not deny that the once-mighty Zero had lost its sting, that the enemy's new fighters far outclassed us in the air. In the Marianas and other sea-air engagements, the Grumman F6F Hellcat had clearly established its superiority in almost every performance respect.

From the South Pacific came disturbing reports of new models of the Lockheed P-38 Lightning which were great improvements over the first F-38s to enter combat late in 1942. With new engines, the Lightnings had gained greatly in all-around performance. Once the big twin-boomed fighter was brought into a dogfight, the Zero's superior maneuverability gave our pilots an excellent chance. Otherwise, the Lightning's great speed, its sensational high-altitude performance, and especially its ability to dive and climb much faster than the Zero presented insuperable problems for our fliers. For the P-38 pilots, flying at great heights, chose when and where they wanted to fight... with disastrous results for our men.

No less troublesome was the Corsair, a powerful gull-winged American Navy fighter which operated mostly from land bases. Not as maneuverable as the Hellcat, the Corsair nevertheless was much faster than the Zero and had tremendous diving speed.

Our Army pilots in Burma reported encountering another new enemy plane, the P-51 Mustang, which outperformed the Zero on an even greater range. The Mustangs made their combat debut as escorts for the four-engined Liberator bombers in November of 1943, and the performance of the new models was simply astounding. The Army pilots flying the Hayabusa (Oscar) were outflown and outfought consistently by the sleek American plane.

And it was only too obvious to all that we were totally unprepared for the great Superfortresses which had first struck at Kyushu from their China airfields. The light Army fighters which intercepted these planes were woefully ineffective against the fast, heavily armed, armored bombers. If the B-17 had been a formidable opponent, the B-29 was insuperable.

Now that the Marianas were in American hands, and rapidly being transformed into great airfields, all Japan expected heavy attacks by the B-29s.

The defensive concepts adapted by the high command came too late, and were also inadequate. The majority of our fighters were Zeros, well adapted to our offensive tactics earlier in the war, but virtually useless against the B-29s. Most of our bomber pilots still flew the Mitsubishi Betty, now too old, too slow, and possessed of the unhappy trait of exploding violently into flame under enemy fire.

The loss of Saipan furnished the impetus to discard the cobwebs in our planning. The high command screamed for the new fighters, designed specifically to overcome the Zero's shortcomings.

In September I began test-flying two new fighter planes. The Shiden (Lightning in Japanese), known by its code name of George to the enemy, was designed as an interceptor to outfight the Hellcat. It lacked the Zero's range and was heavier, but it possessed great speed and four 20-mm. cannon. It afforded pilots safety through armor plating and excellent structure. I found it surprisingly maneuverable for its heavy weight; it gained this flexibility partially through an automatic flap system.

Unfortunately, the Shiden's flight characteristics were treacherous and demanded an experienced pilot. Too many men with little time behind the controls of fighter planes never lived to fly the Shiden into combat. Their familiarization flights killed them.

The Raiden (Thunderbolt in Japanese), called Jack by the Americans, was designed specifically to fight heavy bombers like the B-29. For this purpose its performance was excellent, and many of our pilots compared the airplane to Germany's great Focke-Wulf FW-190 fighter. Four 20-mm. cannon gave the Raiden an excellent punch against a bomber, and its ability to fly at more than 400 miles an hour—extraordinary in those days—overcame the Zero's trouble in this respect. Even with its cannon and heavy steel armor plate, the Raiden could outclimb the Zero.

It was well suited to bomber attack but, like the Shiden, demanded high skill from its pilots. The overemphasis on speed and armament made the plane loggy in aerobatics. Compared to the Zero in this respect, it flew like a truck. We suffered appalling losses in training. Later, when the Hellcats and Mustangs roamed over Japan proper, those pilots in Raidens who opposed the enemy fighters discovered all too late the airplane's inability to maneuver.

Moreover, the production of these new models proved painfully slow. Despite the orders of the high command, the old Zero remained our fighter mainstay.

The test pilot assignment afforded me the opportunity once again to visit with my family. I left Yokosuka early one Sunday morning to travel to my uncle's house, passing through Tokyo on the way.

During my absence, the city had deteriorated further. Although no bombings had occurred since the Doolittle attack of 1942, the city appeared drab and lifeless. Most of the stores were closed, their windows empty. The significance of this was clear. There were no goods to sell, and the owners were away, working in war plants. The few stores which remained open hardly resembled the colorful and well-stocked establishments I once knew. Few goods were on display, and for the most part these were crude substitutes. The Allied blockade of Japan was pinching the national stomach severely.

Often I passed official demolition crews tearing down long stretches of buildings and private homes. Hundreds of men ripped and broke up buildings in order to clear wide firebreaks in the heart of the city, in anticipation of the bombings which all Japan feared. The families being forced from their homes stood in small groups on the street, watching with sorrowful faces as the labor gangs ripped their homes to pieces.

I had seen bombing before. To me the demolition work was no more than a pitiful attempt, a wasted effort which would do little good against masses of incendiary bombs. Tokyo's wooden homes and commercial buildings would flare up like matchboxes.

Most of the men on the streets wore overalls, or the wartime civilian standard suit, patterned after military uniforms. Not once did I see a single woman wearing her "Sunday Best," the colorful kimonos of prewar days. Instead, they were attired in black slacks, in the drab and nondescript Monpe, baggy and colorless kimono pants.

Nearly every street corner had its long queues of women and children, shuffling patiently in line as they waited for rations. The shortage of wholesome food was obvious. Faces were pinched and bleak, eloquent testimony to the ersatz food being forced on the civilians.

Tokyo was depressingly morbid, and I could not get out of the city quickly enough. Not everything had changed. Corner radios blasted at the ears painfully, trumpeting war songs and chanting phony victories. Posters marred the faces of buildings everywhere in the city, exhorting the people to greater production, to bear with the shortages until Japan won the war.

I felt ill at ease. Never had I dreamed I would see such abject misery in the faces of my own people.

I waited for several minutes before the door to my uncle's home. Someone was playing the piano . . . it could only be Hatsuyo. I listened for a while, hearing the first music in months.

The music stopped when I knocked at the door. I heard Hatsuyo running to greet me.

Her smile was a beam of sunshine. "Saburo! Oh, how wonderful you look!" she exclaimed. For several moments she stared at me. "We all prayed for your return, Saburo," she said quietly. "We have been most fortunate. Here you are again, well, and an officer."

The familiar house was the same. It was still a home to me, more welcoming than any others because of Hatsuyo. "You look beautiful," I said, "the most beautiful thing I have seen in many long months. But why are you so dressed up? You look radiant," I marveled. She wore a tasteful kimono dress, every line neat and perfect on her slim body.

She laughed at me. "Saburo, sometimes you are a fool! Don't you know that this is a special occasion? I have kept this dress waiting for you, waiting patiently to wear it when I received a newly commissioned officer." She smiled. "Here; see these sleeves? I must apologize for the kimono, my cousin." The sleeves had been cut to half length.

"The government has ordered us to cut off the long dancing sleeves," she cried gaily, whirling about the room with her arms out before her. "Don't you know," she whispered in mock seriousness, "that the dancing sleeves are unfit for the emergency!"

I smiled at her. "Hatsuyo, where is everyone?" I asked. "Isn't the family at home?"

She shook her head. "Only I am here to welcome you, Saburo. Father will be out the rest of the day. He has volunteered for home defense work, and is receiving his refresher training in the Army Reservists Corps at a high school nearby. Michio will be working overtime in his factory tonight."

Her face clouded. "Mother is out, too, Saburo. She is trying to buy something for you, from . . . from the black market.

She wants so much to have something special to welcome you!"

I stared at Hatsuyo. If my aunt were caught, she would be in serious trouble with the police. "Why did she do that?" I gasped. "Doesn't she know what could happen to her?"

"I know, I know, Saburo. But she wanted so much to make your welcome more pleasant! "

I shook my head. "Well, let us hope that everything is all right. I should have told her when I called that none of the men ever visit a civilian home today without bringing their own meals." I showed her my lunchbox, as well as gifts I had purchased from the Yokosuka Post Exchange.

Hatsuyo was embarrassed. One does not normally bring home toilet necessities as gifts. "Thank you, Saburo," she blushed. "Times are not normal, and I. . . thank you."

She quickly changed the subject. "Come here and sit down, Saburo. Now, tell me everything that has happened since we last saw you. What happened at Iwo Jima? We have heard nothing on the radio, except that there has been terrible fighting at Saipan."

I stammered clumsily. We were under strict orders not to discuss what had happened at Iwo Jima. The catastrophe suffered by our forces was classified as top secret, and no one outside of the military knew what really had taken place.

I changed the subject, talking excitedly about the new interceptors I had flown in tests. "If we have enough of these new fighters, we may be able to turn the tide," I said. "They have marvelous speed, and their four cannon should be enough to destroy any plane flying." This was not exactly true, I realized. If things kept up at the training fields, with the student pilots crashing daily, we'd have precious few of the new planes to get into the air when the time for combat arrived.

A half hour went by while we discussed everything but the subject which interested me most. I stole side glances at Hatsuyo, studying her profile, watching the way she talked, the way her eyes shone when she became excited, the way she moved her arms, her poise in walking, the way her cheeks wrinkled when she smiled.

I talked with Hatsuyo, but I spoke without paying any attention to the words. I was in love with her, I wanted to tell her how I felt, I wanted to shout the pent-up words. More than two months ago, when it seemed I was only minutes away from eternity, when Iwo Jima faded over the horizon and I saw a vision of Hatsuyo, I vowed that, if by some miracle I lived, I would tell her my feelings.

Now ... I couldn't! Nothing had changed. I was still a pilot, even if I had achieved officer's status. I knew I would fly in combat again, and the burning Zeros I had seen falling before the Hellcats' guns left a fiery imprint on my mind. I knew the odds were against me, that the very next time I flew into battle I could be one of those men hurtling toward earth, out of control, burning alive.

Then, suddenly, she interrupted me. "Saburo," she spoke quietly, "did you know that Fujiko-san has been married?"

I hadn't known. "After it was all over," she continued, "Fujiko-san married a pilot. A flier. Like yourself," she added defiantly.

I started to speak, but she went on. "Saburo, why aren't you married yet? You are no longer a youngster, you know. You are twenty-seven years of age. You have become someone. You are an officer now. You should take a wife."

"But, I tell you, Hatsuyo, I don't know any women I like that much!" I protested.

"Didn't you love Fujiko-san?"

I didn't know what to say. A clumsy silence settled over us. Hatsuyo walked across the room and turned on the radio, tuning in to the afternoon symphonic hour. The music eased the awkwardness of the moment.

She returned and sat by me again. "Well," she smiled, "perhaps, Saburo, we should recommend some young women who would better suit your taste."

Hatsuyo was making me uncomfortable. She refused to look away, but stared directly into my eyes. I became flustered and started to speak, but could only stammer.

I rose quickly and walked to the window, staring out. The beautiful flowers were gone. Vegetables had replaced them, I noticed.

"There are many women as beautiful as Fujiko-san, Saburo," Hatsuyo said. She had walked after me and now stood almost directly behind me.

"Hatsuyo!" I shouted, whirling around, "I don't want to talk about it again. Please!" My outburst startled her. "We've talked this over so many times. The facts don't change. Nothing has changed. I am a flier, don't you understand? Every time I go up, there is the chance that I will never return! Every time! Sooner or later it is certain to happen. Sooner or later!"

I was upset and distressed. Why did she have to talk about marriage again? I hated myself for the way I was talking, I hated myself for not telling her how I felt.

"There is not a pilot today who does not expect to die, Hatsuyo," I explained. "Our luck has to run out. Skill has nothing to do with it. It is.."

"You talk like a child. Saburo." Her eyes flashed in anger. She spoke so quietly I could hardly hear her. "You prattle on and on, and you know nothing of what you're saying. You do not know a woman's heart."

She raised her arms in exasperation. "You talk of flying, of dying, Saburo. You talk of nothing else. You do not talk of living!"

She stalked away, turning off the radio with an angry gesture. She ignored me and sat before the piano, her fingers moving idly over the keys.

I was speechless. For several minutes I stood rooted in one spot, unable to speak a word. Finally I caught my voice again. "Hatsuyo, I—I don't know. Maybe, if...Is it my fault, can I help it if we are in a war?" I cried. "Why do you always talk like this?

"It is enough for me to see you here, in this house," I went on. "I want—oh, I don't know," I stammered. "All I want to know, all I wish is that you will live long and happily."

She slammed her hands down on the keys and whirled around. "I don't want to live long! What is it to live long and—and ..." she placed her hand over her heart, "to be empty in here? None of us, here at home—or even a flier—can live forever. Don't you understand that, Saburo?"

Her anger startled me. "A woman is happy," she spoke in a hush, "only if she lives with the man she loves. Even—even if it's for a few days and no more."

She turned away bitterly, venting her anger on the piano. I stood transfixed, utterly at a loss as to what to say or do.

CHAPTER THIRTY

ON OCTOBER 27, ten days after the first American troops stormed ashore on the Philippines, Imperial Headquarters issued this historic communique:

"The Shikishima Unit of the *Kamikaze* Special Attack Corps, at 1045 hours on 25 October 1944, succeeded in a surprise attack against the enemy task force, including four aircraft carriers, thirty nautical miles northeast of Suluan, Philippine Islands. Two Special Attack planes plunged together into an enemy carrier, causing great fires and explosions, and probably sinking the warship. A third plane dove into another carrier, setting huge fires. A fourth plane plunged into a cruiser, causing a tremendous explosion which sank the vessel immediately afterward."

This was the thunderous beginning of the *Kamikazes*. The first suicide mission was led by Lieutenant S. G. Yukio Seki, who flew at the head of five Zero fighters, each carrying a 550-pound bomb. Seki was a bomber pilot with less than 300 hours flight time; the other four pilots had logged no more hours in the air. Yet, of the five, only one plane missed its target in the death dive.

Four Zero fighters provided escort for the five bomb-carrying aircraft. I discovered later that the flight leader of the escort group was my friend Hiroyoshi Nishizawa, by then a Warrant Officer. Nishizawa adroitly avoided interception by more than twenty prowling Hellcats, taking his nine planes through the wild storms to reach the enemy fleet.

After the dives of the five *Kamikaze* planes, Nishizawa returned with his flight to his base at Mabalacat on Cebu, and reported the mission as an outstanding success.

Everywhere in the Navy, pilots talked about the unprecedented attack. And it had been carried out with such brilliant results, by contrast with our disastrous losses at Iwo Jima. As a fighter pilot I was never inclined to approve of suicide missions, but now there was no denying the tremendous blow which had been struck at the American fleet off the Philippines. Even I had to acknowledge the fact that the suicide dives appeared to be our only means of striking back at the American warships.

From that day on, *Kamikaze* became a byword of our language, a term which assumed new meaning. We knew every time the *Kamikaze* planes took off that our men were going to die. Many of them never even reached their objectives, blasted from the sky by the enemy interceptors and the incredible walls of antiaircraft fire thrown up by the ships.

But there were always those which did get through, which plummeted like avenging spirits from the sky, sometimes with wings tom off, at other times engulfed in flames. One after the other, sometimes in pairs, often as many as six, ten, and sixteen, they roared off their runways for the last time, then plunged into their objectives.

The *Kamikazes* gave us tremendous new strength. Their effectiveness was obvious in the number of enemy warships and transports, once inviolate from our attacks, safe behind their ' withering firepower, which now resounded with the roar of flaming gasoline, exploding bombs, the shrieks of men. The *Kamikazes* ripped aircraft carriers from stem to stem, sinking more than all our combined weapons had been able to destroy. They split open cruisers and destroyers, and exacted a terrible toll.

To the enemy our men seemed to be committing suicide.

They were throwing their lives away uselessly. Perhaps it will never be fully understood by Americans, or anyone in the Western world, that our men did not consider that they were throwing away their lives. On the contrary, the *Kamikaze* pilots volunteered en mass for their one-way missions.

This was not suicide! These men, young and old, were not dying in vain. Every plane which thundered into an enemy warship was a blow struck for our land. Every bomb carried by a *Kamikaze* into the fuel tanks of a giant carrier meant that many more of the enemy killed, that many more planes which would never bomb and strafe over our soil.

These men had faith. They believed in Japan, in striking a blow for Japan with their lives. It was a cheap price to pay; , one man, perhaps, against the lives of hundreds or even thousands. Our country no longer had the means to base its strength on conventional tactics. We were no longer possessed of such national power. And a man, every one of these men, who surrendered his mortal soul was not dying. He passed on life to those who remained.

Again, however, it was a case of too little and too late. Not even the stupendous toll reaped by the Kamikazes could halt the terrible power amassed by the Americans. They were too mighty, too many, too advanced. There were too many ships and planes and guns and men.

Perhaps our men who flew for the last time realized this. It is difficult to believe that many of those who flew the Kamikazes did not recognize the hopelessness of Japan's position in the war.

They did not flinch, they did not hesitate. They flew their bomb-laden planes, and died for their country.

There were other developments of more ominous significance for our people.

One of the great B-29s soared over Tokyo for the first time on November 1, 1944, flying to Japan from the new bases on Saipan. The dreaded moment for the people of the capital city was almost at hand, for it was obvious that the tremendous bomber was but a reconnaissance plane, paving the way for others to follow in the near future. The Superfortress cruised leisurely high over Tokyo, and Army and Navy fighters scrambled frantically to intercept the raider. They failed to get close enough to fire a single shot.

On November, and again on the seventh, single B-29's from Saipan visited Japan. For the second and third times, fighter planes scrambled into the air and vainly struggled to reach the great height at which the B-29s cruised. The high command spluttered angrily and cursed the pilots for being so clumsy and inept in the air. "One plane!" they thundered, "one plane, and we can do nothing!"

They did not understand the difficulties of intercepting the Superfortresses at that height. For one thing, our fighters did not have the rate of climb which would allow them to reach more than 30,000 feet in the few minutes available between the time the alarm was received and the time the bombers departed. Even had they reached the more than six miles, the pilots doubted their ability to slug it out with the B-29s, which had amazing speed.

In December the long-awaited blows came. Tokyo, Osaka, Nagoya, Yokohama, and the other great cities of our country reeled beneath the terrible assault of waves of bombers. They went after the aircraft plants in particular, and devastated factory after factory. Too often the flow of new fighters died to a trickle. Spare parts became more and more difficult to find.

The history of the terrible fire raids launched against Japan's greatest cities has been documented in the greatest detail. It is a story well known to the world.

The Superfortresses came at night, and most of the Japanese pilots sat helplessly on the ground cursing the lack of night fighters, the lack of training for night combat. Except for a few fighter planes, which did no more than to annoy the nocturnal raiders, the enemy planes were harassed only by antiaircraft fire.

Everywhere we were losing. Everywhere we were forced to fall back, to retreat. Our air units were being slashed to ribbons, their planes falling in droves, the pilots not dying singly or by twos or threes, but by the dozens. By mid-January our ability to defend the Philippines had vanished. Literally every Japanese warplane in the islands was gone—either shot out of the air by the American fighters it engaged, or expended in the *Kamikaze* attacks, which continued until no planes were left.

Now we were concerned not with the islands, but with the defense of the homeland itself. We knew the B-29s, even with their terrible power to bum and destroy entire cities, were not the last word. More planes, other types of planes, would come.

On January 20, the Imperial Navy organized a new fighter wing—the last of the war—at Matsuyama on Shikoku Island. When I transferred to the new air base, I found Commander Nakajima assigned to the wing as its deputy commander. He had fled the Philippines with fifty fighter pilots to help staff the new group. This was no ordinary wing of fighters; we had the best men in Japan. Our wing commander was Captain Minoru Genda, considered one of the most brilliant naval strategists Japan has ever produced.

Nakajima was the only man I knew personally. When the opportunity presented itself, I dropped into his office to talk about the men we had fought with in the past. It was he who stunned me with the news of Nishizawa's death.

"He was lost," Nakajima said, "under deplorable circumstances on October 26, the day after the first *Kamikaze* attack against the American warships.

"Nishizawa volunteered for the *Kamikaze* mission on the second day, after he had returned from his escort flight of the first five planes to dive into the enemy fleet. He told me that he was convinced that he would soon die. It was strange," Nakajima mused, "but Nishizawa insisted that he had a premonition. He felt he would live no longer than a few days.

"I wouldn't let him go. A pilot of such brilliance was of more value to his country behind the controls of a fighter plane than diving into a carrier, as he begged to be permitted to do." Nakajima described how Nishizawa's fighter was armed with a 550-pound bomb and manned by NAP 1/C Tomisaku Katsumata. At least Nishizawa had the benefit of knowing that his plane had fulfilled the mission he wanted to fly. Katsumata plunged directly onto the deck of an American carrier off Surigao, exploding the fuel tanks of planes waiting for take off, turning the carrier into a raging furnace.

That same day Nishizawa took off in an old, unarmed DC-3 transport to fly himself and several other pilots to Clark Field, where they could pick up some Zero fighters. The transport took off early on the morning of October 26 from Mabalacat. It was never heard from again.

"Only one thing could have happened," Nakajima reflected. "His plane must have been caught by the Hellcats operating in that area. Unarmed and flying an old transport, he didn't have a chance. Most likely he went down somewhere over Cebu. I still find it hard to believe, Saburo, that such a great pilot had to die like that, helpless, unable to fight. . . ."

There was nothing to say. So Nishizawa, too, was gone. The Devil, the scourge of enemy planes at Lae and Rabaul, had gone the same way as Sasai and Ota and all the others.

"If anything, Nishizawa fought even harder in the Philippines," Nakajima said. "He no longer bothered to count his victories in the air!"

Nishizawa was like that. Nakajima believed that he had shot down more than 100 enemy planes in the air combat. There was no question, either to Nakajima or myself or to any man who knew and who had fought with him, that Nishizawa was Japan's greatest ace, a pilot of unparalleled skill and ability. And he had been killed flying an unarmed transport plane! The news of his death affected me strangely. I returned to my quarters and took out pen and paper. At least, I thought, I would A not die without first saying to Hatsuyo what I had longed to say, what I felt she wanted also to know.

"I have been reassigned to combat duty," I wrote. "From this day on we shall be fighting against what appear to be overwhelming odds. Today I heard that my very close friend, Hiroyoshi Nishizawa, was killed in the Philippines. Nishizawa was the greatest pilot our country has ever known. I feel that if he has met his end, then I, handicapped by the loss of an eye, am certain to follow him soon.

"Perhaps this letter will be the last one I shall ever write to you. It is impossible to tell, Hatsuyo. But I cannot wait any longer to tell you what I have wanted to say for so long.

"The last time we spoke, you told me I did not understand a woman's heart. You were wrong, Hatsuyo. So very wrong.

"Do you recall our days as children together? Those were wonderful times, filled with fun and laughter. You and I lived as sister and brother, and even then our fondness for each other was strong.

"What I have long wished to tell you, Hatsuyo, was that in my heart you have been the dearest person on this earth to me.

I know now that I have looked upon you as my only love. Perhaps it is wrong to say so, perhaps it is not the way I would like it to be said, but I believe you were always there in my heart.

I did not know it then as I have known it for these last months.

"I have long loved you, Hatsuyo, and loved you deeply. There has been no outward sign from me to you, although this has been the hardest thing in my life ... to keep away from you the way I really felt. I love you now. I have waited so long to tell you these words! The war has created a great barrier between us. I realize that my feelings have never been shown, that this love I have for you has been throttled and kept inside.

"We are, after all, cousins. Perhaps it is best for both of us that marriage lies beyond our grasp. But now I have said what was necessary. I pray for only one thing, my love. May you live long, and may happiness be yours forever."

The next morning our combat training began in earnest. The pilots shouted uproariously when they watched the dozens of gleaming new fighters landing on the field—the Shiden, the airplane which I had test-flown not too long ago. The men went wild with joy as they took the fighters off the ground. Speed! Four cannon! Armor plate! Tremendous climb! Diving speed! Maneuverability!

It was all there, all wrapped up in one fighter plane. This was no longer the Zero, outclassed in almost every respect by the Hellcat. The pilots couldn't wait to return to the air; they wanted to know every trick their planes had, everything they could do. Their morale soared to new heights. "Bring on the Hellcats!" they shouted. They were out for blood again.

The majority of the fliers in the new wing were veterans of many battles. There were aces among their ranks. We were the elite of all the fighter units in the Imperial Navy, which was why we had been supplied the new planes. Despite the impelling need for volunteers in the *Kamikaze* units, these men together were the strongest air weapon Japan had produced, and Commander Nakajima rejected all applications for transfer to the *Kamikaze* operations.

Adore than ten days had passed without a reply to my letter to Hatsuyo. I could not understand why she failed to answer me. There was nothing I could do; I could not afford to allow sentiment to interfere with my duties, especially now. On the twelfth day after I had sent the letter, I was giving a lecture to new pilots on dogfighting techniques. When the class was over, an orderly approached to inform me that I had two visitors waiting to see me. I left at once for the guest room.

I found Hatsuyo and her mother awaiting me. As soon as I entered the room Hatsuyo rose from her chair. "I have come, Saburo," she said quietly. "I have come here to become your wife."

I stood frozen to the floor, struck dumb.

"If you are prepared to die, Saburo, then it is the same with me. If we are to be given only days or weeks, then we shall have them together. That is God's will for us."

"*Hatsuyo!*" I cried. It was impossible. It couldn't be true! It was all too wonderful to happen to me!

My aunt spoke. "Saburo, there is no reason why you and Hatsuyo should not be wed. The fact that you are cousins should not stand between you. You are both sound mentally and physically. It is my daughter's wish—and mine—that this marriage shall come to pass."

I was delirious with joy. But before we could proceed further with any wedding plans, there was the matter of writing my mother and asking for her approval, as the eldest of my family. Her letter offered her blessings, but contained the unhappy news that she would be unable to attend the ceremony. Kyushu's rail facilities had been torn into wreckage, and no passengers were being carried. She requested my aunt to attend to all necessary details.

When I first arrived at Matsuyama, the president of a large aircraft factory in the city had offered me a spacious upstairs room in his large home. He told me that he had followed my actions in combat from the time I shot down my very first plane in China, and that he wished me to live with his family. I declined the offer, not because I did not wish to accept his generosity, but for another reason entirely. I felt it would be unfair for me to enjoy the comforts of a large home while the men with whom I flew remained in shabby barracks.

Now, however, I needed a place to live for Hatsuyo and myself. Rather embarrassed, I informed Commander Nakajima of my marriage plans. He broke into a wide smile and told me to stand exactly where I was, not to move an inch. He picked up his desk phone and dialed the company president direct. I was to move in as soon as the marriage took place, he said, then hung up. Nakajima had known of the generous offer, and refused to entertain any objections.

Hatsuyo and I were married the evening of February 11, 1945, on our country's Foundation Day. It was a modest ceremony, attended only by my aunt and the company president's family. The plans for the wing pilots to attend were changed at the last moment, when an air-raid alert occurred early in the evening. The other men remained by their planes, ready to scramble, while the marriage took place. We had not anticipated that our wedding music would be the spine-shivering shriek of hundreds of air-raid sirens.

After the ceremony, Hatsuyo and I walked together through the blackout to a Shinto shrine. There we knelt and reported to God of our marriage.

A honeymoon, of course, was out of the question under the circumstances. On the following Sunday we invited the fifty pilots of the wing to a reception. They had laughed loudly at my report of the "Siren's March" the night of the ceremony. The reception more than made up for the lack of festivities on our wedding night. Many of the pilots brought with them their own instruments, guitars and accordions, and belatedly played for us a joyous wedding march. I was the happiest man in the world. The pilots exclaimed over and over again about the beauty of my bride. It was a wonderful, wonderful night.

My aunt had a surprise for all of us. She had scoured the remote provinces and somehow managed to purchase additional food for the occasion. The fifty men fell to their meals with gusto. The party continued late into the night. All the men gathered in a large group and sang song after song for us. Hatsuyo led the chorus with the piano, and the men with instruments gathered around her to form an impromptu orchestra.

Those were the happiest hours I had ever known. I was drunk with happiness. All that had happened before now seemed unimportant; it was trifling, compared to the wondrous joy and elation which swept through me now.

I could not take my eyes off Hatsuyo. She was a dream come true, a princess of fairy tales, radiant, beautiful. She was my wife.

CHAPTER THIRTY-ONE

IN MARCH of 1945, for the first and only rime in its history the Japanese Navy departed from its rule of "no precedents" in announcing a special citation to two naval fighter pilots. Only the critical military situation could have influenced our Imperial staff to perform such an act. The citations awarded to NAP 1/C Shoichi Sugita and to me, both of us part of the Matsuyama Wing, were intended to bolster the flagging morale of many pilots.

Sugita, twenty-four years old, was a brilliant flier. Most of his combat activity took place at Truk and in the Philippines, during which he claimed a total of 120 air kills as of January 20, when he returned to Japan.

This figure, however, appears considerably to exceed the actual number of his air victories, which I personally believe totaled about eighty planes. Sugita admitted to me that many of the victories were questionable and had not been confirmed, since battle circumstances made it impossible to provide an accurate check. Most of the dogfights occurred when Sugita fought defensively against superior numbers and when he was unable to take the time to watch a plane actually crash, bum completely in the air, disintegrate, or to be abandoned by its pilot. The fact that we did not carry gun cameras was a handicap to the man who lacked actual proof that his target was destroyed.

When a nation is winning its war, every step is taken to double check all air fighting claims, as we did during our easy conquests in Moresby Alley. But when the situation has deteriorated into a series of defensive battles against a superior enemy, accuracy invariably suffers. No one, however, could dispute Sugita's brilliance in the air.

After watching him in combat, I was so impressed that I felt he could be regarded as the equal of no less an ace than Nishizawa.

Sugita demonstrated his superb skill in spectacular fashion on March 19, when the Matsuyama Wing intercepted enemy carrier fighters during an attack in force against the great Kure naval base. Prior to this air assault, Japan proper had been raided several times by carrier planes, and with virtually no opposition.

Today it was different, although the American pilots thought otherwise. The radiomen at Matsuyama listened in to the conversations of the enemy pilots as they appeared from the south. One would have thought they were thousands of miles from imminent combat, for they discussed openly their formations and attack altitudes.

All available fighters at Matsuyama—forty planes—took off at once. The Shidens, about to receive their baptism of fire with our wing, cruised in wide circles just above the height maintained by the enemy formations. Sixty pilots, myself included, remained on the ground because of a shortage of operational planes. I had an excellent view from the control tower, from which I trained my binoculars on the planes.

The battle exploded the moment the Hellcats came within range. Two flights of Shidens screamed down from their vantage point 1,500 feet above the Grummans. Sugita plummeted, like a stone. Coming out of his dive, he rolled in against a Hellcat and snapped out a burst. The four cannon proved their effectiveness in dramatic fashion. Flames burst out from the fighter's engine as it careened wildly through the air, out of control. Sugita rolled away and came out directly behind a second Hellcat, sending his cannon shells into the fuselage and cockpit. The Grumman skidded crazily and plummeted for the ocean. A third fighter raced in against the Shiden. Sugita gave him no chance. His fighter soared upwards, hung on a wing, then came around in a beautiful diving turn. The Hellcat fell apart in the air.

Sugita's fighter flashed away, heading for the main dogfight. It was a spectacular battle. Every man on the ground cheered and shouted as one Hellcat after the other went down. This time it was different . . . this time the Hellcats fought for their lives! Obviously the appearance of the Shiden fighters, which were much faster than the Hellcats, which possessed greater climbing speed and firepower, and which were manned by some of the best pilots in Japan took the enemy fliers completely by surprise.

An hour later a jubilant Sugita returned to the field singing the praises of his new plane. He claimed four fighters definitely shot down—kills confirmed by the other pilots—as well as three probables. Sugita couldn't stop talking about the Shiden; only his lack of ammunition, he said, prevented him from downing more planes.

The Matsuyama Wing provided the only spark of hope for the entire day. Nowhere else over Japan could our pilots claim a victory. Indeed, the Hellcats had run wild over all other opposition, and our victories appeared to be the only losses suffered by the Americans. Later we received copies of an American report of the air battle, which registered considerable surprise at the high performance of the Shiden fighter. The American pilots were shocked at the new airplane's ability to withstand tremendous damage from the heavy machine guns of the Hellcats.

Within a month, however, disaster struck our wing. The greatest pilot still living in Japan, Soichi Sugita, was killed. The Matsuyama Wing had transferred to Kanoya in southern Kyushu to oppose the American planes supporting the invasion of Okinawa. On April 17, without any warning, mass formations of enemy fighter planes screamed down on our field. We had only a glimpse of them at about 12,000 feet as they thundered down. We were caught flat-footed. Apparently the enemy planes, both Corsairs and Hellcats, had flown from aircraft carriers in Okinawa waters. We had no radar at Kanoya, and the fighters were already diving when the alarms clamored.

On the field the battle command flag, "Go Out and Fight," fluttered in the wind over the Command Post. Several pilots ran for their planes, but Captain Genda shouted to us to get off the field and into the shelters. It was obviously too late to attempt a take-off.

His orders went unheard by Sugita, Shoji Matsumara, and another pilot. All three men had seen the enemy fighters before the alarm sounded, and had ran for their own planes. Even as the Corsairs and Hellcats screamed low over the field, Sugita and his wingman, with Matsumara directly behind, were taxiing into take-off position. Two enemy fighters screamed down from the right and to the rear. Sugita's wingman went first. The Shiden's wheels were barely off the ground when a Corsair fired a long burst into the fighter. The Shiden reeled wildly under the impact of the bullets of six heavy machine guns, tumbled wing over wing through the air, and struck the ground with a tremendous blast.

Moments later another fighter streaked in. Tracers spit through the air. I stared in horror as the bullets hurled dirt upwards as they moved across the runway and poured into Sugita's taxiing fighter. Sugita never even had a chance to take evasive action with his plane still on the ground.

In a moment the tracers had found the Shiden's fuel tanks and the fighter exploded into a roaring ball of fire. Flame and smoke billowed behind the still-moving plane. There was no movement within the cockpit. I could not believe my eyes. The greatest pilot in Japan, an ace more than fourteen times over, was dead before my eyes.

The destruction of Sugita's plane saved Matsumara's life. The thick clouds of smoke which trailed the burning fighter enveloped Matsumara's plane, shielding him from the enemy fighters. (Today Shoji Matsumara is an F-86 Sabre jet fighter pilot in the new Japan Air Force. He finished his war flying with the destruction of six Hellcats and Corsairs during the final days of combat.)

Those were terrible days. The great aces of Japan, their numbers already diminished by American guns, fell one after the other. Two months after Sugita went to his death, Kinsuke Muto, the man who had fought with me at Iwo Jima, was gone. Muto scored at least thirty-five victories in the air; indicative of his superb flying ability and fearless actions in combat were the four B-29s officially credited to him.

Muto had flown brilliantly in the spring of 1945, when he was based at Yokosuka. On February 26 he completed a sensational day in the air by attacking in an obsolete Zero twelve Corsair carrier fighters strafing Tokyo. Muto took off from the fighter base at Atsugi and lost no time in plunging into the enemy formation. The startled pilots scattered before the unexpected attack of a single Zero, and two Corsairs tumbled to earth, wrapped in flames, before the American fliers could turn against Muto's plane. In a savage, incredible dogfight which ran from Atsugi to over Yokosuka, Muto confounded the enemy pilots with brilliant aerobatics. Despite their frantic efforts, the Corsairs failed to keep Muto in their sights long enough to send the Zero down. By constantly attacking, almost seeming to ram during his wild flying, Muto kept the Corsairs off his own neck while he shot down two more of the enemy. Finally, out of ammunition, he dove away from the fight.

Four months later he was dead. He transferred to Okinawa in June, still flying the old Zero fighter. He was last seen attacking a Liberator bomber near Yaku Shima. As our other pilots reported the battle, Muto closed in to point-blank range, pouring a stream of fire into the four-engined bomber. He never saw the Mustang which dove with tremendous speed against him, firing a long burst which tore the right wing off his plane.

We had hardly recovered from the shock of Muto's loss when the death of another of our greatest aces stunned all pilots. Lieutenant S/G Naoshi Kanno, of the Kanoya Wing, met his end near Yaku Shima in a fighter wrapped from nose to tail in flames. Kanno was famous for his unprecedented successes against the B-17s in the South Pacific, and had no less than a dozen Fortresses among his fifty-two confirmed air victories. He was the first pilot to perfect the rolling and diving head-on attack against the Fortresses, the same firing pass later discovered by the Luftwaffe to be the most effective against the powerful B-17.

So now, to the list of Sasai, Ota, Nishizawa, and others were added more of our greatest—Kanno, Muto, and Sugita.

Now, I, who had been denied permission to fly combat missions while at Matsuyama, was the surviving ace who led all other pilots. My demands for permission to fly the Shidens in combat were denied repeatedly by Captain Genda, who finally ordered me and Hatsuyo back to Yokosuka. In April, chafing at my orders to stay out of the air, I returned to my former base.

CHAPTER THIRTY-TWO

OUR return to Yokosuka involved a wearying, sleepless journey of forty hours by train. We stopped perhaps two dozen times to stand on the tracks outside different cities which even at that moment were receiving terrible punishment by enemy fighters and bombers. The strain of the uncomfortable ride was telling on Hatsuyo, who was visibly fatigued from the halting progress of the train. She never complained, but always smiled at my worried glances, and assured me in a tired whisper that she would be all right.

We were appalled at the ruins and charred wreckage which met our eyes as we passed through the different cities along the route. Vast areas stretched away from each station, blackened and seared by the terrible fire bombs sown by the B-29s. Each of these cities was a wasteland of ash. The wind picked up fine soot and dust and filled the air with its choking substance. Every time we left a city we breathed a sigh of relief, only to encounter almost exactly the same garish scene before our eyes at the next station. Our country was being pounded into wreckage and it was obvious to me as a pilot that we could do little to prevent the appalling destruction from increasing.

To our surprise, the big naval city of Yokosuka was intact. Strangely, the Americans spared it, while the B-29s burned and leveled more than 140 other provincial cities, many of far less strategic value than this naval bastion. Perhaps the fact that Yokosuka harbored none of the huge battleships or aircraft carriers contributed to its immunity from the enemy's bombs. I saw only small motorboats churning across the big port, maneuvering wildly, undergoing special training. The crews were preparing themselves for the final day when our soil would be invaded. These were the counterparts of the *Kamikaze* planes. Each speedboat was crammed full with high explosives, and its crew would race in against enemy transports to destroy themselves with the enemy. Again, there was a price to be paid. But how many men on an American transport or warship could be killed by two or three Japanese smashing their boat against the sides of an enemy vessel?

The Navy provided us with a small three-room dependent house near the Oppama Airfield, in northern Yokosuka. Our life was far from easy, and Hatsuyo did her best to transform our meager supplies of food into something resembling meals.

The huge storage warehouses at Yokosuka were virtually empty, stripped of all their goods by the military. The meals served to officers and enlisted men were no longer different; they were equally poor and ill tasting. We lived at the barest level of subsistence. All Post Exchange and Dependent Purchase centers had long ago been boarded up for lack of supplies.

Most of the stores in the city proper had been closed for months. Even though it had escaped the bombing which had smashed other cities, Yokosuka was dreary and almost lifeless. The few people who trudged the streets were hungry and destitute.

And still the B-29s came in ever greater numbers, and carrying more and more bombs. The raids we had thought to be the ultimate in destruction were eclipsed less than twenty-four hours later in assaults which beggar description. Literally *millions* of fire bombs cascaded down from the skies, causing conflagrations the like of which the earth had never seen before.

All Japan was shocked by a raid on Tokyo which came on the night of March 10. More than nineteen square miles of the city lay gutted the morning after, a fantastic, rotting wasteland. There were reports that as many as 130,000 people had died during the flaming night.

Originally, the Army had been charged with the responsibility of intercepting the great bombers. They never achieved even a fleeting moment of success in this task. After a series of costly and futile attempts to stem the tide of Superfortresses, the Army licked its wounds and abandoned all attempts at interception. They left the sky to the B-29s, and all Army planes were withdrawn from active service. Mechanics swarmed over the fighters and bombers, working to bring them into the best possible condition, preparing them for the day of reckoning when the Americans would invade.

Now the responsibility for defending the homeland lay entirely in the hands of the Navy. Every day our fighters went up to slash at the B-29s, and every day we achieved spectacularly little success. Our men were doing their best, but it was not enough against the Superfortress. From Atsugi, near Yokosuka, Raiden fighters took off on interception flights against the B-29s that resulted in daily wild scrambles. For a short period of time the fighters broke the B-29s' myth of invincibility, and the Raiden's four cannon and flashing speed raised our hopes by blowing several B-29s from the sky.

The enemy's answer was to send swarms of Mustangs over Japan during the daylight raids. The swift enemy fighters tore savagely at our planes and slaughtered them. Where the Raiden shone against the B-29, it was helpless before the swifter, more maneuverable Mustang. Almost every day our new fighters plunged burning from the sky, their wings torn off, their pilots dead.

Out of this terrible massacre there emerged but one shining pilot, a man of superb flying ability. Lieutenant J/G Teimei Akamatsu, who was as different from other pilots as night from day. He was the only Japanese naval pilot I ever knew who had successfully defied almost every regulation in the books. He was the typical swashbuckling hero of fiction, powerfully built, noisy, and always happy. Akamatsu had joined the Navy nearly ten years before my own enlistment, but he failed to achieve the rapid promotions which his fellow pilots coveted. Indeed, he was even broken in rank on several occasions, and threatened with dishonorable discharge. He was incorrigible, but he was a genius in the air, and the Navy was loath to lose a man of his spectacular ability.

Akamatsu stunned his superior officers by his conduct. Instead of attending pilot briefings and waiting on the flight line like the other men, he had his own warning system hooked up in a brothel! He often came racing to the air base in an old car, driving like a demon with one hand, drinking from a bottle held in the other. The sirens were screaming a warning as he bolted from the car to his fighter plane, already warmed up by the mechanics. He took off the moment the cockpit canopy was closed. He was equally as wild in the air as he was on the ground, and was the only pilot who ever successfully engaged both Mustangs and Hellcats in dogfights and emerged the victor. Akamatsu shot down no less than ten of these excellent enemy planes while flying the Raiden, a feat most other pilots considered to be impossible. Akamatsu was fortunate in that at least eight of these kills were verified by other fliers.

To this day no man knows how many enemy planes Akamatsu shot down in combat. He fought continuously for more than six years, cutting his teeth in China, where he bagged several enemy fighters. Then he went on to fight in almost every area of the Pacific, often returning with his plane shot to ribbons, grinning and shouting loudly.

Akamatsu himself does not know his total number of victories. When drunk, he would pound his fist on the table and bellow that he had blown at least 350 Allied planes out of the air. He never boasted when he was sober. Other pilots who had fought with him and managed to survive through the war corrected this figure down to about fifty air kills.

I often saw Akamatsu landing at Oppama when he failed to reach Atsugi because of fuel shortages caused by the wild air melees. It was heartening to everyone on the field to see him climbing out of his fighter, thumbing his nose at the bullet holes, always grinning. He would shout to me and hold up his hand with several fingers upraised, denoting the number of planes he had shot down that day.

More than once Akamatsu took off in a flight of five to eight fighters, and was the only man in the group to survive the battles. Mustangs were his favorite prey, and he had a healthy respect for the American fighter. He cursed the officers who sent up green pilots in the Raiden—they could barely fly the airplane, let alone fight with it.

Akamatsu survived the war. Today he runs a small restaurant in Kochi, his home town in Shikoku Island.

The Oppama air base was mainly a testing field where pilots ran new fighters through their flight checks. I was not given the opportunity to fight for a long time, since the base commander felt that my long experience would be invaluable in testing our new planes. I realized that more combat, however, was only a matter of time. Every man who could fly, every plane which could stagger into the air, would be thrown against the invading fleet.

In June I was ordered to report to Nagoya to test a new fighter plane, the Reppu. There had been rumors about the new aircraft which indicated that the Reppu was the greatest plane which had ever flown. I was anxious to get my hands on the ship to see if the rumors had some substance. Such a fighter would be a blessing to us.

All the rumors were true. The Reppu was a sensational airplane, the fastest I had ever flown. It took my breath away with its tremendous speed, and its rate of climb was astounding. With a powerful engine, a four-bladed propeller, and new superchargers, the Reppu ran away from everything in the air, Japanese or American. It could fly circles in a climb around either the Hellcat or the Mustang, and the engineers told me it would fight at better than 40,000 feet.

Unhappily, for us, the Mitsubishi factories which were to produce the Reppu were blasted into wreckage before production could get under way. Only seven planes were produced; the one existing model, flown by the enemy after the war, astounded the American pilots with its flashing performance.

Before I left for Nagoya, Hatsuyo had made me promise to purchase for her a small dagger. The city was famous for its outstanding swords and daggers, and my wife insisted upon a blade from the craftsmen of that city. Upon my return Hatsuyo silently inspected the gleaming length of steel, cautiously touching the blade. "Saburo, it is not sharp enough." She looked at me. "Tomorrow, at Oppama, will you hone the steel to a fine edge?"

Her serious expression startled me. "What on earth did you want a dagger for, anyway?" I asked.

She took my hands in hers and looked directly into my eyes. "You are my life, Saburo," she said quietly. "All that matters in this world is you. There is only one thing for me to do if you are killed."

She said no more, and I pressed the matter no further. The next day I sharpened the blade on an oilstone until the edge was razor sharp. That night Hatsuyo tested the steel by slicing effortlessly through soft tissue paper. "It is good now," she commented, then slipped the dagger beneath her kimono sash. We never discussed the subject again.

After our departure from Matsuyama, Hatsuyo never touched a piano. I knew that she wanted to play again; she had a wonderful feeling for music and could have passed the hours much more easily with a piano to occupy her during the long days. She declined my offer to borrow the instrument we had at the officers' mess. So long as we were all fighting so hard, she said, it was not right for her to enjoy the pleasure of music by herself. I could appreciate her attitude. All Japan suffered bitterness which rose even above the pain and horror of the bombings. The nation was being torn asunder, our cities lay prostrate and flaming as if trampled by a gigantic foot. There was no doubt in anyone's mind that the end was near, that soon the fighting would be transferred to our soil. There was no possibility of surrender. We would fight to the last man.

On August 6 the reports of a vast and terrible explosion in Hiroshima, later confirmed as an atomic bomb, stunned the pilots at Oppama. The idea that a single plane could inflict so much damage was staggering and too great to absorb all at once.

Then came the hammer blow of the Soviet invasion of Manchuria, which followed almost immediately. This was more personal and more real and far more devastating in its implications.

The second atomic bomb on Nagasaki followed. My mind was hazy from the unbelievable devastation being wrought by the Americans. All of this exceeded the limits of credibility. It couldn't be true, and yet it was.

At three in the afternoon on August 13, all officers at the Oppama base were hurriedly summoned to a secret meeting in the commandant's office. Our commanding officer was pale and visibly shaken. He could hardly stand and supported his weight against his desk. He spoke weakly, in a faltering voice.

"What I am about to tell you is of the utmost importance," he began, "and must be regarded as absolutely top secret. I rely upon your integrity as officers of the Imperial Navy to keep this information strictly to yourselves.

"Japan," here his voice choked, "has decided to accept the enemy's terms. We will abide by the Potsdam Declaration." He stared at us with vacant eyes. "The surrender orders may be announced at any moment. I want all officers to cooperate with me to the fullest. Order must be maintained at this base. There may be hotheads who will refuse to accept the decision to surrender. We cannot afford to have our men violate whatever conditions our country accepts. Remember—and never forget it—that His Majesty's orders come before anything else."

A bomb could have exploded among us, and not a man would have flinched. We were rooted to the floor, unbelieving. We had known that the end would come, but we had not anticipated this. The men walked slowly from the room, dazed, many staring dully ahead of them or at the floor. Some of the officers were crying, others cursing. I myself was incapable of thought or speech. I walked in a fog, crossing the field without looking to either side. For some reason I wanted to be near my plane, and I leaned weakly against the Zero.

A close friend of mine, Ensign Jiro Kawachi, walked up to me. For several minutes we stood next to each other, mute, unable to talk.

It was over.

We had lost.

Japan was about to *surrender.*

"Sakai." I looked up. "Saburo, it . . . it is just about the end now," Kawachi spoke. "We have very little time left. Let us make one more flight together, one last fight."

He kicked the ground idly with his foot. "We just can't quit like this," he protested. "We have to draw blood once more."

I nodded. He was right. We told the maintenance men to move our two Zeros out to the runway, to prepare them for flight. We knew that the Superfortresses would bomb tonight. The weather forecast appeared promising, and there were so many bombers overhead every evening that B-29s could be intercepted almost anywhere. For a long time they had flown over Oppama without opposition, using the field for a landmark. They would not expect fighters.

Kawachi and I kept our plans strictly to ourselves, not even telling the other pilots. After we inspected our fighters, we walked to the tower and sat down to wait. Several hours passed without a word between us. We were lost in our thoughts, the memories of the long years from China onward.

The afternoon passed and we remained seated, almost invisible in the darkness. Shortly before midnight the tower radio spluttered. "Alert. Alert. A B-29 formation is now approaching the Yokosuka-Tokyo area."

We jumped to our feet and ran across the field to our planes. The air base lay in blackness, not a light showing. There was just enough light from the stars to enable us to make our way. When we reached the Zeros, we discovered we were not the only pilots determined to go up for a last mission. At least eight other fighters were lined up at the edge of the runway, fueled and armed.

I was afraid that with only one eye I would not be able to see properly at night in the air, and I asked Kawachi to lead me off the ground. We took off at once, without any further conversation. At any moment, we knew, the commandant might learn of our plans and order the planes held on the ground. The moment we were airborne, I swung in close to

Kawachi's fighter and took up a position off his wing. Eight other Zeros were in the air with us, forming into two flights behind our planes. We climbed steadily, then circled at 10,000 feet over Tokyo Bay.

Kawachi's fighter banked abruptly and pulled away to the east. I flew with him, the two flights close behind. For a few moments I failed to see any other planes in the air. Then Kawachi's cannon started firing, and I made out the big bomber flying northward. I had him now, clear in my sights. I pulled up almost alongside Kawachi's plane and opened fire. We each had four cannon now, and we would need every weapon against the tremendous airplane. I had never seen anything so huge! As I swung around after completing my firing pass, I saw the eight other fighters storming the Superfortress. They appeared like tiny gnats milling around a tremendous bull. How could we hope to shoot down an airplane of such incredible size?

I came in again, climbing and sending my fire into the B-29's underside. The counter-fire was terrible. Tracers spilled into the air from the multiple turrets on the B-29, and I felt the Zero shudder several times as the enemy gunners found their mark. We ignored the bomber guns and kept pressing home the attack. The Superfortress turned and headed south. Apparently we had damaged the big plane, and now he was running for home. I clung to Kawachi and slammed the engine on over-boost. The other eight fighters were already lost far behind us, and it was doubtful that we could keep up with the bomber. It possessed remarkable speed and was, in fact, faster than the Zeros I had flown at Lae.

Kawachi, however, had no intention of losing the big plane in the dark. He cut inside the B-29's wide turn and led me down in a shallow diving attack. This time we had a clear shot, and both Kawachi and I kept the triggers down, watching the tracers and shells ripping into the glass along the bomber's nose. We had him! Suddenly, the Superfortress's speed fell off and the pilot dropped the airplane down for a long dive. We came around in a tight turn, firing steadily in short bursts, pouring the cannon shells into the crippled plane.

The great bomber descended quickly. I saw no fire or smoke. There was no visible damage, but the airplane continued to lose altitude steadily, dropping toward the ocean. We kept after the fleeing plane. O Shima Island suddenly loomed out of the darkness. We were fifty miles south of Yokosuka.

We pulled out of our dives, and climbed to 1,500 feet. A volcano on the island reared 1,000 feet above the water, and we dared not risk a collision in the blackness. I could make out the bomber faintly as it dropped. Presently it ditched with a splash of white foam in the ocean, several miles off O Shima's northern coastline. In less than a minute the B-29 disappeared beneath the water.

Back at the airfield, we learned that at least three cities had been gutted during the night. The fires were still burning fiercely, unchecked, sweeping before the wind.

The war was to end less than twelve hours later. I shook my head in dismay.

The commandant was visibly angry over our flight, but he spared us his wrath. "I suppose I can't blame you," he said, "but we cannot have any repetition of what occurred tonight. From this moment on, all planes are grounded."

He told me that Atsugi was the scene of wild riots, that a near rebellion had occurred on the field. That was the Raiden fighter base where Akamatsu and other pilots were stationed, men who could not accept the idea of a surrender, who tried to get their planes into the air. They lost their heads and defied the officers, swearing that they would refuse to accept surrender, that they would fight until their last breath. Reinforcements were moved in; not until several days after the surrender was a semblance of order restored.

The destruction of the enemy bomber was kept secret for many years, and no record was made of our flight that night. And, of course, no pilot claimed credit for the destruction of the B-29. This is my first disclosure of that battle. We felt I no exultation at shooting down the tremendous bomber. Nothing mattered except that we were surrendering our nation, our people, our homes to the enemy.

I slept fitfully on a mess-hall table until daybreak. The air base was pandemonium itself. Many of the pilots were blind drunk, shouting and cursing wildly.

Other men appeared dazed, as if they were in shock, when the historic dawn of August 15, 1945, arrived. The war was over. It was done. In every office high-ranking officers burned documents and files. Men walked around in a stupor or sat on floors or the ground outside.

Exactly at noon we heard the Emperor personally read the surrender orders to our armed forces, wherever they happened to be. The 2,000 men at Oppama stood rigidly at attention on the field. Most of us had never before heard the Emperor's voice. Many of the men were crying unashamedly.

Suddenly I remembered—I had not been home last night! *Hatsuyo!*

What would she think? If she hears the Emperor's broadcast, she will think I was killed and....

I listened no more, but ran from the room. There were no cars. I grabbed a bicycle and pedaled frantically toward my small home. I was there in a few minutes. I leaped off the bicycle even before it stopped moving. I flung open the door, shouting for her. Hatsuyo ran from her room and flung herself into my arms, sobbing. For several minutes we clung fiercely to one another, unable to speak.

Finally she lifted her head. "Are—are you all right, Saburo?" she whispered. I nodded.

"Oh, my sweet," she cried. "I wept like a child when I heard. It is really over, isn't it? The fighting ... all the bombing, it is all done?"

I shook my head slowly in assent.

"I don't care about anything, Saburo, I don't care! You have won all your battles, my darling, even if we have lost."

A light dawned in her eyes as she looked at me. "You—you will never have to fight again!" she whispered. "It is all over now. Never, never again!"

She drew back suddenly and withdrew the dagger from beneath her sash.

"I will never need it again!" she cried, flinging the shining steel to the floor.

The dagger clattered across the room and came to a stop in the corner.

ILLUSTRATIONS

Over China in 1939. In this fighter (3-107) I scored my first—and my only—victory against the Chinese.

Beneath my Claude at Kiukiang Air Base in Central China, in 1938. About two months before my first kill.

The five leading aces of Japan, when we were assigned in 1942 to the Lae Wing. (Rear, l. to r.) Takatsuka, Sasai, and myself. (Front, l. to r.) Ota and Nishizawa. All these men were killed by war's end, but Nishizawa became Japan's leading ace with 103 kills confirmed.

Lieutenant Sasai, my closest friend, who was killed at Lae after I was wounded and sent back to the homeland.

One of our Zero fighters at Lae in 1942. This was the best fighter plane in the Pacific—and we loved it.

I flew this Zero in 1940. Later, we cut off the radio mast and took out the radios to lighten the fighters.

Late in 1942, we studied several captured American planes. The B-17's tough construction amazed all of us.

My friend Kozai (r.) and I flew together many times in China. We left Hankow in 1941; Kozai died at Midway.

This is the Raiden fighter which I flew as a test pilot. With four cannon, it was designed to attack B-29's.

Recuperating from wounds in my eye and head, at Yokosuka Hospital in September, 1942. My friend (r.) was hit at Midway.

This is my wife, Hatsuyo. She survived the war with me, only to die of poverty and illness two short years later.

Tokyo, 1956.